Faith Renewed

The Judaic Affirmation Beyond the Holocaust

Volume I

**Judaism Transcends Catastrophe
God, Torah, and Israel Beyond the Holocaust**

Faith Renewed

The Judaic Affirmation Beyond the Holocaust

Volume I

Judaism Transcends Catastrophe
God, Torah, and Israel Beyond the Holocaust

Jacob Neusner
Editor

Mercer University Press
Macon, Georgia

ISBN 0-86554-460-3

Faith Renewed:
The Judaic Affirmation Beyond the Holocaust
Edited by
Jacob Neusner

Copyright © 1994
Mercer University Press
Macon, Georgia

Library of Congress Cataloging-in-Publication Data

Judaism transcends catastrophe: God, Torah, and Israel beyond the Holocaust/
Jacob Neusenr, editor.
  x + 196 pp.   6" x 9" (15 x 23 cm.)
  Includes bibliographical references.
Contents: v. 1 Faith renewed: the Judaic affirmation beyond the Holocaust.
  ISBN 0-86554-460-3
  1. Holocaust (Jewish theology) 2. Holocaust, Jewish (1939–1945)—
  Influence. 3. God (Judaism) 4. Jews—Election, Doctrine of.
  5. Suffering—Religious aspects—Judaism. 6. Judaism—Doctrines.
  I. Neusner, Jacob, 1932–
  BM645.H6J83 1994
  296.3'11—d c20   94-38718
                                                               CIP

Contents

Part One—Defining Terms

Part Two—Framing the Issue

Part Three—Bearing Witness

Part Four—The Commanding Voice of Auschwitz

Part Five—Summing Up

Preface

The polemic of this anthology, which is meant to be a highly crafted statement and not merely a collection of this and that, a political portrait of ephemerally important folk, is simply stated: "God after Auschwitz" endures as of old, and that is the God of Sinai, known to us through the Torah. Eternal Israel after Auschwitz has not only survived but has remained faithful to its election, loyal to its covenant, and true to its vocation of exploring what it means to form a kingdom of priests and a holy people. To be born that eternal Israel, or to find a place in that Israel, for those who are there, abides God's ultimate act of grace: so eternal Israel has always affirmed, and so, whether in or after Auschwitz, eternal Israel today confesses. That confession and affirmation adumbrate not intellectual problems but spiritual mysteries; it is how life is defined and lived for me and for all of us who embody in our time and place the remnant of that eternal Israel.

In this anthology, I mean to offer the reader the occasion to take up enduring issues of theology as Judaic theologians in our day have framed those issues. Christianity, as much as Judaism, formulates its religious experience in the theological categories represented here: (1) the encounter with God in history; (2) finding God in the world, or how we meet God in the here and now (here: God); (3) responding to revelation, or God's self-manifestation (here: Torah); (4) forming the community of the faithful, in Christian language, the body of Christ (here: eternal Israel), as well as (5) theological thinking about theology. So far as the two religious traditions, Christianity and Judaism, are conceived within a single, shared structure, what Judaic thinkers define as their discipline and task bears relevance to Christian thinking about the same category, and the contrary also is the case. These are the issues of the five volumes:

(1) for the Holocaust in particular, how a religious reading of the massacre of millions of Jewish children, women, and men has defined the issues of the last half of the twentieth century, the bases for the affirmation of God and beyond the Holocaust (thus: "Judaism transcends catastrophe")

(2) for God, how we know God, where we meet God, the meaning of prayer, other forms of religious encounter and experience

(3) for the Torah, the definition of the Torah as God's self-manifestation; the issues of how we mediate between that form, which is to say, writing of a particular age, and eternal truths that are made manifest

(4) for Israel, we want to know how people have thought about the vocation and election of Israel, not only in the aftermath of the Holocaust and the foundation of the state of Israel, but in more enduring categories as well, and how these categories that endure—this is the way of life that God has given us for our service to God, this is the life of faith that we lead in the Torah—have formed a system for the interpretation of what happens in the here and now

(5) for theology, the account of how theologians have defined their work, the program they have defined for their heirs, the philosophically-minded religious intellectuals of the coming century.

My purpose is to afford access for faithful Christian and Judaic readers to a kind of religious thinking and writing, profoundly in Judaic character, that is possessed of acute relevance but at the same time subjected to wasteful neglect. As I explain in the Introduction, people suppose that "after Auschwitz theology," or "post-Holocaust theology," we must deal with only one question, which is, the problem of evil. But that supposition is only partly right, therefore entirely wrong. In fact, Judaic theology from 1945 is in one way or another a response to the catastrophe of the German murder of millions of Jews by reason of nothing they ever did but only what they were, which is, born of one Jewish grandparent.

No thinker whom we read in these pages wrote a single line in the oblivion of forgetting or ignoring the revelation of absolute evil that has taken place in our time. But the important thinkers, those whose writings will instruct the coming century, brought to the Holocaust the issues of transcendence, the classical categories and enduring doctrines of the Torah the world calls "Judaism." Therefore, I think it is important to afford access here to moments of theological reflection that form in a variety of idioms and voices a single cogent work of sustained, rigorous thought.

In the post-Holocaust writings I aim to show coherence; cogency; consistency; proportion and balance; authority and commanding mastery—in all, the classical tradition of Judaic theology as it has come to expression in diverse, authentic formulations in our time. I do so in the conviction that first-rate minds provide the rest of us with a model and standard for our own religious thought, and much first-rate work is encompassed in these pages.

I address Christian as well as Judaic readers because the issues of Christian theology, framed in their own idiom to be sure, run along the same lines as those facing eternal Israel. We want to know what the world can reveal about God; so do they. We explore the responsibilities of the covenant with God that defines our being; so do they. We want to understand what it means to be "Israel," meaning, the people of God assembled before Sinai and children of Abraham, Isaac, and Jacob; and so, by their own word, do they.

The dilemmas of faith and temptations of unbelief—how can an all-powerful God have made the world to be what it now is, for instance—confront us both. Judaism and Christianity share a common heritage of revelation, Judaism's written Torah (a term explained in the Introduction), and Christianity's Old Testament. Whatever one of us learns about God in the here and now and in revelation is going to lay claim upon the attention of the other, since by our own word both of us maintain that each party worships and loves the same, one, and unique God (along with Islam).

That explains why I chose as my publisher a press conducted by academic colleagues who without apology stand for a clear and explicit religious position; and my publisher has chosen my work because of its comparable recognition that I here make an uncompromisingly religious statement. I take pride in presenting anthology through the medium of this Southern Baptist university press; valuing the written Torah ("the Old Testament") as the word of God, just as eternal Israel does, that university and its press form an appropriate medium for an account of how God speaks in our place and time. And through theologians' intellect, as much as through saints' deeds and prayers, in responding, we answer the call that comes first and provokes response. Our response may not be the one God wants, but it is an authentic response to a call, that in the end, we maintain, comes to us from God.

Religious faith begins with God, not with us, for the world does not witness to God, but, more often than not, against Him. For me it follows that revelation, in the scripture we share, the Torah/Bible, forms the beginning of our diverse religious thought. Theology for each of us follows rules of disciplined and rigorous reflection that God in the Torah/Bible has exemplified and that the words of God in the Torah/Bible embody.

It is not for us to know why God made the world the way it is, or to understand the reason why ancient Israel endures through the three great faiths that identify with it, rather than only through us, Israel after the flesh and (we think) the spirit too. But that is how it is and how it has been for long enough, now, as to defy easy explanation. None of us conceives that theological negotiation is possible; each party believes its torah is the Torah, and that is how God has made us. That Baptists can find in an anthology of Judaic theology a work worthy of their publication forms a tribute to both the Baptists and the intellectual achievement of the theology of Judaism portrayed here.

This is no history of Judaism either, nor do I promise a thumb-nail account of how nearly two thousand years of thought took place prior to the last half of this century. At the outset, I lay out the issues of the Holocaust and then turn to the classical categories. But in each volume, I mean to offer perspective on the issues at hand. Therefore, I begin with a brief account of how, in the formative age of Judaism and its canon, catastrophe has elicited rational refection, and, for volumes two through four, how the categories find definition: God, Torah, and Israel in the definitive documents of Judaism. In volume five, the counterpart is my own position on the next task in the theology of Judaism. In these opening statements, I offer perspectives of what is to follow.

Then I turn to the repertoire of writings on these same topics in our own time, not a survey of popular opinion, which is irrelevant to theology, but a re-presentation of informed thought, which embodies the theological voice. Each speaker is given a brief introduction, in which I explain what I find important in what is to be said.

Readers have taken up not individual thinkers' whole systems, but specimens of thought of a number of thinkers on classical problems.

Since I have placed this anthology into the categorical context of Christian theology, I call attention to four other books co-authored by Bruce D. Chilton and myself on the problem of comparative theology, the first three on the comparison of theological structures and the fourth on the comparison of theological systems of Judaism and Christianity. These are as follows:

Christianity and Judaism: The Formative Categories. I. Revelation. The Torah and the Bible. Philadelphia: Trinity Press International, 1995.

Christianity and Judaism: The Formative Categories. II. The Body of Faith: Israel and Church. Philadelphia: Trinity Press International, 1996.

Christianity and Judaism: The Formative Categories. III. God in the World. Philadelphia: Trinity Press International, 1997.

Judaeo-Christian Debates. Communion with God, the Kingdom of God, the Mystery of the Messiah. Minneapolis: Fortress Press, 1997.

These works are free-standing but may prove of interest to Judaic and Christian readers interested in the comparison and contrast of the two great traditions of Scripture.

No work of mine can omit reference to the exceptionally favorable circumstances in which I conduct my research. I edited these three volumes as part of my labor in research scholarship, expressed through both publication and teaching at the University of South Florida, which has afforded me an ideal situation in which to conduct my scholarly life. I express my thanks for not only the advantage of a Distinguished Research Professorship, which must be the best job in the world for a scholar, but also of a substantial research expense fund, ample research time, some stimulation, and cordial colleagues. In the prior chapters of my career, I never knew a university that prized professors' scholarship and publication and treated with respect those professors who actively and methodically pursue research.

The University of South Florida and all ten universities that comprise the Florida State University System as a whole exemplify the high standards of professionalism that prevail in publicly-sponsored higher education in the U.S.A. and provide the model that privately-sponsored universitas would do well to emulate. Here there are rules; achievement accounts; and presidents, provosts, and deans honor and respect the University's principal mission: scholarship alone—both in the classroom and in publication. Here at last I find integrity, governing in the lives of people true to their vocations and their mission.

Jacob Neusner
Distinguished Research Professor of Religious Studies
University of South Florida, Tampa

Introduction

This five-volume anthology systematically presents, in the words of great theologians of Judaism in the generation after the Holocaust, how the enduring issues of the Judaic faith transcended catastrophe and shaped the mind of the age beyond. For it is now clear that from 1945 to today we have witnessed one of the remarkable moments in the history of theology in the West, Judaic and Christian alike: the power of rigorous thought to think about events that, before they actually took place, none could even have imagined. The theological minds of eternal Israel in our own day have met a challenge of which few prior generations could have even taken the measure: transcending radical evil, or, in classical terms, meeting Satan and yet affirming the living God made manifest in the Torah.

The past half-century has witnessed the unfolding of one of the great religious dramas of all time: how people survived evil beyond imagining and affirmed their heritage of faith. When Israel, the Jewish people, looked backward from 1945, so far as the eye could say lay ruins: villages and towns where the Torah had been proclaimed for a thousand years, now bereft of the presence of holy Israel; great cities, once vital with the vivid affairs of eternal Israel, now destroyed. With everything that flourished in 1939, homes, families, entire societies, suddenly a mass of ashes and an empty empire of death, who could then have predicted what in fact took place? For it was not the mass-apostasy that the failure of faith might have provoked, but the determination, among religious Jews (Judaists) and secular ones alike, to reaffirm, renew, rebuild. What happened then was not to have been predicted at all: the rebirth of the eternal Israel, the reaffirmation of its loyalty to God's word in the Torah, the renewal of faith in the one and only God of all ages. Not only did the remnants of the people, Israel, emerge from death factories where Satan ruled, they renewed their lives by forming a new political entity, the State of Israel, and by rebuilding throughout the world any religious community of Israel that embodies Judaism, that is, the Torah, in the here and now.

The covenant with God affirmed, the holy life of the faith resumed, the hope for the salvation of Israel and humanity through the Messiah represented, the people of Scripture sets forth as God's first love renewed and its sustained, and sustaining, life of loving loyalty and obedience to God's Torah. Satan vanquished, a calamity in many ways unique in history survived, Israel's remarkable rebirth marked the transcendence of catastrophe such as the world has seen only seldom. Had Israel then cast off its covenant with God and thrown its lot in with Satan, the rest of humanity would have deplored but understood its tragic end. But this is not what has happened. With the turning of the century and the daily passing of the generation that accomplished the physical feat of surviving, the time has come to take note of what has taken place among us all. An entire people, overcoming despair and renewing hope, embodied the faith of Job: even though He has slain so great a part of us, yet shall we all trust in Him. It is on that foundation, and only on that foundation, that holy Israel has surpassed death and tasted resurrection.

To that religious experience, theology devotes its best intellectual energies in the pages of these five volumes. Here we see how the first rate thinkers of the people, Israel, addressed the crisis of the day, on the one side, but also took up the disciplines and tasks of the classical theological heritage of the Torah, on the other. If no generation in the history of Judaism has confronted so critical a catastrophe, none was better served by its thinkers. The anthology shows the ways in which the important Judaic theologians writing in English have thought about the five issues that could not be avoided and had to be met head on: the defining hour of the Holocaust; then the three principal categories of the theological structure of Judaism: God, Torah, and Israel, meaning the eternal people to whom God spoke at Sinai; and then the challenge of the coming century.

We here encounter not descriptions of opinion or historical accounts of what various people have thought about the Holocaust, God, Torah, and eternal Israel, and the tasks of theology for generations to come. Rather we read in their own words the theologians' propositions, arguments, passionate advocacy of particular positions. This is theology not recorded but lived in vivid intellects, how thoughtful, rigorous, demanding and restless minds have taken up the critical, anguished issues of a living faith at its time of crisis. The writers assembled here show diverse capacities of learning, acumen, perspicacity, and wit; some write one way, some another. But all of them do precisely what theologians in the traditions of Islam, Christianity, and Judaism are expected to achieve, namely the formulation in well-crafted prose of faith seeking understanding through processes of rationality. They give sustained and vigorous argument concerning the solution of conceptual problems of a religious character. More than mere philosophers of religion speaking about matters in general, mediating commanding revelation (for Judaism, the Torah) and rigorous, worldly reason, these writers reshape conviction and conscience into intellectually compelling statements of an entirely rational order.

A generation of theologians of Judaism, the one from World War II to the end of the Cold War, which faced the enormous intellectual challenges of the Holocaust, the founding of the State of Israel, now completes its work. The earlier figures, represented by the names of Berkowitz, Herberg, and Heschel, have gone to their rest, and the later ones, represented by Borowitz, Fackenheim, and Vogel, now bring their thought to fruitions and wisely undertake their valedictory statements. The next generation has yet to coalesce; we simply cannot at this time predict the shape and structure of thought; Judaic theology out of the most recent generations proves still ephemeral and has yet to find either its voice or its agenda. But in the moment of ebb tide, as the waters eddy and seek their new force, a backward perspective illuminates; we can at least take the measure of the high tide that has flowed out. So it is time to inquire into how rigorous religious intellectuals asked themselves the urgent questions precipitated by the greatest catastrophe Israel, the eternal people, has ever faced.

This anthology of five volumes about theological thinking about the Holocaust, God, Torah, eternal Israel, and Judaic theology of the second half of the twentieth century and beyond allows us to take stock of what has happened in the Judaic intellect. The anthology demonstrates that the classic and enduring—chronic in a healthy sense—issues of religious truth, not solely the critical and painful—acute—issue of evil and theodicy, elicited intelligent and profound thought over the past half-century. Not only so, but much that has been written endures as a legacy and a heritage for the thoughtful among the faithful in the century that is now dawning. It is meant to showcase important discussions on the principal categories of the theology of Judaism in the period from World War II to the end of the Cold War.

What makes such an anthology urgent is not only the passing of a generation. It is also that, in general, Jews present themselves as a wholly secular social entity, and the media of religious expression common among their Christian neighbors do not define how Jews make their religious statement. It is the simple fact that while the Hews are a social entity of a single religion, Judaism, or no religion at all (acceptance of any religion other than Judaism marks a person, in functional terms, as no longer a part of the Jewish people), the proportion of Jews who also are Judaists, that is, practitioners of Judaism, varies but hardly encompasses the entire community. Not only so, but even among Judaists, serious encounter with the intellectual heritage of Israel takes place only in modest proportion. Faith without learning (an oxymoron in Judaic piety) is very common; faith surpassing understanding, which two generations from 1945 to the present in fact embodied, is not fully grasped.

It follows that, because of the prevailing secularity of the Jews' pubic discourse, the modest place accorded to Judaists in the scheme of the Jews' ethnic existence, and the uncomprehending disdain for the reality of God's presence in and through eternal Israel, many, Jewish and gentile, have missed the astonishing intellectual events of our time. If attentive to the better publicized theological discourse, the more discerning will have judged the theological response to the Holocaust shallow and predictable. If God is all-powerful, then what does the Holocaust tell us about God? And if God is not all-powerful, then the Holocaust proves there is no God. So the issue of theodicy has exacted—and not only from theologians by any means—many sleepless nights. Many people now suppose that the only theological issue important in Judaism is theodicy, which is to say, theologies that focus upon "God after Auschwitz."

All Judaic theology from 1945 onward, I think for centuries to come, will have to qualify as "after Auschwitz"-theology, not only for chronological reasons, but for substantive ones. We have learned facts about this world that, before the rule of Satan, we culd never have conceived. A central religious task of rigourous thinking will always require confrontation with these facts, as much as, for the prophets, the demise of Northern Israel and the destruction of Jerusalem in 586 precipitated deep thought on how God acts in history. But what the catastrophe teaches, how eternal Israel has responded, the commanding voice of Sinai, the renewed encounter with the living God in prayer and acts of service—these all together form that theology in the shadow of the Holocaust. The reason is that, beyond the shadows, there has been much illumination: eternal Israel, responding to the living God, renewed its covenant in the Torah.

That is the story of the rebirth of Judaism throughout the world, on the one side, and the message, too, of the theologians whom we meet in these five books. In an exact sense, for all who mourn for Israel's millions, murdered by the Germans from 1933 through 1945, every breath is an act of affirmation of Israel. That is why we refer to "Holocaust theology." We presently understand that every piece of religious expression, encompassing the entirety of Judaic theological writing, forms a response to the issue of the Holocaust; there is no other fact of transcendent religious character that compares in our time, or, many would maintain, in al time. Here I show a different picture. It encompasses not only the reaffirmation of God beyond the gates of Hell. It extends also to how thinkers have worked on a wide front, all of them under the shadow of the catastrophe of the Holocaust, but all of them engaged by classic issues and the revealed Torah. True, that statement contradicts how people presently assess the condition of eternal Israel and of Judaism. Any observer, following public life, would have supposed there has been paralysis in the encounter with the classic challenges to systematic thought.

I here make manifest that that is not the case. I show how thought has taken place in the main lines of theology of Judaism not despite the Holocaust nor solely in response to the Holocaust but in re renewal of the religious life of reflection in the aftermath of the Holocaust: how people mediated between new experience and received truth. The enduring categories of thought—God, Torah, Israel—continue to form the definitive outline of truth. For that forms the challenge to thought, which is to say, the religious mind transcends events and transforms them into enduring truth, making occasion into eternity.

For the secular Jews, these questions come to formulation in secular speech: fiction, poetry, film, music; and they are given a secular articulation in politics and social thought. For the religious Jews, there is yet another response. It takes two forms, the inchoate, profound expression of live as it is lived under the covenant with the Almighty: the life of faith and trust, hope, patience, and service, which the Torah teaches. And, it takes the second form of reflection on the meaning and truth of that life, reflection in the form of not only prayer or poetry or artful gesture, but sustained and rigorous thought, lucidly set forth in crafted prose. Secular Jews dominate the public square. But religious ones—Judaists, not only Jews—have also found voices, and in this anthology, these voices gain their hearing.

In this same context—the distinction between the secular and the religious in the life of the Jews—a further complication must be introduced. When in the theology of Judaism we speak of "Israel," we do not mean the State of Israel in particular but the eternal, holy people. That people, of whom Scripture speaks, to whom God gives the Torah, of course encompasses the Jewish part of the population of the State of Israel, but is not limited to that one sector of the Jewish people, not at all.

In fact, the name, "Israel," bears a variety of meanings. In the Torah, "Israel" always speaks not of a place nor yet of a state but only, invariably, of the people Israel, the extended family of Abraham and Sarah, Isaac and Rebecca, Jacob and Leah and Rachel; the kingdom of priests and the holy people. In all Judaic theology, and in all Jewish ethnic writing, before 1948, when people spoke of "Israel" they meant the Jewish people. All other usages in which "Israel" appeared referred to the same sense, e.g., in Hebrew, "land of Israel," did not mean, "the land, Israel," but "the Land that belongs in particular to Israel, the people." In the liturgy of Judaic prayer, "Israel" refers to the elect people of Israel, to whom God gave the Torah, wherever they live, it does not refer to a particular place or to a particular group of Jews as distinct from all others.

The confusion between the received, theological meaning carried by the word "Israel" began in 1948, when the Jewish state, founded by the Zionist movement, to which, as a matter of fact, most of the Jews in the world and in the Land of Israel subscribed, called itself "the State of Israel." Now that formulation, "the State of Israel" by contrast quite properly speaks of the Jewish state, located in the Land of Israel (as the Jewish people have always known that place). When the Psalmist speaks of "The guardian of Israel does not slumber nor sleep," he means, of course, "the guardian of the holy people," and not "the guardian of the Land of Israel," or obviously of "the political entity, the State of Israel." "Israel" as the holy people to whom God revealed the Torah, identified in the here and now as Israel the Jewish people, obviously should not to be confused with the contemporary State of Israel, a this-worldly fact, to be sure bearing profound religious meaning to Judaism. Since the people refer to the State of Israel simply as "Israel," I distinguish the State of Israel from the holy people of Israel of whom the Torah speaks by referring to the latter as "eternal Israel." That will sidestep the difficulties in sense and meaning brought about by calling a secular state by a name that bears its own, distinct theological referent.[1]

So it is time to distinguish the ethnic from the religious, the secular from the theological, out of the voices of a half-century of pained and anguished reflection upon, not merely response to, the catastrophe of the ages that took place between 1933 and 1945. For those who see Israel not as an ethnic group alone but as God's people, those who interpret the world not in its own terms alone, but as testimony to the Almighty, those who distinguish this world's facts from eternal truths, those who view humanity "in our image, after our likeness," the issues surpass ethnic testimony about sound social policy or political action. Judaists, without apology, without shame, see the world under the aspect of God's rule, find in the Torah surpassing truth, appreciate the Israel of this world in its transcendent setting.

The profoundly secular character of the Jews' public life and therefore shared discourse in the USA and Europe obscures the equally deep, rooted religious faith of Judaists' inner life. This book and its four companions give testimony to the living faith, Judaism—which calls itself "the Torah," which sees itself as the "Israel" of which the Torah speaks and which identifies itself as the statement of eternal God, creator of heaven and earth, ruler of all worlds, and ultimate redeemer of humanity. Specifically, they show how Judaic thinkers, rooted in the absolute and unshakable givenness of God's presence in history and rule over Israel, responded in rigorous, rational, theological ways to the defining moments of our day.

Theology in this context refers to systematic and rigorous reflection on religious questions as faith seeks understanding through processes of rationality and gives sustained and vigorous argument concerning the solution of conceptual problems of a religious character. In Judaism, theology has taken a variety of forms, important ideas expressing themselves through patterns of behavior as much as through propositions of belief. But in times past, and in our own day, rigorous and systematic religious thought has yielded a harvest of sustained, proportioned, coherent theological writing. This anthology means to portray how Judaic theology in the past half-century has conducted its work of making sense of the world measured by the dimensions of (1) the Holocaust events themselves; (2) the revealed Torah; (3) the one, unique, and only God who is made manifest in the Torah at Sinai; (4) the eternal, holy nation, Israel, God's first love; and (5) the presence, in eternal Israel, of rigorous, philosophically-insistent intellects and their theological program for time to come.

Knowing what we have learned in this awful century, how do we read the Torah, think about the power and mercy of God, make sense of the mystery of Israel? And what tasks face us in the coming generation?

The Holocaust

What makes the theological adventure of Judaic religious thought compelling and of broad interest to a wide audience of religious faithful, Christian and Judaic alike, over the past fifty years? The gates of the death factories, built by the Germans in World War II, closed finally in 1945. No event in the history of humanity bears more profound implications for our understanding of Torah, Israel, and God, not the fall of Man and Woman, not the Golden Calf, not the exile of the lost tribes, not the destruction of the Temple in 586 B.C.E. nor again in 70 C.E., not the massacre of Rhineland Jewries in the First Crusade, nor the expulsion of the Jews from Spain, nor the advent of Communism, nor the empowerment of Fascism and Nazism. Seen by themselves or all together, these turnings in time made sense on the received cartography of the known ways, God's and humanity's. But the received solutions to the problem of evil—Job's or Jeremiah's for instance—for many proved insufficient, incommensurate to what now has happened. Consequently, Judaic thinkers writing in the American language faced a challenge of reflection, critical thought, and sustained, rigorous intellection. Some directed their attention to the problem of evil and the issue of theodicy.

God, Torah, Israel

But others took up the ancient discipline of rationality in quest of religious truth and broadened the discussion. The Holocaust for them presented the occasion, even the provocation. But it did not define the issues. These, for eternal Israel had been determined at Sinai, when, God having made the world and brought Israel into being and assembled the holy people before the mountain, completed the trilogy by giving the Torah. Creation, revelation, redemption defined the workings of the unfolding system that Sinai set forth, while God, Torah, and Israel constituted the structure by which all reality, here and above, natural and supernatural, would be ordered. So for those who surpassed the occasion, the Holocaust stood for a new beginning in the unending encounter, in intellect, with the living God of Sinai's Torah.

Now, a half-century later, it is time to take stock of the work of a generation that has run its course. Clearly, two distinct kinds of theology require attention, "Holocaust-theology," and "theology that takes account of the Holocaust." The former, as is clear, rightly insists that all thought within the Torah finds its defining program in the catastrophe of 1933–1945 (whether or not completed by the miracle of 1948 to the present day represented by the creation of the State of Israel, the Jewish state, in the Land of Israel). The latter carry forward the classical program of Judaic theological thought—how to live the holy life that God has commanded to covenanted Israel, how to reflect intelligently on the defining categories of that sanctified community's existence, God, Torah, Israel. Among these latter thinkers, the Holocaust found full recognition; but those events were not permitted to silence thought or impose upon the full and transcendent program of intellectual reflection constraints of what are, ultimately, an adventitious character. For they did not permit episodes to define eternal issues, but only to contribute new facts to the contemplation of those issues. So far as the Holocaust contained defining moments on the character of humanity and the holiness of Israel, it was to make, and it did make, its full, ample, and necessary contribution. But the Holocaust for this second set of writers, the more classical ones in education and sensibility, was to be faces within the received and eternal framework of the Torah.

Ample evidence, part of which is laid out in these five anthologies, demonstrates that, transcending catastrophe, great intellects of Judaism accomplished two remarkable tasks of an intellectual character, and they did so forthrightly and courageously.

First, they faced head-on what came to be called "the Holocaust." A formidable corpus of writing by systematic thinkers of Judaism took up the problems of religious belief presented by the events of 1933–1945, when millions of Jews, men and women and upwards of a million children, were murdered my reason of not their faith but the mere fate of having been born into a Jewish family. In fiction, poetry, film, music, as well as in the media if sustained and rigorous thought in the form of ideas carefully crafted and persuasively set forth, the issue of the catastrophe was formed. Certainly, no generation has ever confronted a more insistent or formidable challenge than finding ways to think theologically about the unthinkable.

The faithful of Christianity and Judaism alike have found in the results not only important religious ideas, commensurate to the enormous dimensions of the challenge, but also the occasion for the renewal of faith. That is why the religious response to the Holocaust has rightly won for itself so rich a response of public appreciation. These anthologies do not have to provide a reprise of that protracted chapter in post-Holocaust theology of Judaism. But within the demanding discipline of reasoned thought abut religious questions that theology comprises, a specific, theological formulation of matters was set forth. And that has to be appreciated to make sense of everything else. The achievement of the theologians—as distinct from philosophers, poets, film makers, composers, novelists, moralists, and publicists—was to insist that the Holocaust ask not a thin question of theodicy, but a thick question of encounter: God was there, the Torah was there, with eternal Israel in Auschwitz.

Second, some of these same thinkers and others as well in the same period, under the shadow of the same tremendous events, furthermore took up the received agenda of Judaic theology, that is, the program of mediating between revelation, the Torah, and the present hour that defines the work of theology in that religious tradition. From the formation of the classical and authoritative writings of Judaism, called all together "the Torah," to our own day, each generation has taken up the labor of making its own what the ages had handed on, the fundament of faith for which the Torah stands. The past half-century has witnessed a remarkable display of how enduring and historically-rooted intellectual traditions have taken over and made their own the newest of humanity's, and eternal Israel's, discoveries. When thinking about God, Torah, and Israel, the three generative categories of thought, the Judaic theologians took up an age-old discipline of continuous reflection, always aware of the catastrophe in Europe, but never struck dumb by it. This corpus of religious thinking of a rigorous character in Judaism shows us how Judaism not only faced the Holocaust, but also, through appeal to enduring theological disciplines, transcended it as well. And it is to that labor if intellectual transcendence that these three anthologies are devoted.

What justifies the work in the proportions that characterize these anthologies—the Holocaust forming only part of the portrayal of the encounter with God in our time—is simple. While ready access to the first of the two massive enterprises of Judaic theology, both in its conventional form and in the unconventional formulations of the second half of the twentieth century, is easily gained in numerous and widely-appreciated works, to the second labor, the more classical, few have afforded an opening. That is to say, we may readily find anthologies of Judaic theological and Jewish ethnic responses to the Holocaust, and many of these have rightly enjoyed a massive hearing. But the paramount status rightly accorded to the theological challenge of the Holocaust has tended to obscure this other kind of theology that the generation beyond the Holocaust has formulated.

That is the theology that has continued the ages-old discussion of the enduring issues of Judaic faith to which the greater part of these volumes is devoted. Theologians of mighty power met the challenge, only to find their work neglected in favor of other kinds of expression, because of the paramount secularity characteristic of the Jewish world. For the secular taste, the Holocaust validated atheism; God could not stop those events, so God is not God; or God could stop them but did not do so, so God is evil. For the religious perception, God is always, everywhere, eternally God, without qualifications, condition, or apology. In the context of the iron, incorruptible faith of eternal Israel from its origins to today, silence before the unknowable hardly defined a task beyond accomplishment. So the secular reading of the Holocaust prevailed in public life.

But of course for those of us who find our being in God's Israel and the purpose of our being in God's Torah, the Holocaust is reduced in its dimensions when treated as an event only in this world's terms. So reading the Holocaust in the narrowly political, secular, and ethnic reading of the catastrophe—or in terms essentially secular people assume pertain to theology impoverishes. More happened at Auschwitz and the other capitals of evil embodied than this world contains. And we have known the reality of pure evil from of old; for our paradigm, if there is no ultimate evil, there also is no meaning to the ultimate redemption. And God is diminished. But in the structure of a this-worldly reading of existence that predominates in Israel, the Jewish people, as distinct from eternal Israel in the here and now, how the received, enduring dimensions of the Torah are to be measured has scarcely attracted attention.

The issues of religious encounter with the living God that religious Jews—practitioners of Judaism, called Judaists—find urgent but secular, ethnic Jews scarcely acknowledge are not addressed in theodicy alone, or in declarations that there was a God but he died in Auschwitz and similar formulations. Consequently, when people take up the examination of the theology of Judaism in the generation now completing its work, they take for granted one issue defines discourse. That issue is the one of theodicy, framed as "God after Auschwitz." People have taken for granted that, when we turn to theology, all we shall discuss is what we can know about God in light of the revelations of systematic murder of the people, Israel, in Europe. That is a legitimate issue it is not the only one.

It is a broadly held impression that, in the aftermath of the murder of nearly six million Jews in Europe in World War II and also the creation of the State of Israel, the theology of Judaism has given itself over to the enormous problem of theodicy presented by the former, and the political concerns defined in response to the creation and maintenance of the latter. So God is no longer God in creation, revelation, and redemption, as Judaism has always encountered God. God is now subject to human judgement, requiring explanation and defense. But we in holy and eternal Israel have known more about God than the works of this day's history. We have defined our existence in more dimensions than the political and the empowered. Not only so, but theologians, who undertake in each generation to mediate the Torah to the acutely-present moment, have set forth rigorously argued systems, or components of systems, that provide rational and philosophically-defensibly re-presentations of the received and revealed Torah of Sinai.

It is time to right the balance. That is not by an opposite and equal distortion, namely, re-presenting the theology of Judaism in the last half-century under the aspect of Sinai but not of Auschwitz. No theologian of Judaism has imagined such a vision; it were folly. All theologians of Judaism from 1945 onward have written in full consciousness of the events of 1933 to 1945, and every one of them in every line acknowledged those events. No religious thinking in Judaism has aimed at obscuring or diminishing the dreadful power of the ultimate revelation of evil—the counterpart and opposite of Sinai. But all of those represented in these pages have conducted the theology of Judaism in a different way.

The Holocaust-theologians start where they finish: at Auschwitz. The theologians who transcend catastrophe and move, as time moves, beyond the Holocaust, conduct their thought in a different realm. They surpass calamity and transcend the Holocaust by continuing the ancient and lasting conversation with the Torah, speaking of this morning's headlines in the language of eternity. Specifically, theologians who carry on beyond the Holocaust do so by placing that theology of Judaism in its own, enduring context, under the aspect of Sinai that of course illuminates all life, all time, all being, even unto death. What some have called "the commanding voice of Auschwitz" then is taken in to the commanding voice of Sinai. In this setting, one immense event casts its shadow over all that has come before and over all that will follow; but it is not the whole of time, nor does it set forth the entirety of truth.

Theology

I have throughout used a term not defined at all, "theology." An entire volume in this anthology, the final one, is devoted to the Judaic definition of theology. But to begin with, we turn to the definition of the particular kind of thinking that is represented in these anthologies: theological thinking, not philosophy, not "Jewish thought" (which rarely is defined but generally means Jews thinking about Jewish things), and not history, literature, or anything else but itself.

To state matters simply: theology philosophically sets forth religion. That statement paraphrases the definition of Ingolf U. Dalferth,

> Theology is not philosophy, and philosophy is not a substitute for religious convictions. But whereas religion can exist without philosophy, and philosophy without religion, theology cannot exist without recourse to each of the other two. It rationally reflects on questions arising in pre-theological religious experience and the discourse of faith; and it is the rationality of its reflective labor in the process of faith seeking understanding which inseparably links it with philosophy. For philosophy is essentially concerned with argument and the attempt to solve conceptual problems, and conceptual problems face theology in all areas of its reflective labors.[2]

Accordingly, by the definition of theology that is before us, what we here examine is contemporary Judaic theologians' systematic and rigorous reflection on religious questions, faith seeking understanding through processes of rationality, and sustained and vigorous argument concerning the solution of conceptual problems of a religious character.

To understand the claim of this anthology, a clear definition of theology is required at the very outset. For that purpose I reverse the elements of the definition provided by Dalferth. The predicate becomes the subject in this way:

(1) *where* we have rational reflection on questions arising in religious experience and the discourse of faith,

(2) *there* we have theology.

When we find reflective labor on the rationality—the cogency, harmony, proposition, coherence, balance, order, and proper composition—of statements of religious truth, e.g., truth revealed by God, then we have identified a theological writing. In these pages I present numerous, sustained examples of reflective labor on the rationality of statements of religious truth and consequence: God commands; the Torah teaches; eternal Israel endures. Those three theologoumena encompass the entire theology that Judaism has maintained and today sustains as God's truth. They form Judaism in its theological manifestation.

Concern with argument, the attempt to solve conceptual problems—these characterize that writing. By themselves, of course, they do not mark a writing as theological. Argument concerning conceptual problems yields theology when the argument deals with religion, the conceptual problems derive from revelation. Only the source of the givens of the writing—revelation, not merely reasoned analysis of this world's givens—distinguishes theology from philosophy, including, as a matter of fact, philosophy of religion. But that suffices.

To make this point clear, let me refer to the canonical documents and how they make their points. Take for example that splendid formulation of religion as philosophy, the Mishnah. The Mishnah states its principles through method of natural history, sifting the traits of this-worldly things, demonstrating philosophical truth—the unity of one and unique God at the apex of the natural world—by showing on the basis of the evidence of this world, universally accessible, the hierarchical classification of being. That is a philosophical demonstration of religious truth. The Talmud of Babylonia states its principles through right reasoning about revealed truth, the Torah. The Torah (written, or oral) properly read teaches the theological truth that God is one, at the apex of the hierarchy of all being. That is a theological re-presentation of (the same) religious truth. But that representation in the two Talmuds (and in the Midrash-compilations, not treated here) also exhibits the traits of philosophical thinking: rigor, concern for harmonies, unities, consistencies, points of cogency, sustained argument and counter-argument, appeal to persuasion through reason, not coercion through revelation. In our time, as through the past centuries, in Judaism, the methods of philosophy applied to the data of religious belief and behavior produced theology. The method of philosophy shapes the message of religion into a restatement characterized by rationality and entire integrity.

Since I have made references to the received and classical documents of Judaism, a very brief account of the sources out of which all authentic Judaism thought proceeds is here required. That is important for the understanding of the opening chapter of each of these volumes, which provides the starting point of all Judaic theological thought, which is, the canonical definition of the several categories that form Judaism. A brief account of that authoritative canon must start with the end-product, which is, the Torah as defined at the end of the formation of Judaism.[3] Many people, both Christian and Jewish, take for granted that "Judaism" is pretty much the same thing as "the Old Testament," and if they know the word "Torah" at all, they mean by it "the Pentateuch," the Five Books of Moses: Genesis, Exodus, Leviticus, Numbers, and Deuteronomy.

But Judaism is no more the religion of the Old Testament alone than Christianity is the religion of the New Testament alone. "Torah" for Judaism is the counterpart to "Bible" for Christianity. Just as Christianity reads the Old Testament in the light of the New, so Judaism reads what it knows as "the written Torah" in the complementary and fulfilling setting of "the oral Torah." So to understand the enduring conversations about religious truth that theologian of Judaism conducts, we have to acquire a very exact knowledge of the sources of religious truth that the Torah comprises. What then is this "Torah" that forms "the Bible" for Judaism?

It is the Torah in two media, written and oral. That Torah, called in due course "the one whole Torah of Moses, our rabbi," was formulated and transmitted by God to Moses in two media, each defining one of the components, written and oral. The written is Scripture as we know it, encompassing the Pentateuch, Prophets, and Writings. The oral part of the Torah came to be written down in a variety of works, beginning with the Mishnah, ca. 200 C.E. The canon of the Judaism the theology of which is described here is made up of extensions and amplifications of these two parts of the Torah. The written part is carried forward through collection of readings of verses of Scripture called Midrash-compilations. The oral part is extended through two sustained, selective commentaries and expansions, called talmuds, the Talmud of the Land of Israel, also called the Yerushalmi (c.a. 400 C.E.), and the Talmud of Babylonia, also called the Bavli (ca. 600 C.E.).

In literary terms, then, the formation of Judaism reached its fruition in extensions of the oral Torah and the written Torah. For the oral Torah, the formative age came to its conclusion when the Talmud of Babylonia set for the theological statement of Judaism by expressing the religious convictions of the Talmud of the Land of Israel in accord with a profound reconsideration of the philosophical norms of the Mishnah, around 200. C.E. Joining the method of the Mishnah to the messages of the prior Talmud, the framers of the second Talmud thereby defined the theological, including the legal, norms of Judaism. For the written Torah, the Midrash-compilations of the successive ages, corresponding to the two Talmuds and associated with them, carry forward the same modes of discourse and express in their ways the same hermeneutics.

The Talmud's distinctive hermeneutics, which contains within itself the theology of the Judaism of the dual Torah, is exposed not in so many words but in a page-by-page repetition; it is not articulated but constantly (even tediously) instantiated; we are then supposed to draw our own conclusions. The unique voice of the second of the two Talmuds, the Talmud of Babylonia, which bears the hermeneutic, speaks with full confidence of being heard and understood; and that voice is right; we never can miss the point. For the hermeneutic itself—insistence on the presence of philosophy behind jurisprudence, law behind laws, total harmony among premises of discrete and diverse cases pointing to the unique and harmonious characters of all existence, social and natural—properly understood, bears the theological message: the unity of intellect, the integrity of truth.

As the Mishnah had demonstrated the hierarchical classification of all natural being, pointing at the apex to the One above, so the second Talmud demonstrated the unity of the principles of being set forth in the Torah. The upshot is that Judaism would set forth the religion that defined how humanity was formed "in our image, after our likeness," not to begin with but day by day: in the rules of intellect, the character of mind. We can be like God because we can think the way God thinks, and the natural powers of reason carry us upward to the supernatural origin of the integrity of truth—that sentence sums up what I conceive to be the theological consequence of the Talmud's hermeneutics.

The Talmud of Babylonia therefore forms the pinnacle and the summa—what we mean when we speak of "Judaism"—because from the time of its closure to the present day it defined not only Judaic dogma and its theological formulation but also Judaic discourse that carried that dogma through to formulation in compelling form. Not only so, but the entire documentary heritage of the first six centuries of the Common Era was recast in that Talmud. And that body of writing was itself a recapitulation of important elements of the Hebrew Scriptures and in its basic views indistinguishable in theological and legal character from elements of the Pentateuch's and Prophets' convictions and requirements. Scripture itself ("the written Torah") would reach coming generations not only as read in the synagogue on the Sabbath and festivals, but also, and especially, as recast and expounded in the Talmud in the school houses and courts of the community of Judaism.

Other received documents that had reached closure during that long period of time—the Mishnah, the Tosefta, the Talmud of the Land of Israel itself, the score of Midrash-compilations—furthermore flowed into the Talmud of Babylonia. So each prior writing found its proper position, in due proportion, within the composite of the Bavli. And the Bavli made of the entire heritage of the revealed Torah, oral and written, not a composite but a composition, whole, proportioned, coherent. That is what I mean by "the Talmudic re-presentation," that is, the second Talmud's re-presentation of the Torah given by God to our rabbi, Moses, at Mount Sinai.

That re-presentation was accomplished through one medium: a governing, definitive hermeneutics, the result of applied logic and practical reason when framed in terms of the rules of reading a received and holy book. I need not hide my conviction that the persuasive power of the Talmud's hermeneutics explains the Talmud's success in taking the primary position in the canon of Judaism. That conviction admittedly is subjective, resting as it does on the unprovable premise that ideas and attitudes account of conduct and social policy. But it is the indubitable fact that the second Talmud effected the re-presentation of all that had gone before. Given the Talmud's priority of place among all Judaic writings, before and since for all time, I set forth an objective fact when I maintain that the Talmud also stated in its distinctive way, through its particular hermeneutics, the authoritative theology of the Judaism for which it formed the summa. Religious belief and right behavior to express that belief—both would find definition in its pages, exposition and exegesis in accord with its modes of analytical thought. With the Bavli, the theological text had been inscribed; all the rest was commentary.[4] The commentary would flourish from then to now; the exegesis of that exegesis would define the future history of Judaism.

For the later history of Judaism, from late antiquity to the present day, theology would take a distinctive, and I think, unique form. It provoked rigorous arguments, rather than merely laying out well-defined propositions. In this way it guided the conduct of theological thought, rather than merely defining its propositions and syllogistic goals. When the sages of Judaism chose to make their statements of norms, they began in the Talmud, worked within its categories, framed their ideas in accord with its intellectual discipline, and spoke in its language about its problems. They did so in the (descriptively-valid) conviction that the Talmud had made the full and authoritative statement of the Torah of Sinai, oral, covering the Mishnah and Midrash-compilations, and written, covering Scripture, as well. That is why everything to come would validate itself as a commentary to the text set forth by the Talmud out of all the prior texts that all together comprised the Torah.

It remains to explain that a well-known Judaism is not treated here. Specifically, in this setting, I do not address "the Judaism of Holocaust and Redemption," which from 1967 to the very recent past enjoyed enormous power in the life of American Jews. It was the Judaic religious system formed around the events of the Holocaust in Europe and the creation of the State of Israel, and it held that the principal task of the Jews (not "eternal Israel") is to remain Jewish (without a supernatural definition of what that meant, that is, without a Judaism) and to support through political and philanthropic activity the State of Israel. It was enormously influential among American Jews, accounting to them why they should remain different from gentiles, but defining the difference in this-worldly terms, with no bearing on the conduct of everyday life and affairs. Profoundly secular in every way, that Judaism elicited the kind of devotion that, under other circumstances, religions ordinarily do.

But as a matter of fact, by any definition of religion and theology, that Judaism was no religion and had no theology. It was itself an element in the political and sociology of Americans in general and in its surviving pockets still is a chapter of the politics and sociology of Jewish Americans. "Holocaust and Redemption" writing has no place in the theology of Judaism, except as rigorous theologians have transformed the issues, as they have, into the occasion for profound theological reflection. "The Judaism of Holocaust and Redemption" formed a Judaic system—an account of the way of life, world view, and definition of the social entity of a particular version of "Israel," but even though powerful in Reform and Conservative Judaisms, it was not a Judaic religious system, lacking as it did a serious confrontation with God and with issues of transcendence and holiness.[5]

Clearly, my focus is on issues of faith seeking understanding, the rational, philosophical construction of religious belief. It is not on the facts of who said what; I do not describe what pretty much everybody has thought, and I entirely ignore the institutional embodiments of the faith in the partisan seminaries and organizations of synagogues: Reconstructionist, Orthodox, Reform, Conservative, humanistic, and the like. In these pages the sects of contemporary Judaism play no role at all, because the issues that divide them are trivial and personal. Not only so, but locally-important theologians are not surveyed, since the criteria of selection emphasize the excellence of thought, not the ephemeral influence of the thinker. None of the worldly facts of episodic popularity bears theological consequence; all form mere accidents of local politics and sociology.

Episodically-famous personalities, joined to such institutions and occasions of ritual celebration by them, mean nothing. Mediocrity lays no claim upon the future. We are not here to celebrate platitudes and banalities. Conventional thinking fails the challenges of classical faith, and routine and full minds do not require a hearing that is not compelled by politics. Writers in the English language, and those whose works translated into English, that are not treated here are not neglected; they are rejected. Nor do I choose to pay attention to what by the standards of the Torah are simply heresies, on the one side, or rationalizations for apostasy, on the other. That is why I ignore some local icons, whose writing I find merely homiletical, on the one side, and theologians whose theology consists of the announcement that there is no God, on the other. For different reasons, neither class of theologians of Judaism deserved a hearing when the faithful come together rigorously to analyze the faith.

At stake here are issues alone. And I should maintain the catholic character of the writing, coming as it does from theologians identified with Orthodox, Reform, Conservative, and other Judaisms, resident in the English-speaking world or overseas, justifies that decision. Here ar no party platforms nor partisan voices, celebrated here but unknown there, but rather, sober efforts at purveying truth—God's truth, so far as, in this world, we gain access to it. That is why this anthology presents not a historical-biographical repertoire covering everybody who was around at that time, but a sampler of vivid thinking and provocative, engaged writing. I bear sole responsibility for the judgments represented by inclusion and exclusion; nothing is tacit.

I have chosen writing that means to persuade, not merely inform; writing from heart to heart; writing that sets forth in the medium of words a deeply-felt religious sentiment, attitude, emotion, or conviction. In these pages readers meet embodiments of faith, hope, love for God, in the words of exemplary figures. That is why readers may expect to be not merely informed as to information but invited to participate in the thought and argument of interesting minds in important questions. When people go to a museum formed as a storehouse, they acquire information; they are left inert and unchanged. But when they go to a museum designed to teach, instruct, and engage, they enter into the experience of what is placed on display. They are affected and changed. Here they describe in vigorous advocacy of propositions, fully analyzed, amply documented, the encounter with God that has brought regeneration and renewal after the unparalleled catastrophe of our century.

Endnotes

[1] I have spelled out the many meanings imputed to "Israel" in various Judaic religious systems in my *Judaism and its Social Metaphors. Israel in the History of Jewish Thought* (New York: Cambridge University Press, 1988).

[2] Ingolf U. Dalferth, *Theology and Philosophy* (Oxford: Basil Blackwell Ltd., 1988) vii.

[3] By "Judaism" throughout these pages I mean one Judaic system in particular, the Judaism of the dual Torah, oral and written. The canon of that Judaism in particular is what is described in this and following paragraphs. Other Judaic systems have flourished and do today. Here the focus is upon the system that predominated and now continues, in a variety of modulations, to define Judaism for most practitioners of (a) Judaism, and to provide a principal source for all the others. That operative definition is descriptive, of course. All of the Judaic theologians represented in this anthology appeal to that one canonical literature and acknowledge its authority and authenticity as represented of God's revelation to eternal Israel.

[4] We of course should not ignore the fact that the labor of extension, amplification, application, and commentary in the richest sense went forward, and now goes forward, in a variety of directions. But no contemporary Judaic system begins elsewhere than in the Talmud and the oral part of the Torah represented by it. In the seminaries of all Judaic systems, and in the synagogues of all contemporary Judaisms, the Torah is presented in both the written and the oral components, though, I hasten to add, different Judaisms take up, each its own position on what fits into that entire Torah and how the Torah ia to be received and re-presented.

[5] Reading that Judaism in its correct, secular framework, I have dealt with that matter at some length in *Stranger at Home. Zionism, "The Holocaust," and American Judaism* (Chicago: University of Chicago Press, 1980).

Chapter 1

Four Responses to Catastrophe in Formative Judaism*

Jacob Neusner

Before we consider contemporary responses to the Holocaust, we gain perspective by examining how, at the time of the destruction of the Temple of Jerusalem in 70 C.E., several Judaic systems interpreted the events of the day. These are the responses of Apocalyptic thinkers, the Essenes of Qumran, the Christians, who at that time formed part of the people, Israel, and the Rabbis who in time would define the Judaism of the dual Torah. Two points are striking.

First, all Judaic thinkers took for granted that the tragic events conveyed God's will and judgement. The heritage of prophecy guided each group, and the message of prophecy left no room for doubt on that point. But, second, each Judaic system drew conclusions consistent with its larger view of matters, and while everyone's positions rested on a single, common premise, no response to catastrophe went over the ground of any other. The catastrophe presented the occasion for deep thinking about not the past but the future, and the two great religions that began at that time—Christianity and Judaism, as the West would come to know them—responded to the crisis with fresh and original thought.

When we consider the reading of the Holocaust that occupies this volume, we shall find ourselves at home among thinkers who transformed crises into the occasion of renewal and so accomplished the rebirth, beyond the gates of Hell, of Israel, the eternal people.

***

The destruction of the second temple marked a major turning in the history of Judaism in late antiquity. The end of the cult of animal sacrifice, which from remote times had supplied a chief means of service of God, placed the worldly modes of divine worship upon a quite new foundation. The loss of the building itself was of considerable consequence, for the return to Zion and the rebuilding of the Temple in the sixth and fifth centuries B.C.E. had long been taken to mean that Israel and God, supposed by prophecy to have been estranged from one another because of idolatry in first-temple-times, had been reconciled. Finally, the devastation of Jerusalem, the locus of

*From "Emergent Rabbinic Judaism in a Time of Crisis: Four Responses to the Destruction of the Second Temple," *JUDAISM* 21, 3 (1972): 313-27. Reprinted by permission of American Jewish Congress.

cult and Temple piety, intensified the perplexity of the day, for, from ancient times, the city, as much as what took place in its Temple, was holy. The cultic altar, the Temple and the holy city, by August, 70, lay in ruins—a considerable calamity.

My purpose is to survey some of the several ways in which individuals and groups of Jews of that day responded to calamity. I do not propose new interpretations of individual texts or promise to present previously unknown facts, but, rather, hope, by putting together a number of hitherto unconnected data, to facilitate the comparison of the different forms of Judaism of the period.

The Political Problem

What kind of issue faced the Jews after the destruction of the Temple? It was, I contend, a fundamentally social and religious issue, not a matter of government or politics.

For most historians of the Jews, it is axiomatic that the destruction of Jerusalem and its Temple in 70 C.E. marked a decisive political turning-point. For example, current rhetoric uses the year 70 as the date for the end of "Jewish self-government." Precisely what is meant by that rhetorical flourish is difficult to determine. If one means the end of Jewish independent government in Palestine, then that came to an end with the procurators, and, one might say, even with the advent of Herod. So the importance of the date must be located elsewhere. The Jews continued to govern themselves, much as they had in procuratorial times, though through different institutions, long after 70 C.E. Patriarchal government finally ended at the start of the 5th century—a matter of Byzantine policy—but by that time large numbers of Jews had already left the land, and their institutions of self-government persisted in the countries of their dispersion.

Then we must say that the significant event was the destruction of the Temple. But long before 70 the Temple had been rejected by some Jewish groups. Its sanctity, as we shall see, had been arrogated by others. And for large numbers of ordinary Jews outside of Palestine, as well as substantial numbers within, the Temple was a remote and, if holy, unimportant place. For them, piety was fully expressed through synagogue worship. In a very real sense, therefore, for the Christian Jews, who were indifferent to the Temple cult, for the Jews at Qumran, who rejected the Temple, for the Jews of Leontopolis, in Egypt, who had their own Temple, but especially for the masses of diasporan Jews who never saw the Temple to begin with, but served God through synagogue worship alone, the year 70 cannot be said to have marked an important change.

The diasporan Jews accommodated themselves to their distance from the Temple by "spiritualizing" and "moralizing" the cult, as with Philo. To be sure, Philo was appropriately horrified at the thought of the Temple's desecration by Caligula, but I doubt that his religious life would have been greatly affected had the Temple been destroyed in his lifetime. For the large Babylonian Jewish community, we have not much evidence that the situation was any different. They were evidently angered by the Romans' destruction of the Temple, so that Josephus had to address them with an account of events exculpating Rome from guilt for the disaster. But Babylonian Jewry did absolutely nothing before 70 C.E. to support the Palestinians, and, thereafter, are not heard from. The Babylonian and Mesopotamian Jews' great war against Rome, in Trajan's time, was not the result of the Temple's destruction, but, in my opinion, of Trajan's evident plan to rearrange the international trade routes to their disadvantage. Nor does one hear of any support from the diaspora for Bar Kokhba, so apparently no one was ready to help him reestablish the Temple in a new Jerusalem. At any rate, the political importance of the events of 70 cannot be taken for granted. It was significant primarily for the religious life of various Palestinian Jewish groups, not to mention the ordinary folk who had made pilgrimages to Jerusalem and could do so no more.

We shall examine four responses to the challenges of the destruction of Jerusalem, the end of the Temple, and the cessation of the cult. These responses had to deal with several crucial social and religious problems, all interrelated. First, how to achieve atonement without the cult? Second, how to explain the disaster of the destruction? Third, how to cope with the new age, to devise a way of life on a new basis entirely? Fourth, how to account for the new social forms consequent upon the collapse of the old social structure?

The four responses are of, first, the apocalyptic writers represented in the visions of Baruch and II Ezra; second, the Dead Sea community; third, the Christian church; and finally, the Pharisaic sect.

When the apocalyptic visionaries looked backward upon the ruins, they saw a tragic vision. So they emphasized future, supernatural redemption, which they believed was soon to come. The Qumranians had met the issues of 70 long before in a manner essentially similar to that of the Christians. Both groups tended to abandon the Temple and its cult and to replace them by means of the new community, on the one hand, and the service or pious rites of the new community, on the other. The Pharisees come somewhere between the first and the second and third groups. They saw the destruction as a calamity, like the apocalyptics, but they also besought the means, in both social forms and religious expression, to provide a new way of atonement and a new form of divine service, to constitute a new, interim Temple, like the Dead Sea sect and the Christians.

The Apocalyptic Response

Two documents, the Apocalypse of Ezra and the Vision of Baruch, are representative of the apocalyptic state of mind. The compiler of the Ezra apocalypse (II Ezra 3–14), who lived at the end of the first century, looked forward to a day of judgment, when the Messiah would destroy Rome and God would govern the world. But he had not removed the inclination to do evil, so men could not carry out God's will:

> For we and our fathers have passed our lives in ways that bring death. . . . But what is man, that thou art angry with him, or what is a corruptible race, that thou art so bitter against it? . . . (Ezra 8:26)

Ezra was told that God's ways are inscrutable (4:10-11), but when he repeated the question, "Why has Israel been given over to the gentiles as a reproach?" he was given the answer characteristic of this literature—that a new age was dawning which would shed light on such perplexities. Thus he was told:

> . . . if you are alive, you will see, and if you live long, you will often marvel, because the age is hastening swiftly to its end. For it will not be able to bring the things that have been promised to the righteous in their appointed time, because this age is full of sadness and infirmities. . . . (4:10-26)

An angel told him the signs of the coming redemption, saying:

> . . . the sun shall suddenly shine forth at night and the moon during the day, blood shall drip from wood, and the stone shall utter its voice, the peoples shall be troubled, and the stars shall fall. . . . (5:4-5)

And he was admonished to wait patiently:

> The righteous therefore can endure difficultcircumstances, while hoping for easier ones, but those who have done wickedly have suffered the difficult circumstances, and will *not* see easier ones. (6:55-56)

The pseudepigraphic Ezra thus regarded the catastrophe as the fruit of sin, more specifically, the result of man's *natural* incapacity to do the will of God. He prayed for forgiveness and found hope in the coming transformation of the age and the promise of a new day, when man's heart would be as able, as his mind even then was willing, to do the will of God.

The pseudepigraph in the name of Jeremiah's secretary, Baruch, likewise brought promise of coming redemption, but with little practical advice for the intervening period. The document exhibited three major themes. First, God acted righteously in bringing about the punishment of Israel:

> Righteousness belongs to the Lord our God, but confusion of face to us and our fathers. . . (Baruch 2:6)

Second, the catastrophe came on account of Israel's sin:

> Why is it, O Israel . . . that you are in the land of your enemies? You have forsaken the fountain of wisdom. If you had walked in the way of the Lord, you would be dwelling in peace forever. (3:10-12)

Third, as surely as God had punished the people, so certainly would He bring the people home to their land and restore their fortunes. Thus Jerusalem speaks:

> But I, how can I help you? For He who brought these calamities upon you will deliver you from the hand of your enemies. . . . For I sent you out with sorrow and weeping, but God will give you back to me with joy and gladness forever . . . (4:17-18, 23)

Finally, Baruch advised the people to wait patiently for redemption, saying:

> My children, endure with patience the wrath that has come upon you from God. Your enemy has overtaken you, but you will soon see their destruction and will tread upon their necks. . . . For just as you purposed to go astray from God, return with tenfold zeal to seek Him. For He who brought these calamities upon you will bring you everlasting joy with your salvation. Take courage, O Jerusalem, for He who named you will comfort you. (4:25, 28-30)

The saddest words written in these times come in 2 Baruch:

> Blessed is he who was not born, or he who having been born has died
> But as for us who live, woe unto us
> Because we see the afflictions of Zion and what has befallen Jerusalem . . .
> (10:6-7)

> You husbandmen, sow not again.
> And earth, who do you give your harvest fruits?
> Keep within yourself the sweets of your sustenance.
> And you, vine, why do you continue to give your wine?
> For an offering will not again be made therefrom in Zion,

Nor will first-fruits again be offered.
And do you, O heavens, withhold your dew,
And open not the treasuries of rain.
And do you, sun, withhold the light of your rays,
And you, moon, extinguish the multitude of your light.
For why should light rise again
Where the light of Zion is darkened? . . .
(10:9-12)

Would that you had ears, O earth,
And that you had a heart, O dust,
That you might go and announce in Sheol,
And say to the dead,
"Blessed are you more than we who live."
(11:6-7)

Yohanan ben Zakkai's student, Joshua, met such people. It was reported that when the Temple was destroyed, ascetics multiplied in Israel, who would neither eat flesh nor drink wine. Rabbi Joshua dealt with them thus:

> He said to them, "My children, On what account do you not eat flesh and drink wine?"
> They said to him, "Shall we eat meat, from which they used to offer a sacrifice on the altar, and now it is no more? And shall we drink wine, which was poured out on the altar, and now it is no more?"
> He said to them, "If so, we ought not to eat bread, for there are no meal offerings any more. Perhaps we ought not to drink water, for the water-offerings are not brought anymore."
> They were silent.
> He said to them, "My children, come and I shall teach you. Not to mourn at all is impossible, for the evil decree has already come upon us. But to mourn too much is also impossible, for one may not promulgate a decree for the community unless most of the community can endure it. . . . But thus have the sages taught: 'A man plasters his house, but leaves a little piece untouched. A man prepares all the needs of the meal, but leaves out some morsel. A woman prepares all her cosmetics, but leaves off some small item.'"
> (b. *Bava Batra* 60b)

The response of the visionaries is, thus, essentially negative. All they had to say is that God is just and Israel has sinned, but, in the end of time, there will be redemption. What to do in the meantime? Merely wait. Not much of an answer.

The Dead Sea Sect

For the Dead Sea Community, the destruction of the Temple cult took place long before 70 C.E. By rejecting the Temple and its cult, the Qumran community had had to confront a world without Jerusalem even while the city was still standing. In so stating matters, I am repeating the insight of my sometime colleague. Professor Yigael Yadin, who remarked to me that the spiritual situation of Yavneh, the community formed by the Pharisaic rabbis after the destruction of the Temple in 70, and that of Qumran, are strikingly comparable.

Just as the rabbis had to construct—at least for the time being—a Judaism without the Temple cult, so did the Qumran sectarians have to construct a Judaism without the Temple cult. The difference, of course, is that the rabbis merely witnessed the destruction of the city by others, while the Qumran sectarians did not lose the Temple, but rejected it at the outset.

The founders of the community were Temple priests, who saw themselves as continuators of the true priestly line, that is, the sons of Saddok. For them the old Temple was, as it were, destroyed in the times of the Maccabees. Its cult was defiled, not by the Romans, but by the rise of a high priest from a family other than theirs. They further rejected the calendar followed in Jerusalem. They therefore set out to create a new Temple, until God would come and, through the Messiah in the line of Aaron, would establish the Temple once again. As Bertil Gartner points out (in *The Temple and the Community in Qumran and the New Testament. A Comparative Study in the Temple Symbolism in the Qumran Texts and the new Testament* [Cambridge: University Press, 1965], 15), "Once the focus of holiness in Israel had ceased to be the Temple, it was necessary to provide a new focus. This focus was the community, which called itself 'the Holy place' and 'the holy of holies.'" Thus, the Qumran community believed that the presence of God had left Jerusalem and had come to the Dead Sea. The *community* now constituted the new Temple, just as some elements in early Christianity saw the new Temple in the body of Christ, in the Church, the Christian community. In some measure, this represents a "spiritualization" of the old Temple, for the Temple, as Gartner points out, was the community, and the Temple worship was effected through the community's study and fulfillment of the Torah. But, as Gartner stresses (18), the community was just as much a reality, a presence, as was the Jerusalem Temple; the obedience to the law was no less real that the blood sacrifices. Thus, the Qumranians represent a middle point, between reverence for the old Temple and its cult, in the here and now, and complete indifference to the Temple and cult in favor of the Christians' utter spiritualization of both, represented, for example, in the Letter to the Hebrews.

If the old Temple is destroyed, then how will Israel make atonement? The Qumranian answer, Gartner tells us, is that "the life of the community in perfect obedience to the Law is represented as the true sacrifice offered in the new Temple." The community thus takes over the holiness and the functions of the Temple (44) and, so, is the "only means of maintaining the holiness of Israel and making atonement for sin."

> When these things come to pass in Israel according to all these laws, it is for the foundation of the holy spirit, for eternal truth, for the atonement of the guilt of sin and misdeeds, and for the well-being of the land by means of the flesh of burnt offerings and the fat of sacrifices, that is, the right offerings of the lips as a righteous sweet savour and a perfect way of life as a free-will offering, pleasing to God . . . (Manual of Discipline 9:3ff.)

The response of the Dead Sea sect, therefore, was to reconstruct the Temple and to reinterpret the nature and substance of sacrifice. The community constituted the reconstructed Temple. The life of Torah and obedience to its commandments formed the new sacrifice.

The Christian Community

The study of Judaism in the late antiquity comprehends a considerable part of early Christian experience, simply because for a long time in Palestine, as well as in much of the diaspora, the Christian was another kind of Jew and saw himself as such. Moreover, the Christians, whether originally Jewish or otherwise, took over the antecedent holy books and much of the ritual life of Judaism. For our purposes they serve, therefore, as another form of Judaism, one which differed from the rest primarily in regarding the world as having been redeemed through the Word and Cross of Jesus. But one must hasten to stress the complexity of the Christian evidences. Indeed, the response of the Christians to the destruction of the Temple cannot be simplified and regarded as essentially unitary.

Because of their faith in the crucified and risen Christ, Christians experienced the end of the old cult and the old Temple before it actually took place, much like the Qumran sectarians. They had to work out the meaning of the sacrifice of Jesus on the cross, and whether the essays on that central problem were done before or after 70 is of no consequence. The issues of August, 70, confronted Qumranians and Christians for other than narrowly historical reasons; for both the events of that month took place, so to speak, in other than military and political modes. But the effects were much the same. The Christians, therefore, resemble the Qumranians in having had to face the end of the cult before it actually took place, but they were like the Pharisees in having to confront the actual destruction of the Temple, here and now.

Like the Qumranians, the Christian Jew criticized the Jerusalem Temple and its cult. Both groups in common believed that the last days had begun. Both believed that God had come to dwell with them, as he had once dwelled in the Temple (Gärtner, 100). The sacrifices of the Temple were replaced, therefore, by the sacrifices of a blameless life and by other spiritual deeds. But the Christians differ on one important point. To them, the final sacrifice had already take place; the perfect priest had offered up the perfect holocaust, his own body. So for the Christians, Christ on the cross completed the old sanctity and inaugurated the new. This belief took shape in different ways. For Paul, in 1 Cor 3:16-17, the Church is the new Temple, Christ is the foundation of the "spiritual" building. Ephesians 2:18ff. has Christ as the corner-stone of the new building, the company of Christians constituting the Temple.

Lloyd Gaston (in *No Stone on Another: Studies in the Significance of the Fall of Jerusalem in the Synoptic Gospels* [Leiden: E.J. Brill, 1970], 97ff.) has persuasively argued that the Jerusalem Christians probably did not continue to worship in the Temple. Jesus was fundamentally indifferent to the cult, and, for him, Gaston claims (p. 240), the functions of the old Temple were to be fulfilled in the new Temple which Jesus had come to found. That new Temple was, as at Qumran, the community, not himself alone. Gaston says that the church, from the beginning, was uninvolved in the cult of the Temple. For the Christians long before 70, as much as for those coming later on, the Temple had ceased to exist as a holy place. But, unlike the Qumranian community, the Christian Jews continued to revere Jerusalem as the holy city—an important distinction. The Temple, before 70, served as the focus of Israel's national cult; it was, therefore, to be used as a place of proclamation of the Gospel. But while the early Christians felt a solidarity with Israel the people, with Jerusalem, and with the Temple, to them the cult of the Temple was meaningless, for the forgiveness of sins had taken place once for all through the last sacrifice, which rendered the continuation of the cult a matter of indifference.

Perhaps the single most coherent statement of the Christian view of cult comes in Hebrews. Whether or not Hebrews is representative of many Christians or comes as early as 70 is not our concern. What is striking is that the Letter explores the great issue of 70, the issues of cult, Temple, sacrifice, priesthood, atonement, and redemption. Its author takes for granted that the church is the Temple, that Jesus is the builder of the Temple, and that he is also the perfect priest and the final and most unblemished sacrifice. Material sacrifices might suffice for the ceremonial cleansing of an earthly sanctuary, a sacrifice different in kind and better in degree is called for (F. F. Bruce, "Hebrew," *Peake's Commentary on the Bible,* ed. Matthew Black and H. H. Rowley [London: Thomas Nelson and Sons, Ltd., 1962], 1015). It is Jesus who is that perfect sacrifice, who has entered the true, heavenly sanctuary and now represents his people before God: "By his death he has consecrated the new covenant together with the heavenly sanctuary itself." Therefore, no further sacrifice—his or others'—is needed.

The Pharisees Before 70

We know very little about the Pharisees before the time of Herod. During Maccabean days, according to Josephus, our sole reliable evidence, they appear as a political par- ty, competing with the Sadducees, another party, for control of the court and govern- ment: Afterward, they all but fade out of Josephus's narrative. But the later rabbinical literature fills the gap—with what degree of reliability I do not here wish to say—and tells a great many stories about Pharisaic masters from Shammai and Hillel. These circles of disciples seem to have flourished in the first century, down to 70 and beyond.

The legal materials attributed by later rabbis to the pre-70 Pharisees are thema- tically congruent to the stories and sayings about Pharisees in the New Testament Gospels, and I take them to be accurate in substance, if not in detail, as represen- tations of the main issues of Pharisaic law. After 70, the masters of Yavneh seem to have included a predominant element of Pharisees, and the post-70 rabbis assuredly regarded themselves as the continuators of Pharisaism. Yohanan ben Zakkai, who first stood at the head of the Yavnean circle, was later once said to have been a disciple of Hillel. More credibly, Gamaliel II, who succeeded Yohanan as head of the Yav- nean institution, is regarded as the grandson of Gamaliel, a Pharisee in the council of the Temple who is mentioned in Acts 5:34 in connection with the trial of Paul. In all, therefore, we shall have to regard the Yavnean rabbis as successors of the pre-70 Pharisees and treat the two as a single sect, or kind, of Judaism.

What was the dominant trait of Pahrisaism before 70? It was, as depicted both in the rabbinic traditions about the Pharisees and in the Gospels, concern for certain matters or rite, in particular, eating one's meals in a state of ritual purity as if one were a Temple priest, and carefully giving the required tithes and offerings due to the priesthood. The Gospels' agenda on Pharisaism also added fasting, Sabbath- observance, vows and oaths, and the like, but the main point was keeping the ritual purity when they carried out the requirements of the cult. To be sure, the Gospels al- so included a fair amount of hostile polemic, some of it rather extreme, but these intra-Judaic matters are not our concern. All one may learn from the accusations, for instance, that the Pharisees were a brood of vipers, morally blind, sinners, and un- faithful, is one fact. Christian Jews and Pharisaic Jews were at odds.

The Pharisees, thus, were those Jews who believed that one must keep the purity laws outside of the Temple. Other Jews, following the plain sense of Leviticus, sup- posed that purity laws were to be kept only in the Temple, where the priests has to enter a state of ritual purity in order to carry out the requirements of the cult, such as animal sacrifice. They also had to eat their Temple food in a state of ritual purity, but lay people did not. To be sure, everyone who went to the Temple had to be ritually pure, but outside of the Temple the laws of ritual purity were not observed, for it was not required that noncultic activities be conducted in a state of Levitical cleanness.

But, as I said, the Pharisees held, to the contrary, that even outside of the Temple, in one's home, one had to follow the laws of ritual purity in the only circumstance in which they might apply, namely, at the table. They therefore held one must eat his secular food, that is, ordinary, everyday meals, in a state of ritual purity *as if one were a Temple priest*. The Pharisees thus arrogated to themselves—and to all Jews equally—the status of the Temple priests and did the things which priests must do on account of that status. The table of every Jew in his home was seen to be like the table of the Lord in the Jerusalem Temple. The commandment, "You shall be a kingdom of priests and a holy people," was taken literally. The whole country was holy. The table of every man possessed the same order of sanctity as the table of the cult. But, at this time, only the Pharisees held such a viewpoint, and eating unconsecrated food as if one were a Temple priest at the Lord's table thus was one of the two significations that a Jew was a Pharisee, a sectarian.

The other was meticulous tithing. The laws of tithing and related agricultural taboos may have been kept primarily by the Pharisees. Here we are not certain. Pharisees clearly regarded keeping the agricultural rules as a chief religious duty. But whether, to what degree, and how other Jews did so, is not clear. Both the agricultural laws and purity rules in the end affected table-fellowship: *How and what one may eat.* That is, they were "dietary laws."

We see, therefore, that the Dead Sea Sect, the Christian Jews, and the Pharisees all stressed the eating of ritual meals. But while the Qumranians and the Christians tended to oppose sacrifice as such, and to prefer to achieve forgiveness of sin through ritual baths and communion meals, the Pharisees before 70 continued to revere the Temple and its cult, and afterward they drew up the laws which would govern the Temple when it would be restored. In the meantime, they held that (b. *Berakhot* 55a), "As long as the Temple stood, the altar atoned for Israel. But now a man's table atones for him."

The Pharisees never opposed the Temple, though they were critical of the priesthood. While it stood, they seem to have accepted the efficacy of the cult for the atonement of sins, and in this regard, as in others, they were more loyal to what they took to be the literal meaning of Scripture. More radical groups moved far beyond that meaning, either through rejecting its continued validity, as in the Christian view, or through taking over the cult through their own commune, as in the Qumran view.

While the early Christians gathered for ritual meals, and made them the climax of their group life, the Pharisees apparently did not. What expressed the Pharisees' sense of self-awareness as a group apparently was not a similarly intense, ritual meal. Eating was not a ritualized occasion, even though the Pharisees had liturgies to be said at the meal. No communion-ceremony, no rites centered on meals, no specification of meals on holy occasions, characterize Pharisaic table-fellowship.

Pharisaic table-fellowship thus was a quite ordinary, everyday affair. The various fellowship-rules had to be observed on a wholly routine circumstance—daily, at every meal, without accompanying rites, other than a benediction for the food. Unlike the Pharisees, the Christians' myths and rituals rendered table-fellowship into a much heightened spiritual experience: *Do these things in memory of me.* The Pharisees told no stories about purity laws, except (in later times) to account for their historical development (e.g. who had decreed which purity-rule?). When they came to the table, so far as we know, they told no stories about how Moses had done what they now do, and they did not "do these things in memory of Moses our rabbi."

In the Dead Sea commune, table-fellowship was open upon much the same basis as among the Pharisees: appropriate undertaking to keep ritual purity and to consume properly grown and tithed foods. As we know it, the Qumranian meal was liturgically not much different from the ordinary Pharisaic gatherings. The rites pertained to, and derived from, the eating of food and that alone.

The Dead Sea sect's meal would have had some similarity to the Christian Eucharist if it had included some sort of narrative about the Temple cult, stories about how the sect replicated the holy Temple and ate at the table of God, how the founder of the community had transferred the Temple's holiness out of unclean Jerusalem, how the present officiants stood in the place of the High Priest of Jerusalem, how the occasion called to mind dome holy event of the past, and comparable tales. But we have no allusions to the inclusion of such mythic elements in the enactment of the community meal. Josephus's Essenes have a priest pray before the meal and afterward: "At the beginning and the end they do honor to God as the provider of life." This seems to me no different from the Pharisaic table-rite. The primary difference is the prominence of priests in the life of the group. The table-fellowship of Qumranians and Pharisees thus exhibits less of a ritual embodiment of sacred myth than does that of the early Christians.

On the other hand, both Christians and Pharisees lived among ordinary folk while the Qumranians did not. In this respect the common-place character of Pharisaic table-fellowship is all the more striking. The sect ordinarily did not gather *as a group* at all, but in the home. All meals required ritual purity. Pharisaic table-fellowship took place in the same circumstances as did all non-ritual table-fellowship: common folk ate everyday meals in an everyday way, among ordinary neighbors who were not members of the sect. They were engaged in workaday pursuits like everyone else.

The setting for law-observance was the field and the kitchen, the bed and the street. The occasion for observance was set every time a person picked up a common nail, which might be unclean, or purchased a *se'ah* of wheat, which had to be tithed—by himself, without priests to bless his deeds or sages to instruct him. Keeping the Pharisaic rule required neither an occasional exceptional rite at, but external to, the meal, as in the Christian sect, nor taking up residence in a monastic commune, as in the Qumranian sect in Judaism. Instead, it imposed the perpetual ritualization of daily life, on the one side, and the constant, inner awareness of the communal order of being, on the other.

The Pharisees after 70: The Rabbinic Reformulation

The response of the Pharisees to the destruction of the Temple is known to us only from rabbinic materials, which underwent revisions over many centuries. A story about Yohanan ben Zakkai and his disciple, Joshua ben Hananiah, tells us in a few words the main outline of the Pharisaic-rabbinic view of the destruction:

> Once, as Rabban Yohanan ben Zakkai was coming forth from Jerusalem, Rabbi Joshua followed after him and beheld the Temple in ruins.
> "Woe unto us," Rabbi Joshua cried, "that this, the place where the iniquities of Israel were atoned for, is laid waste!"
> "My son," Rabban Yohanan said to him, "be not grieved. We have another atonement as effective as this. And what is it? It is acts of lovingkindness, as it is said, *For I desire mercy and not sacrifice*."
>
> [Hos. 6:6] (*Avot de Rabbi Natan*, Chap. 6)

How shall we relate the arcane rules about ritual purity to the public calamity faced by the heirs of the Pharisees at Yavneh? What connection between the ritual purity of the "kingdom of priests" and the atonement of sins in the Temple?

To Yohanan ben Zakkai, preserving the Temple was not an end in itself. He taught that there was another means of reconciliation between God and Israel, so that the Temple and its cult were not decisive. What really counted in the life of the Jewish people? Torah, piety (We should add, Torah as taught by the Pharisees and, later on, by the rabbis, their continuators.) For the zealots and messianists of the day, the answer was power, politics, the right to live under one's own rulers.

What was the will of God? It was doing deeds of lovingkindness: "I desire mercy, not sacrifice" (Hos. 6:6) meant to Yohanan, "We have a means of atonement as effective as the Temple, and it is doing deeds of lovingkindness." Just as willingly as men would contribute bricks and mortar for the rebuilding of a sanctuary, so they ought to contribute renunciation, self-sacrifice, love, for the building of a sacred community. Earlier, Pharisaism had held that the Temple should be everywhere, even in the home and the hearth. Now Yohanan taught that sacrifice greater than the Temple's must characterize the life of the community. If one were to do something for God in a time when the Temple was no more, the offering must be the gift of selfless compassion. The holy altar must be the streets and marketplaces of the world, as, formerly, the purity of the Temple had to be observed in the streets and marketplaces of Jerusalem. In a sense, therefore, by making the laws of ritual purity incumbent upon the ordinary Jew, the Pharisees already had effectively limited the importance of the Temple and its cult. The earlier history of the Pharisaic sect thus had laid the groundwork for Yohanan ben Zakkai's response to Joshua ben Hananiah. It was a natural conclusion for one nurtured in a movement based upon the priesthood of all Israel.

Why did Yohanan ben Zakkai come to such an interpretation of the meaning of life of Israel, the Jewish people? Because he was a Pharisee, and the Pharisaic party had long ago reached that same conclusion. Though it had begun as a political party, not much different from other such groups in Maccabean times, toward the end of the Maccabean period the party faced the choice of remaining in politics and suffering annihilation, or giving up politics and continuing in a very different form. On the surface, the Pharisees' survival, the achievement of Hillel and his response to the challenge of Herod, tells us that the choice had been made to abandon politics. But that is not the whole answer.

The Pharisees determined to concentrate on what they believed was really important in politics, and that was the fulfillment of all the laws of the Torah, even ritual tithing, and the elevation of the life of the people, even at home and in the streets, to what the Torah had commanded: *You shall be a kingdom of priests and a holy people.* A kingdom in which everyone was a priest, a people all of whom were holy —a community which would live as if it were always in the Temple sanctuary of Jerusalem. Therefore, the purity laws, so complicated and inconvenient, were extended to the life of every Jew in his own home. The Temple altar in Jerusalem would be replicated at the table of all Israel. To be sure, only a small minority of the Jewish people, to begin with, obeyed the law as taught by the Pharisaic party. Therefore, the group had to reconsider the importance of political life, through which the law might everywhere be effected. The party which had abandoned politics for piety now had to recover access to the instruments of power for the sake of piety. It was the way toward realization of what was essentially not a political aspiration.

The Outcome

Of the four responses briefly outlined here, only the ones associated with the Christians and the Pharisees produced important historical consequences. The visionaries who lamented the past and hoped for near redemption enjoyed considerable success in sharing their vision with other Jews. The result was the Bar Kokhba War, but no redemption followed; rather, severe repression for a time. Then the Pharisees' continuators, the rabbis led by the patriarch, gained complete control within the Jewish community of Palestine, and their program of attempting to make all Jews into priests, which to them meant into rabbis, was gradually effected.

The Qumran community did not survive the war, but its viewpoint seems to have persisted within the complex of Christian churches. For the Christians, the events of August, 70, were not difficult to explain. Jesus had earlier predicted that the Temple would be destroyed; the Jews' own words had convicted them, as Matthew, writing in the aftermath of 70, claims, "Our blood be upon our own heads." But the new Temple and the new cult would go forward. The picture is complex, involving Jesus, become Christ, or the Church, embodying the new Temple, but the outcome is clear. The events of 70 served to confirm the new faith, and the faith itself supplied a new set of images to take over and exploit the symbols of the old cult.

The destruction of the Temple, Jerusalem, and the cult therefore marked a considerable transformation in the antecedent symbolic structures of Judaism. The ancient symbols were emptied of their old meanings and filled with new ones; they continued formally unchanged but substantively in no way the same.

Part One
Defining Terms

Chapter 2

The Holocaust
in the Context of Judaism*

Jonathan Sacks

The fact remains that the problem of evil comes to the surface with a special urgency when we contemplate the Holocaust. The issue of the character of humanity, capable of such events, compelled attention. Jonathan Sacks here focuses our attention on the issue of the radical evil of humanity, and he does so with all the necessary specificity. The Holocaust here becomes concrete and immediate, the issue of where was God is framed in authentic, human terms. The further issue of Israel's covenant with God is spelled out, and a review of proposed explanations—sins and atonement, repentance and reconciliation—reminds us of the classical responses to catastrophe and evil, now not abstractions but immediate events and present moments.

It is no credit to German Protestant Christianity that, in 1948, meeting at Darmstadt, Evangelical Lutheran theologians invoked the explanation that the Holocaust was the work of God, penalizing Israel, the holy people, for its rejection of Jesus Christ. The Christianity that could justify the Holocaust as the penalty for Jews' enduring loyalty to the Torah hardly showed the world a winning face. Indeed, coming from the very people who three years earlier were active participants in the German war effort, that appeal to Israel to accept salvation from the hand of murderers and their accomplices underscored the mystery of the moment: How could people of conscience, speaking in the name of Christianity, so profoundly miss the very point of their own existence? Their appeal carried with it a self-righteous justification: The Holocaust really did God's work, and so did the Germans. A Christianity of such character won justifiably little respect in the world beyond Germany and certainly did not speak for Roman Catholic or much of Protestant Christian theological opinion. But it does form part of the theological record.

*From "The Valley of the Shadow," *Crisis and Covenant: Jewish Thought after the Holocaust.* Copyright © 1992 by Modern Jewish Studies Fund and Jonathan Sacks. Reprinted by permission of Manchester University Press.

Sack's introduction to Holocaust theology sets the stage for our sustained read-ing of the two principal constructive theologians, Eliezer Berkovits and Emil Facken-heim, for whom the Holocaust formed the center of thought.

***

Judaism has its silences, Elie Wiesel once said, but we don't speak about them. After the Holocaust, the *shoah*, there was one of the great silences of Jewish history.

A third of world Jewry had gone up in flames. Entire worlds—the bustling Jewish townships of Eastern Europe, the talmudic academies, the courts of Jewish mystics, the Yiddish-speaking masses, the urbane Jews of Germany, the Jews of Poland who had lived among their Gentile neighbours for 800 years, the legendary synagogues and houses of study—all were erased. A guard at Auschwitz, testifying at the Nuremburg trial, explained that at the height of the genocide, when the camp was turning 10,000 Jews a day into ashes, children were thrown into the furnaces alive. When the destruction was over, a pillar of cloud marked the place where Europe's Jews had once been; and there was a silence that consumed all words.

More had died in the Final Solution than Jews. It was as if the image of God that is man had died also. We know in retrospect that Jews—both victims and survivors—simply could not believe what was happening. Since the Enlightenment they had come to have faith that a new order was in the making. The age-old teachings of contempt for the chosen-or-rejected people were at an end, they believed, and in their place would come a rational utopia.

It is hard in retrospect to imagine that sense of almost religious wonder which German Jews felt for the country of Goethe, Beethoven and Immanuel Kant. The Christian anti-Judaism might mutate into the monster of racial anti-Semitism, that a Vatican might be silent as the covenantal people went to its crucifixion; that chamber music might be played over the cries of burning children; that the rational utopia might be *Judenrein*: these, for the enlightened Jews of Europe, were the ultimately unthinkable thoughts. Since the early nineteenth century, humanity had seemed to many Jews a safer bet that God; and it was that faith that was murdered in the camps. Where was man at Auschwitz?

But where, too, was God? That He was present seemed a blasphemy; that He was absent, even more so. How could He have been there, punishing the righteous and the children for sins, their own or someone else's? But how could He *not* have been there, when, from the valley of the shadow of death, they called out to Him?

Jewish faith sees God in history. But here was a definitive, almost terminal, moment in Jewish history, and where was God's hand and His saving, outstretched arm? It seemed as if the *shoah* must have, yet could not have, religious meaning.

Wiesel has written of that time: 'Never shall I forget those moments which murdered my God and my soul and turned my dreams to dust. Never shall I forget these things, even if I am condemned to live as long as God Himself.' But to whom could one speak of these things so much larger than man, if not to God? It was a crisis of faith without precedent in the annals of belief. If God existed, how was Auschwitz possible? But if God did not exist, how was humanity after Auschwitz credible?

Covenant and Refutation

There is a line of theological reasoning which argues that a single moment of innocent suffering is as inexplicable as attempted genocide. Abraham, faced with the proposed destruction of the cities of the plain, had prayed, 'Far be it from You to do such a thing, to bring death upon the innocent as well as the guilty, so that innocent and guilty fare alike. Far be it from You! Shall not the Judge of all the earth deal justly?'[1] Abraham began his famous dialogue with the possibility that there might be fifty innocent individuals; he stopped short at ten. But logic would pursue the argument further. The death of one child is much a crisis for religious beliefs as the *shoah*.

That is true. But it is to miss an essential feature of Jewish belief. There is theology, but beyond that there is covenant, the bond between God and a singular people. The Torah—the Hebrew Bible—reveals a single universal God who created the world and sits in judgement over the whole of human history. But with Abraham and the exodus and the revelation at Sinai, God chooses to associate His name with the fate of a particular extended family: the seed of Abraham, the children of Israel, the Jewish people. It is through them that His presence would be peculiarly manifest. Their way of life would set them apart as a holy nation. Their history would seem to be more than the morally indifferent play of cause and effect. It would read as a succession of commentaries to the covenant. Its deliverance and exiles, sufferings and salvation, its sheer improbable persistence, would invite the adjective 'miraculous'. The people of Israel would, in its own existence, bear testimony to the existence of God.

So the eternity of God is mirrored in the eternity of the Jewish people. The frightening sequence of curses at the end of the book of Leviticus ends with the verse, 'Yet in spite of this, when they are in the land of their enemies, I will not reject or abhor them so as to destroy them completely, breaking My covenant with them.'[2] The prophet Jeremiah declared, 'This is what the Lord says, He who appoints the sun to shine by day, who decrees the moon and the stars to shine by night, who stirs up the sea so that its waves roar—the Lord Almighty is His name: "Only if these decrees vanish from My sight," declares the Lord, "will the descendants of Israel ever cease to be a nation before Me.' "[3]

The faith of Israel cannot be summarised in a set of theological statements which might be true whatever happened in space and time. It is peculiarly tied to the physical existence of the people of Israel. Theological propositions normally resist falsification. They are ways of interpreting events; hence they are not given to refutation by events. But the central premiss of Judaism carries with it the risk of refutation. If there were no Jews, Judaism would have proven to be false. The survival of the Jewish people is the promise on which the entire covenant rests. An early rabbinic commentary put the point audaciously: ' "You are My witnesses, says the Lord, and I am God" (Isaiah 43:12)—that is, if you are My witnesses, I am God, and if you are not My witnesses, I am, as it were, not God.'[4]

Jews had faced inquisitions and pogroms before. They had even, in the book of Esther, known what it was to be condemned by Haman's decision 'to destroy, kill and annihilate all Jews—young and old, women and children—on a single day'.[5] But redemption had always come, or if not redemption, refuge. In the Holocaust their was neither. Jews came face to face with a systematic programme of extinction.

The demonic character of the Final Solution was not missed by Jewish thinkers. George Steiner has traced the intellectual progression from Nietzsche's 'death of God' to the planned death of the people of God.[6] Josef Mengele, the doctor of Auschwitz, openly joked that he had replaced God as the judge of 'who shall live and who shall die'. Franz Stangl, the Treblinka Kommandant, insisted that pious Jews be made to spit on Torah scrolls, and that when they ran out of spittle more should be supplied by spitting into their mouths. In the ghettoes and camps, Jewish sabbaths and festivals were singled out for special actions of cruelty and extermination.

Emil Fackenheim has argued convincingly that the Holocaust eclipses all previous trials of faith.

> The children of Auschwitz were tortured and murdered, not because of their faith nor despite their faith nor for reasons unrelated to the Jewish faith. The Nazis, though racists, did not murder Jews for their 'race' but for the Jewish faith of their great-grandparents. . .
> . At some time in the mid-nineteenth century, European Jews, like Abraham of old, brought a child sacrifice; but unlike Abraham they did not know what they were doing —and there was no reprieve. It is as if Satan himself had plotted for four thousand years to destroy the covenant between God and Israel, and had at last found the way.[7]

The *shoah*, then, did not simply raise six million times over the traditional question of theodicy: why do the innocent suffer? It raised the ultimate question of Jewish existence. The covenant had promised that though individuals might be lost, the people as a whole would eternally survive. A *Judenrein* universe, a world free of Jews, would have refuted the ground of all Jewish hope from the days of Abraham. Not only the present and future, but the Jewish past too would have died.

So, for many years after the *shoah*, the silence outweighed words. The questions were too painful to ask. It was as if, like Lot's wife, turning back to look on the destruction would turn one to stone.

The Search for Explanation

None the less there were, even while the events were taking place, attempts to find theological meaning. Rabbi Elchanan Wasserman, one of the greatest representatives of the Eastern European *yeshiva* world, published a pamphlet setting forth the traditionalist response to catastrophe. It's title, 'The Footsteps of the Messiah', indicated its theme.[8] Jews were being punished for their sins. In the wake of the Enlightenment they had abandoned their holy destiny and pursued false gods. They had lost faith in providence and were turning instead to secular salvation: socialism, nationalism and Zionism. A momentous day of judgement was approaching, a period the talmudic sages had described as the 'footsteps' or 'birth pangs' of the Messiah. An early rabbinic teaching had portrayed this as a time when 'insolence will increase, respect will diminish . . . the wisdom of the sages will decay, sin-fearing men will be despised and truth will be concealed'[9] All these descriptions applied to the present. The suffering of Jews was a call from God to return to faith, the commandments and Torah study.

Rabbi Wasserman remained true to his belief. Arrested by the Nazis in 1941, he went to his death with these words, addressed to those who were to be shot with him:

> It seems that in Heaven we are regarded as righteous, for we are being asked to atone with our bodies for the sins of Israel. We must immediately repent, for the time is short. . . . We must bear in mind that in truth we are among those who 'sanctify God's name' [the rabbinic description of martyrdom]. Let us go [to our deaths] with heads held high, and let us not, God forbid, have any improper thoughts, for an improper thought invalidates a sacrifice. . . . The fire which will burn our bodies will be the fire that restores the Jewish people.[10]

But the traditional categories of punishment, sin, sacrifice and atonement came under increasing strain as the full implications of the Final Solution began to dawn of Jews. One writer reports a searing debate that took place in a synagogue in the ghetto on the eve of Yom Kippur, the Day of Atonement. As the cantor pronounced his blessing, 'Who has kept us alive, and sustained us and brought us to this time', a pious Jew began to cry, 'Lies, lies, it's all lies.' A lapsed Jew, a former *yeshiva* student who had become an atheist, stood up and replied, 'Jews, you know what I blasphemer, a mocker of Israel, a lost soul. And I tell you, yes, there is a God in Heaven. Here we have seen fulfilled the words of the prophets and their curses, all of which have fallen on us.' He opened the Torah and read: 'And it shall come to pass if you will not hearken to the voice of the Lord your God, to take care to fulfil all His commandments and His statutes which I command you this day, that all these curses shall come upon you and overtake you.'[11] But the pious Jew replied, 'My teachers, you have heard that God destroys His people because of their sins. Isn't it foolish to believe that? If this were a punishment from heaven because of our sins, why did all the rabbis, the pure and holy righteous ones who were full of Torah and good deeds, why did they die?'[12]

It was not only that divine punishment failed to explain the deaths of the innocent, the children and the righteous. It also pointed in contradictory directions. For *which* sins was a generation being afflicted? The late Rabbi Joel Teitelbaum, leader of the Chassidic community of Satmar and himself a survivor of Bergen Belsen, declared that the Holocaust was a punishment for Jewish political activism. The Jewish people had, according to the Talmud, taken an oath to wait patiently in exile until God Himself redeemed them. But secular Zionism had broken this promise by forcing the course of Jewish history and bringing premature ingathering to the holy land. The *shoah* was a punishment for Zionism.[13]

An Israeli thinker, Menachem Hartom, pursued the same logic to its opposite conclusion. Throughout its history, he argued, the Jewish people had regarded exile as punishment, as not-being-at-home. That is, until emancipation. Then, for the first time, Jews argued the Europe was where they belonged. Some abandoned the hope for a return to Israel; others deferred it to a metaphysical end of days. For the first time Jews ceased to be Zionists. For this they suffered a devastating retribution. Germany, the country more than any other that Jews had worshipped, became the avenger. The *shoah* was a punishment for anti-Zionism.[14]

Worse than this contradiction was the fact that traditional theodicy could be used, in Christian hands, to justify the concentration camps as punishment of Jews for remaining Jews. In 1948, a mere three years after the *shoah*, a German Evangelical Conference met at Darmstadt. It proclaimed that Jewish suffering in the Holocaust was the work of God. It issued a call to Jews to cease their rejection and ongoing crucifixion of Jesus. Genocide was the punishment for deicide.[15] Nor was this sentiment restricted to Christians who approved of the Final Solution. The great Christian theologian Karl Barth, himself an opponent of the Nazi regime, wrote during the Holocaust that the fate of the Jews was testimony to the stark judgement of God. 'This,' he wrote, 'is how Israel punishes itself for its sectarian self-assertion.'[16]

Such theodicy, as the Christian theologian A. Roy Eckardt has pointed out, inverts the values of God Himself. It fails to comfort the afflicted and afflict the comforted. It comforts the comforted and afflicts the afflicted. Among those who died were 90 per cent of East European Jewry, the last surviving strongholds of traditional Jewish piety. The machines of death indifferently consumed sages and saints, those who had devoted their lives to faith. More than a million children were gassed, burned, shot, tortured or buried alive. At some point the religious imagination rebels against adding to the evil of their death the indignity of saying that it was justified.

A Broken Covenant?

Was Jewish faith, then, itself fractured by the Holocaust? There were thinkers who did not shrink from drawing this conclusion. Emil Fackenheim has argued that if the Holocaust is unique—and he has strenuously contended that it is—then it resists understanding through traditional categories. Because Judaism embodies a philosophy of history, it cannot make itself immune to 'epoch-making events' which confront faith with experiences that it cannot fully assimilate. If we were to incorporate the *shoah* into the narrative of Jewish history, as just one more chapter in the chronicle of exiles, destructions, inquisitions and pogroms of the past, we would be hiding from the singularity that made this experience like no other. The traditional hermeneutic of Jewish self-understanding is 'ruptured'. After Auschwitz we can no longer speak of an unbroken continuity between the Jewish past and present.[17]

Irving Greenberg has drawn similar but more radical conclusions. May we, he asks, morally give voice to the old certainties of faith? 'No statement, theological or otherwise, should be made that would not be credible in the presence of the burning children.'[18] Believers and unbelievers alike are caught in a dialectical tension. We can no longer believe in God with a simplicity we once had. But having seen the brutal-ities of demonic secularism, we can no long *not* believe in God. We are condemned to oscillate between moments when the Redeemer is present, and moments when that vision is obliterated by memories of the blood and burning. Most strikingly, he has suggested that the very terms of the covenant have fundamentally changed. The mission to which God called the Jewish people turned out to be a suicide mission. Morally speaking, Heaven can have no further claims on the covenantal people. 'If the Jews keep the covenant after the Holocaust, then it can no longer be for the rea-son that it is commanded or because it is enforced by reward or punishment.' It has become a *voluntary* covenant.[19]

But if faith is ruptured or momentary, why continue to have faith at all? One American Jewish theologian, Richard Rubenstein, drew the ultimate inference. If there is a God of history, her argued, we must see the *shoah* as a punishment for sin. But there is no sin that could warrant the deaths of a million children. There can be no vindication of the ways of Providence. Therefore there is no God of history. For Rubinstein, and ancient heresy had been proven true: there is no justice and no judge.[20]

Few followed Rubinstein in his abandonment of faith. For even if a backward-looking explanation in terms of sin and punishment failed to do justice to the tragedy, there was another traditional approach, namely to look forward and attempt to under-stand the Holocaust not in terms of divine punishments but divine *purpose*. The Holocaust was not the end of the Jewish people. Three years later, a no less epic event took place, the creation of the State of Israel. Emerging from the shadow of death, Jews had returned to the promised land. And was this not precisely what the Torah had foretold? 'When all these blessings and curses I have set before you come upon you and you take them to heart wherever the Lord your God disperses you among the nations . . . then the Lord your God will restore your fortunes and take you back in love. He will bring you together again from all the peoples where the Lord your God has scattered you.'[21]

The covenant had not been broken: it had been reconfirmed. To be sure, there were many different ways of understanding him. For some, the transition from exile to homecoming recalled the biblical model of the exodus. The twentieth century echoed ancient Egypt. There too there had been threatened genocide followed by redemption. For others it recapitulated the ending of the book of Job. Life had been taken away; now it was restored. These readings emphasised the divine presence in history. Others focused on the human response. The people of Israel had renewed its faith in the covenant by reconstituting its existence as a nation in the land of its beginnings.

The connection between the Holocaust and the State of Israel could be read in many ways, but that there *was* a connection seems to many Jews inescapable. Jacob Neusner has spoken about *shoah u-gevurah* or 'Holocaust and [Israeli] heroism' as the decisive metaphor of contemporary Jewry.[22] This suggests that for the most part Jews have not discovered, in the events of the twentieth century, the meaninglessness of history or the shattering of the covenant. Instead they have found the meaning of the Holocaust in a wider historical context, in a narrative of exile and return.

More recently, others have discerned another narrative. For the Holocaust was followed not just by the return of Jews to the land of Israel but by a revival of religious observance and the study of Torah. Throughout the Jewish world there has been a renaissance of Jewish learning and of *yeshivot*, the traditional centres of study. Since the 1960's, too, there has been a movement among the young of *teshuvah*, journeying back to religious roots. Bernard Maza[23] has suggested that the Holocaust be understood in this context and that the key biblical paradigm lies in the prophecy of Ezekiel: 'You say, "We want to be like the nations, like the peoples of the world. . . . But what you have in mind will never happen. As surely as I live, declares the Lord God, I will rule over you with a mighty hand and an outstretched arm with outpoured wrath." '[24]

The Holocaust drew Jews back to their religious destiny as a holy people after the ravages of assimilation. The talmudic sages in a similar vein had argued that the messianic age would be preceded by collective repentance, and if nothing else brought this about, providence would send a 'ruler whose decrees will be as harsh as those of Haman' to bring Jews back to God.[25] What joins Maza's reading to those that trace a connection between the Holocaust and Israel is the insistence that events disclose their meaning only in retrospect. Unlike those who speak of sin and retribution, they attach significance to what followed the *shoah*, not what preceded it.

The Hiding of the Face of God

These views, ranging from affirmation to qualification or denial, turn upon a relatively straightforward view of the concepts of providence, punishment and divine action in history. However, the biblical and rabbinic literature is more nuanced and complex than these theologies suggest. This fact gave rise in turn to other approaches to the Holocaust.

One strand within rabbinic thought, for example, maintained that the problem of suffering is intrinsically unfathomable from a human perspective. In the mishnaic period, Rabbi Meir has said that Moses' request to understand the ways of providence was denied by God.[26] Maimonides argued that the message of the book of Job was that there was an unbridgeable distance between God's governance of the universe and human understanding.[27]

This in itself would not amount to an approach to suffering, but to it was added a deep tenacity of faith. A famous talmudic passage tells of how a group of rabbis, witnessing the devastation of Jerusalem and the ruins of the Temple, started to weep. Rabbi Akiva, however, comforted them, saying that the fact that the prophecies of destruction had come true was itself a guarantee that the prophecies of consolation would also come true.[28] To have faith in the midst of tragedy is to see it pointing, however obscurely, toward future redemption.

In this way, rabbinic Judaism learned to keep its mourning within bounds. The Talmud recalls a dialogue between R. Joshua and those who, grief-stricken at the destruction of the Temple, refused ever again to enjoy life. He said: 'My sons, come and listen to me. Not to mourn at all is impossible, because the blow has fallen. To mourn overmuch is also impossible, because we do not impose a hardship on the community which the majority is unable to bear.'[29] We may not deny evil, but neither may we be overpowered by it.

These themes are brought together in Michael Wyschogrod's penetrating critique of Emil Fackenheim's Holocaust theology:

> The God of Israel is a redeeming God: this is the only message we are authorised to proclaim, however much it may not seem so to the eyes of non-belief. Should the Holocaust cease to be peripheral to the faith of Israel, should it enter the Holy of Holies and become the dominant voice that Israel hears, it could not but be a demonic voice that it would be hearing. There is no salvation to be extracted from the Holocaust, no faltering Judaism can be revived by it, no new reason for the continuation of the Jewish people can be found in it. If there is hope after the Holocaust, it is because to those who believe, the

voices of the Prophets speak more loudly than did Hitler, and because the divine promise sweeps over the crematoria and silences the voice of Auschwitz.[30]

A second axis of Jewish thought stresses not the inexplicability of suffering but the centrality of human responsibility and free will. This implied a paradoxical notion of divine power. God, as it were, withdraws from the arena of human action to allow scope for human choice. In giving man the freedom to choose to be good, He necessarily gives him the freedom to do evil. God teaches us what goodness is. But He does not intervene to force us to do one thing or refrain from doing another. As Maimonides put it, God sometimes changes the course of nature, but never of human nature.[31]

This was no abstract principle. It had tragic implications, and these were reflected in a series of remarkable rabbinic interpretations of scripture in the wake of the Roman destruction of the second Temple. The mishnaic teacher Abba Chanan, for example, paraphrased the verse 'Who is a Mighty One like You, O Lord?' (Psalm 89:9) to read, 'Who is like You, mighty in self-restraint? For You heard the blasphemy and the insults of that wicked man [Titus], but You kept silent!' In the school of R. Ishmael, the verse 'Who is like You, O Lord, among the mighty [*elim*]?'(Exodus 15:11) was amended to read, 'Who is like You, O Lord, among the silent ones [*illemim*]?'[32] God sees the suffering of His children and yet remains mute. Divine might consists precisely in a willingness to leave the stage of history to human freedom. Strength is self-restraint, and true power the renunciation of power. But because of this such tragedies as the destruction of the Temple can take place. Human freedom is conferred at a terrible price, but there is no alternative.

Eliezer Berkovits chose this line of approach to the Holocaust. Seen in the religious context of freedom and responsibility, it tells us not about God but about man. For Berkovits, Auschwitz represented the moral disintegration of Western civilisation. It was the culmination of centuries of theologically-inspired hatred of Jews as the bearers of God's word. It disclosed what had always been present as a possibility: that men might choose ultimate evil. But it also revealed, at the same time, that in the face of ultimate evil individuals might choose ultimate good. Those Jews who went to their death 'sanctifying the name of God' reached the highest possible religious affirmation. He who faces death because of his faith stands alone with God. 'If at this moment he is able to accept his radical abandonment by God as a gift from God that enables him to love his God with all his soul, "even when He takes his soul from you", he has achieved the highest form of *kiddush ha-Shem*' [sanctification of God's name].[34]

The Holocaust taught the terrible vulnerability of those who believed that true strength is the renunciation of strength, but at the same time it revealed the awesome power of faith that could not be murdered by the most systematic assault on it ever undertaken. The Jewish people is the 'suffering servant' of God. It is the living witness to God's presence in history. The attempt to eliminate the people of God was an attempt to eradicate the presence of God from the human situation. The fact that after Auschwitz the Jewish people still lives and can still affirm its faith is the most powerful testimony that God still lives.

Yet another dimension of Jewish thought spoke about the divine withdrawal from history not as a timeless feature of human freedom but as a specific phase in the history of the covenant. The Torah speaks of the 'hiding of the face' of God. But it does so in a particular context, namely the *exile* of Jews from their land. From the opening chapters of Genesis to the closing speeches of Deuteronomy, human transgression is seen in terms of dislocation, moral and physical. Adam and Ever are exiled from Eden. Moses warns that if the children of Israel sin they too will be exiled. This in turn deepens the alienation between man and God, until man experiences God in His absence, not His presence. 'Then My anger shall be kindled against them in that day, and I will forsake them and I will hide My face from them, and they shall be devoured, and many evils and troubles shall come upon them, so that they will say in that day: "Are not these evils come upon us because our God is not among us?" And I will surely hide My face in that day. . . .'[35]

Seen in this light, divine providence is not a timeless concept but part of the narrative of the unfolding of the covenant. When the people Israel is faithful to the divine word, it lives securely in this land and experienced the providence of God. At such times one can speak of divine reward and punishment. But when it abandons God it is sent into exile, which is not punishment as such but something worse, the *withdrawal* of providence. God 'hides his face'. The moral distinction between these two states of affairs was spelled out by the medieval Jewish philosophers. When God punishes, He punishes only the guilty. But when He withdraws His providence, he 'leave man to chance', in Maimonides's phrase. At such times even the innocent may suffer, for tragedy is then the result not of divine but of human action. Exile is the absence of providence.

This had been the fate of the Jewish people. Only when constituted as a nation on their own land were their affairs governed by direct divine reward and punishment. Sent into dispersion with the destruction of the second Temple, Jews were handed over to the mercy or mercilessness of the nations with only this promise to console them: that a remnant would survive, and surviving, return to God and their land.

Traces of such a view are to be found in the writings of Maimonides, Nachmanides, Gersonides and Abarbanel between the twelfth and sixteenth centuries, and they have been tentatively explored in a post-Holocaust context by Rabbis Joseph Soloveitchik and Normann Lamm.[36] From this perspective the *shoah* was not the acting-out of a possibility of evil always latent in the human situation, but a kind of denouement of exile. The subsequent creation of the state of Israel, though not in any way a compensation for or redemption of the Holocaust, none the less marked the beginning of the end of that long chapter of Jewish homelessness. With the recreation of Jewish national life, not only Jews, but as it were God Himself, had re-entered history.

Each of these strands in Jewish thought might be described as rationalist. But there were also profoundly mystical traces in the rabbinic literature. According to one talmudic passage, in the wake of the destruction of the Temple, God Himself wept and lamented, 'Woe to Me for I have destroyed My house, burned My temple and exiled My children.'[37] Implicit in the idea of a personal God is the concept of divine pathos. God suffers in the suffering of man. Throughout the prophetic and rabbinic literature there is a constant tension between God's justice and His compassion. Justice may require punishment, but God is with those who are punished and grieves with them. Exile may be decreed, but God's presence is with His children even in exile.

These sentiments received remarkable expression in the mystical writings of Rabbi Kalonymos Shapiro during the Holocaust itself. Imprisoned in the Warsaw ghetto where he died in 1943, Rabbi Shapiro continued to deliver discourses to his disciples which he committed to writing and subsequently buried so that they would not be discovered and destroyed by the Nazis. They were eventually discovered and published under the title *Esh Kodesh*, 'The Fire of Holiness'. In them he develops to the full the idea of divine weeping and pain. Because God is infinite, His sufferings are infinite and threaten to overwhelm the world. Drawing on rabbinic texts, Rabbi Shapiro speaks of a hidden place where God retreats to mourn in secret, for were a single tear of divine weeping to enter the world, evil could no longer exist. 'This explains why the world remains standing on its foundation and was not destroyed by God's cry of suffering over the afflictions of His people . . . because His great suffering never penetrated the world.' But just this fact of divine pathos means that man is not alone in his afflictions. Through the highest mystical striving, he can commune with God in the secret chamber of weeping. In the midst of evil, God mourns the fate of man and man mourns the fate of God.[38]

These views testify to an important feature of Jewish thought, namely that *not all theology of suffering is theodicy*, an attempt to explain evil in terms of divine justice or providence. Because Judaism is a religion of morality and history, it has been absorbed by the problem of evil at every stage of its development. The suffering of the righteous form the lietmotiv of prophetic and rabbinic reflection. But a religious response does not necessarily take the form of an explanation, let alone and explanation that presupposes insight into divine actions and intentions. Wyschogrod, Berkovits, Soloveitchik and Shapiro articulate different aspects of a faith that endured the paradox of a world in which evil is real and inexplicable and yet where God can be discerned and addressed.

The most profound expression of this faith is in the book of Job, where God speaks to a sufferer of pains he has not deserved in the form of questions, not of answers. Underlying these questions is a rejection of the idea that the world was created to yield to the devices and desires of man. Faith is not certainty but the courage to live with and for God in the presence of uncertainty and to hear the voice of God even in the heart of the whirlwind.

One writer on the Holocaust records that in his researches he met a rabbi who had been through the camps and who miraculously seemed unscarred. He could still laugh. 'How,' he asked him, 'could you see what you saw and still have faith? Did you have no questions?' The rabbi replied, 'Of course I had questions. But I said to myself: if you ever ask those questions, they are such powerful questions that God will send you a personal invitation to Heaven and give you the answers. And I preferred to be here on earth with the questions than in Heaven with the answers.' That too is theology of a kind, with roots deep in the biblical tradition.

Holocaust and Halakhah

But there was a further Jewish response to suffering, different in kind from those we have considered. It was best expressed by Rabbi Joseph Soloveitchik, who discerned two different stances through which evil could be experienced, one passive, the other active. Man suffers: he is an object to whom things happen. But he also acts: he is a subject through whom things happen. As object, he asks 'Why has this happened?' As subject, he asks a different question: 'What then shall I so?' The two stances generate two views of history, as *goral* and *ye'ud*, fate and destiny. The first, in which man-as-object seeks to understand what has happened to him, has its p;ace in Jewish thought as we have seen. But the second, in which man-as-subject seeks to discern how to act, is characteristic of what Soloveitchik sees as the primary mode of Jewish consciousness—*halakhah* or Jewish law. The halakhic personality refuses to be transformed by tragedy from subject to object. Instead it asks: 'What shall the sufferer do to live in the midst of his suffering?'[39]

In this context the most striking literature to have emerged from the Holocaust is not theological but halakhic: the considered rulings of Jewish law given by rabbis in the ghettos and concentration camps in response to never-before-imagined questions.[40] May a father purchase his son's escape from the ovens, knowing that the quotas will be met and another child will die in his place? May a Jew in the Kovno ghetto recite the morning benediction, 'Blessed are you, O Lord, Who has not made me a slave'? How should one celebrate Passover, the festival of freedom, in a concentration camp?

Over one who uninterruptedly studies God's word, said the rabbis, even the angel of death can win no victory. Rarely can this proposition have been more poignantly vindicated than among the pious Jews of Auschwitz, Treblinka and Bergen Belsen who discovered that even there the word of God was not silent. It had an awe-inspiring resonance.

One particular example is worthy of attention. On 29 October 1941, 30,000 Jews assembled from the Kovno ghetto to face selection for death. One of those present, Reb Elya, posed a question to a rabbi among the crowd, Rabbi Ephraim Oshry. What is the correct form of blessing to be said on going to one's death for the sanctification of God? The rabbi considered two possible textual variants and gave his ruling. Reb Elya then went through the crowd teaching others the correct form of the blessing over martyrdom. In the presence of the Gestapo two Jews, disciple and teacher, were able to stand discussing the Talmud, concerned that the moment of death be dedicated to Heaven by the precise word of blessing.[41]

Judaism had had its chronicles filled with martyrs before. But death then had held the dignity of choice. In the early Middle Ages Judah Halevi had remarked that throughout the religious persecutions of the past Jews could 'escape degradation by a word spoken lightly', but they refused to do so. What made the Holocaust different was that for the first time Jews had no choice. Yet by insisting on making a blessing over a death that seemed to defy all meaning, Reb Elya was making an ultimate affirmation. There is no point at which evil can turn man from subject to object, no situation which cannot be the occasion of a religious act.

Survival and Redemption

But there is one final theme in Jewish thought whose invisible presence is crucial to an understanding of post-Holocaust Jewish history. In this case, though, let us approach it obliquely through a dialectical encounter between modern theology and an historic moment.

It was in 1967, in the weeks surrounding Israel's Six Day War, that an extraordinary transformation took place in jewish sensibilities. In the anxious weeks before the war, with Israel surrounded and apparently abandoned, facing the threat of being driven into the sea, it seemed as if a second Holocaust was in the making. It was then that the memory of the first, so traumatic for two decades, broke through with terrible force, in the form of an imperative: *never again*.

Israel's sudden victory released a flood of messianic emotion. For some it seemed as if the beginning of redemption had arrived. When the mood subsided a deeper sense began to form: that the State of Israel was a powerful Jewish affirmation of life, a determination never again to suffer the role of victim. Virtues which had long been at the heart of Judaism in exile—powerlessness, passivity, martyrdom, trust—had been overthrown. They now seemed, in retrospect, to be unwitting compliance in genocide. A quite new way of speaking about the Holocaust began to emerge.

Its most articulate spokesman was Emil Fackenheim, and he gave the mood of the moments its most famous expression. The *shoah* was not to be understood. But it was to be responded to. Auschwitz yielded a command. Fackenheim invoked the traditional concept of the 613 commandments that constituted biblical Judaism. There had now been added a 614th command: 'The authentic Jew of today is forbidden to hand Hitler yet another, posthumous victory.'[42]

The imperative was Jewish survival as such. He explained: 'I confess I used to be highly critical of Jewish philosophies which seemed to advocate no more than survival for survival's sake. I have changed my mind. I now believe that in this present, unbelievable age, even a mere collective commitment to Jewish group-survival for its own sake is a momentous response with the greatest implications.' It was, he said, 'a profound, albeit as yet fragmentary, act of faith in an age of crisis to which the response might well have been either flight in total disarray or complete despair'.[43]

Fackenheim spoke to a new Jewish consciousness. There was a sense, shared by many, that the universalist vision that had driven Jews of the nineteenth century to 'normalise' the Jewish situation was over. Jews had been singled out by the Final Solution, nor for what they did or what they believed but for what they were. Israel itself had become isolated in the Middle East. A biblical phrase first uttered by the prophet Balaam suddenly came to seem an inexorable fate Israel was 'a people that dwells apart, not reckoned among the nations'.[44]

Only after 1967 could this be seen as something other than a tragic fate. The state of Israel's victory, her determination to survive and the intense involvement of Jews everywhere in her fate, all combined to place Jewish peoplehood and survival at the centre of the religious drama. It was as if, by re-entering history and exercising power, Jews had exorcised the ghosts of powerlessness. Successfully emerging from a second trauma they could at last articulate their thoughts about the first.

But there was a further stage in the dialectic. In the twenty years since Fackenheim's commandment to survive, it has become clear that not all sectors of the Jewish world have heeded its call. In the Diaspora, Jewish birth-rates fell to below-replacement levels. The momentum of assimilation has accelerated. Intermarriage rates have risen. Frustrating Hitler has failed as an effective rationale for Jewish survival.

One group of Jews, though, has obeyed Fackenheim's command to the letter. They have had children in great numbers. They have rebuilt their lost worlds. They have proved themselves the virtuosi of survival. The irony is that they are a group who would deny the entire basis of Fackenheim's thought. They are the ultra-religious, for whom piety, not peoplehood, is the dominant value, and to whom secular survival is not Jewish survival at all.

There is a point at which theology had direct bearing on demography. Fackenheim has written poignantly about what it means to have Jewish children after the Holocaust. More than a million children died, not because of who they were but because of who their grandparents were. 'Dare we *morally* raise Jewish children,' asks Fackenheim, 'exposing our offspring to a possible second Auschwitz decades or centuries hence? And dare we *religiously not* raise Jewish children, completing Satan's work on his behalf?' He adds, 'My soul is aghast at this impossible choice, unprecedented in the annals of faith anywhere.'[45]

But in this last statement Fackenheim is significantly mistaken. The Talmud records that just such a dilemma was faced by the Jews in the second century C.E., having experienced the destruction of the Temple, the brutal suppression of the Bar Kochba rebellion and the Hadrianic persecutions. A statement in the name of Rabbi Ishmael reads: 'From the day that a government has come to power which issues cruel decrees against us and forbids us to observe the Torah and its commands . . . we ought by rights to bind ourselves not to marry and beget children, with the result that the seed of Abraham our father [the Jewish people] would come to an end of its own accord.'[46] This haunting passage tells us that there were profoundly religious Jews like Rabbi Ishmael who believed that on rational grounds one should not bring Jewish children into a world which had experienced a nightmare. But Rabbi Ishmael added that were this to be issued as a ruling it would not be obeyed, for the faith of ordinary Jews transcends logic.

Does this mean that it is an irrational faith? The rabbis implicitly posed the question elsewhere in the form of a projected dialogue between to biblical figures, Amram and his daughter Miriam, at the time of Pharaoh's decree that every male Israelite child should be cast into the river and drowned.[47] Amram and the other Israelite men, according to rabbinic tradition, thereupon divorced their wives and refused to have children. Amram's daughter protested. The decision, she said, was worse that Pharaoh's decree. It condemned both boys and girls. It deprived them of both this world and the next. Amram relented and he and his wife had a son: Moses. The implication is clear. From faith comes redemption. Trust in the future in neither rational nor irrational. Rather it is, in crisis, the critical test of religious courage.

Against the backdrop of falling Jewish marriage-and-birth-rates Orthodox jews, in particular those of the Chassidic and *yeshiva* communities, have dedicated themselves after the Holocaust to having large families. This is surely not unrelated to the fact that they, above all, adhere strenuously to the traditional tenets of Jewish faith. They deny absolutely Fackenheim's claims that the Holocaust is a *novum* in Jewish history, that it reveals a new 614th command, and that after the *shoah* Jews are bidden to survive for survival's sake. Precisely because the dilemmas raised by the Holocaust are not unprecedented, they invite the classic response of Jewish faith, namely to have trust in the future to bring it into being.

Again we are reminded of the book of Job. Job, having heard God in the whirlwind, recovers faith, though it is a faith without answers. The book then ends with a concluding chapter in which Job's fortunes are restored. At the beginning Job's sons and daughters died. At the end, he has new sons and daughters. To some readers this epilogue had seemed unconvincing, as if Job's sufferings could be unwritten by a happy ending. To a post-Holocaust generation the epilogue is disclosed in its full profundity. Job has no answers, but he has been lifted beyond his personal tragedy by the knowledge that he can still speak and be spoken to by God. This gives him the strength to go on living and have children after catastrophe.

That is the kind of faith manifest in traditionalist responses to the Holocaust. Rather than engaging in theological reflection on the Holocaust, the survivors of the Chassidic and *yeshiva* communities on Eastern Europe concentrated on having children to replace a lost generation and rebuilding their shattered townships and institutions in Israel and America, as if to say that death is redeemed only in new life.

The word 'redeemed' brings us finally to the concept that has lain just beneath the surface of our discussion: the resurrection of the dead. Early rabbinic Judaism did not formulate principles of Jewish faith. Its energies went into the articulation of law, not dogma. None the less a Mishnah rules that one who denies the resurrection of the dead has no share in the world to come.[48] This was, for the rabbis, an indispensable requirement of belief. Necessarily so, for Judaism was predicted on the idea of divine justice, yet the sages lived in a world from which it seemed to be absent. *Halakhah* rejected the mystical idea that evil, stripped of our veil of ignorance, would turn out to be good in disguise. To be sure, this idea is present in Judaism. But Jewish law rules that though one must pronounce a blessing over evil as well as over good, they are not the same blessing.[49] The fact of evil could not be denied. If there was justice, it lay in the future. But the existence of divine justice was the faith on which Judaism staked its very being. Therefore if anything was certain, it was that a time would come—in the form of the messianic age or the resurrection of the dead—in which the moral dislocation of the world would be righted. The past would be redeemed.

Whether we speak of the individual birth of Jewish children or the collective rebirth of Israel as a nation, the strongest metaphor to emerge in the wake of the Holocaust is that of resurrection. Rabbi Elchanan Wasserman's dying words have not ceased to reverberate, that 'The fire which burns our bodies will be the fire that restores the Jewish people.' Another rabbi, Yissachar Shlomo Teichtal, shortly before his murder in Auschwitz in 1944, wrote in a similar vein. 'Now if we shall arise and ascend to Zion we can yet bring about a *tikkum* ['mending', restitution] of the souls of the people of Israel who were murdered as martyrs since it is on their account that we are being stimulated to return to our ancestral inheritance. . . . Thus we bring about their rebirth.'[50]

To the biblical paradigms of the 'suffering servant' of Isaiah and the book of Job must therefore be added the vision of Ezekiel who witnessed a valley of dry bones and saw them come to life again: 'Then he said to me: Son of man, these bones are the whole house of Israel. They say, Our bones are dried up and our hope is gone; we are cut off. Therefore prophesy and say to them, This is what the Lord God says: O my people, I am going to open your graves and bring you up from them; I will bring you back to the land of Israel.'[51] This too has been part of the Jewish experience after the Holocaust. The messianic age has not come. The past has not been redeemed. The cries of the victims still haunt the Jewish imagination. But a kind of rebirth has taken place, none the less, and with it that start of the 'mending' of a broken world.

Renewing the Covenant

An analysis of contemporary Jewry and Judaism must begin with the Holocaust because in it, the covenantal people came face to face with the possibility of its own extinction. It took several decades before theologians felt able freely to articulate their thoughts about it. In some circles, silence is still felt to be the best, perhaps the only, response.

The Holocaust reveals to the full the problematic nature of the religious interpretation of history. It has not yielded a single meaning but a vast multiplicity, of which only a narrow range has been touched on here. In the absence of prophecy there are no such things as events which carry with them their own interpretation. And yet Judaism must continue to wrestle with the problem. For one of its primary expressions is narrative: telling the story of the covenantal people through time. Judaism is not simply a faith. It is a faith embodied in a particular people, the way of life it lives and the path it takes through the complex map of history.

Reflection on the *shoah* reveals two significant facts about contemporary Jewish existence. The first is the absence of a shared set of Jewish meanings which aline might have allowed the Holocaust to be incorporated into collective Jewish memory. For the religious believer, the Holocaust confirms his faith; for the unbeliever it confirms his lack of faith. For the radical it creates a *novum* in history; for the traditionalist it recalls earlier catastrophes. For the pietist it testifies to God's suffering presence in the world; for the secularist if proves His absence. These variant readings have shown no tendency to converge over time.

The fundamental divide is between those who see the Holocaust as an unprecedented event which shatters our previous understanding of the covenant, and those who insist that the covenant survives intact even in the valley of the shadow of death. Those who take the first view see *Yom ha-Shoah*, Holocaust Memorial Day, as a seminal addition to the Jewish calendar, a turning point in history. Those who take the second see the Holocaust as a new dimension in an ancient grief, such as that expressed on the ninth of Av, the day of mourning for the destruction of the Temples.[52]

It is important to understand that the ambiguity of the Holocaust is not a feature of the event itself. It is a feature of the pre-understandings that different thinkers bring to it. For many centuries, from the destruction of the second Temple to the threshold of European emancipation, Jews shared a broad framework of belief that allowed them to understand their present situation, why it had come abut and to what it eventually would lead. They were in exile because of their sins, and one day they would return to their land. That shared framework, which experienced stresses from the Spanish expulsion onwards, finally collapsed in the nineteenth century. Those who held to traditional beliefs were now not Jews *tout court*, but a subsection of the community known to their critics as 'Orthodox' Jews. The multiplicity of responses to the Holocaust testifies to the still fragmented nature of Jewish consciousness, which lacks a common language through which a people might reflect on its fate. This preceded the Holocaust itself and has persisted since.

But the second fact is in sharp contradistinction to the first. For the *shoah* confronted Jews with an inescapable reminder that though they might not share a common language, they shared a common fate. The Final Solution made no distinction between Jews. The assimilated half-or quarter-Jew from Vienna or Berlin was cast into the same camp with the pious talmudist from Vilna and the bearded mystic from Berditchev. Jews had different self-definitions. But they were subject to the same other-definition. They might not see themselves, but they were seen by others, as members of the same people.

That fact has significantly shaped post-Holocaust Jewish awareness. The sense of being a people apart and alone, held together in a collective destiny and exercising collective responsibility, has grown. Its focus is the land and state of Israel, symbol and reality of the Jewish determination never again to be homeless, powerless victims. Israel, the land and state, has brought in its wake itractabel problems, political, military, and ethical; and over these, too, Jews have been divided. But this does not detract from its centrality in Jewish life worldwide. Nor is this a political proposition, albeit a controversial one. For the Bible and all subsequent Jewish thought had seen in the return of Jews to their land a new chapter—perhaps the ultimate one—in the covenantal story.

Jewish responses to the Holocaust, then, reveal not only the divisions that still exist in Jewish thought but also a new impetus toward unity: towards a clear and collective sense of peoplehood. For what is striking is that Jews of all kinds, religious and secular, have responded to their threatened destruction with a fierce determination to survive. 'I will not die, but I will live', says the Psalm,[53] and that has been the Jewish response to the journey through the valley of the shadow of death. There may be no common understanding of the Jewish destiny, but there is a common conviction that it must be continued. Faced with its eclipse, the Jewish people has reaffirmed its covenant with history. The story of contemporary Jewry begins with what in retrospect is a not unremarkable fact: that the people of Israel lives and still bears witness to the living God.

Endnotes

[1]Genesis 18:25.

[2]Leviticus 26:44.

[3]Jeremiah 31:35-36.

[4]*Midrash Tehillim* to Psalm 123:1.

[5]Esther 3:13.

[6]George Steiner, *In Bluebeard's Castle*, London: Faber and Faber, 1971, 29-48.

[7]Emil Fackenheim, *The Jewish Return into History*, New York: Schocken, 1978, 47.

[8]Reprinted in Rabbi Elchanan Wasserman, *Kovetz Maamarim*, Jerusalem: E. S. Wassermann, 1963, 106-39.

[9]Mishnah, *Sotah* 9:15.

[10]Reported by Rabbi Efraim Oshry, in Mordecai Eliav (ed.), *Ani Maamin*, Jerusalem: Mossad Harav Kook, 1988, 26-27.

[11]Deuteronomy 28:15.

[12]Cited in Bernard Maza, *With Fury Poured Out*, Hoboken, NJ: Ktav, 1986, 3-4.

[13]R. Joel Teitelbaum, *Vayo'el Moshe*, New York: Jerusalem Publishing Co., 1959; *Al ha-Ge'ulah ve-al ha-Temurah*, New York: Jerusalem Publishing Co., 1967.

[14]Menachem Immanuel Hartom, 'Hirhurim al ha-Shoah', *De'ot* 18 (Winter 5720/1961), 28-31.

[15]I owe this reference to Irving Greenberg, 'Cloud of Smoke, Pillar of Fire: Judaism, Christianity and Modernity after the Holocaust', in Eva Fleischner (ed.), *Auschwitz: Beginning of a New Era?* (New York: Ktav, 1977) 13, note 10.

[16]Karl Barth, 'The Judgement and the Mercy of God', in F. E. Talmage (ed.), *Disputation and Dialogue,* New York: Ktav, 1975, 43.

[17]Emil Fackenheim, *To Mend the World*, New York: Schocken, 1982. Michael Morgan's *The Jewish Thought of Emil Fackenheim*, Detroit, MI: Wayne State University Press, 1987, is a useful anthology of Fackenheim's writings.

[18]Irving Greenberg, 'Cloud of Smoke, Pillar of Fire', 23.

[19]Irving Greenberg, *Voluntary Covenant*, New York: National Jewish Resource Center, 1982.

[20]Richard L. Rubinstein, *After Auschwitz*, Indianapolis, IN: Bobbs-Merrill, 1966.

[21]Deuteronomy 30: 1,3.

[22]See Jacob Neusner, *Stranger at Home*, Chicago: University of Chicago Press, 1981.

[23]Bernard Maza, *With Fury Poured Out*, Hoboken, NJ: Ktav, 1986.

[24]Ezekiel 20:32-33.

[25]Babylonian Talmud, *Sanhedrin* 97b.

[26]Babylonian Talmud, *Berakhot* 7a.

[27]Maimonides, *Guide for the Perplexed*, IIi, 23.

[28]Babylonian Talmud, *Makkot* 24a-b.

[29]Babylonian Talmud, *Baba Batra* 60b.

[30]Michael Wyschogrod, 'Faith and the Holocaust', *Judaism* 20:3 (Summer 1971), 293-4.

[31]Maimonides, *Guide for the Perplexed*, 3:32.

[32]*Mekhilta* 42b; Babylonian Talmud *Gittin* 56b.

[33]Eliezer Berkovits, *Faith after the Holocaust*, New York: Ktav, 1973; *With God in Hell*, New York: Sanhedrin Press, 1979.

[34]Berkovits, *Faith after the Holocaust*, 81.

[35]Deuteronomy 31:17-18.

[36]R. Soloveitchik's views are briefly set out in Abraham Besdin, *Reflections of the Rav*, Jerusalem: World Zionist Organisation, 1979, 37. Norman Lamm's are contained in his *The Face of God: Thoughts on the Holocaust*, New York: Yeshiva University Press, 1986.

[37]Babylonian Talmud, *Berakhot* 3a.

[38]Nehemiah Polen, 'Divine Weeping: Rabbi Kalonymos Shapiro's Theology of Catastrophe in the Warsaw Ghetto', *Modern Judaism* 7:3 (October 1987), 253-70.

[39]Rabbi Joseph Soloveitchik, 'Kol Dodi Dofek', in *Devrei Hagut ve-Ha'arakhah*, Jerusalem: World Zionist Organisation, 1981, 9-16.

[40]See, for example, Irving J. Rosenbaum, *The Holocaust and Halakhah*, New York: KTAV, 1976; Robert Kirschner, *Rabbinic Responsa in the Holocaust Era*, New York: Schocken, 1985.

[41]Rosenbaum, *The Holocaust and Halakhah*, 61-8.

[42]Fackenheim, *The Jewish Return into History*, 22.

[43]*Ibid.*, 21-2.

[44]Numbers 23:9.

[45]Fackenheim, *The Jewish Retun into History*, 48.

[46]Babylonian Talmud, *Baba Batra* 60b.

[47]Babylonian Talmud, *Sotah* 12a.

[48]Mishnah, Sanhedrin 10:1. The Mishnaah goes further and rules that one who denies that the resurrection of the dead is *derived from the Torah* has no share in the world to come.

[49]Mishnah, *Berakhot* 9:2.5.

[50]Quoted in Fackenheim, *To Mend the World*, 255.

[51]Ezekiel 37:11-12.

[52]For a discussion of this controversy, see Irving Greenberg, *The Jewish Way*, New York: Summit Books, 1988, 314-72.

[53]Psalm 118:17.

Part Two
Framing the Issue

Chapter 3

Defining the
Uniqueness of the Holocaust*

Steven T. Katz

The Holocaust theologians, as Fackenheim's brief definition has already made clear, begin their work with the affirmation of the uniqueness of the Holocaust. Precisely what is claimed in this language is carefully spelled out in this classic essay, in which "the singularity of the Holocaust" (using the Hebrew word, shoah) finds its clarification. Katz underlines that no one claims the Holocaust was "more evil" than catastrophes that have overtaken other peoples. He further points to the confused language that has been used to express the conception of uniqueness, and, being a well-trained philosopher, he finds little difficulty in sorting matters out. Finally, he objects to the "mystification" of the Holocaust, by which he means the claim that language does not serve to discuss these awful events to begin with. Katz provides a healthy corrective to the somewhat overwrought character of much of the theological thinking about the Holocaust.

***

Given the confusion, crossed purposes, and misunderstandings that have accumulated around the evidently contentious question of the 'uniqueness' of the *Sho'ah* I should like to clarify six elemental issues that must be understood aright if any real philosophical advance is to be made in the analysis of this matter.

(1) In advancing and supporting the position that the destruction of European Jewry between 1933 and 1945 is phenomenologically unique I am not proposing or endorsing any particular theological conclusion(s). It is not at all clear to me that there is a direct, and preferred, theological meaning to be drawn from the exceptionality of this event, at least not as I interpret this singularity. As I understand the multiple epistemological and metaphysical issues that are raised by this issue both the

theological radicals, for example, Richard Rubenstein, Arthur Cohen, Emil Fackenheim, Yitzchak Greenberg, and on the Christian side, for example, A. Roy Eckardt
and Alice Eckardt, to a degree Jurgen Moltmann, Franklin Littell, Franklin Sherman,
Paul Van Buren, Karl Thieme, Clemens Thoma, and to some degree John Pawli-
kowski, as well as the theological conservatives, for example, Eliezer Berkovitz,
Jacob Neusner, and the Lubavitcher Rebbe, and on the Christian side, for example,
the Protestant Karl Barth, and the Catholic theologians D. Judant and Charles Journet,
have all run ahead of the available evidence and the extant philosophical-theological
argumentation to posit conclusions that are not epistemically or intellectually persuasive. Neither Rubenstein's endorsement of the 'death of God' nor the Lubavitcher's
Rebbe's conservative kabbalistic pronouncements on the *Sho'ah* as a *tikkum* flow necessarily from the event itself. Both these, and other denominational expositions, are
premature and inconclusive. They represent, in essence, *a priori* impositions that are
extrinsic to the Death Camps and rooted in deeply held prior theological positions.[1]

Any theological position, at present, is compatible with the singularity of the
Sho'ah. Religious conservatives who 'intuitively' reject the uniqueness of the Holocaust on the, usually implicit, grounds that such an unequivocal conclusion would
necessarily entail ominous alterations in the inherited normative *Weltanschauung* are
simply mistaken. That is, one can, without self-contradiction, adopt an unexceptional
conservative theological posture (either Jewish or Christian) while, at the same time,
accepting the discrete contention that the destruction of European Jewry was an historical *novum*, given a disciplined understating of the concept of historical *novum*.
Conversely, the theological radicals who hold that the singularity of the *Sho'ah* necessarily entails religious transformations, and within Jewish parameters halachic
changes, have not shown this to be the case. They have merely assumed it to be so,
positing the 'required changes' they take to be obligatory without providing either
halachic or philosophical justification for such innovation. It may be that one or other
of these alternative positions is true, but so far none has made a convincing case for
itself. Therefore, the investigation of the question of the uniqueness of the *Sho'ah*
needs to be separated from theologizing.

(2) In defending uniqueness one must completely avoid simultaneously endorsing
the injudicious claim that the Holocaust is *more evil* than alternative occurrences of
extensive and systematic persecution, organized violence, and mass death. The
character of that historical and phenomenological uniqueness which can be defended
is not tied to a scale, a hierarchy, of evil, that is, of an event X being more or less
malevolent than another event Y, or all previous events E_1 to E_n. This of course, is
not to deny the compelling fact that the *Sho'ah* was a monumental crime, and astonishing act of cruelty, comprised of millions of acts of cruelty, as great as any that has
ever taken place. But in acknowledging this one must at the same time avoid incor-
rectly asserting that the *Sho'ah* is *more* evil than certain other specific events, for
instance, the centuries-long brutality and dehumanization represented by Greco-

Roman and New World slavery, the mass-murder of Armenians in 1915–1917, the vast depopulation of the indigenous peoples of North and South America, the monumental violation of human dignity, the millions of dead, that is the Gulag, or the monstrous transgression that is Cambodia. These other happenings are also morally outrageous, and arguably as morally outrageous as the *Sho'ah*. The insuperable epistemological dilemma that arises here is that there is no argument, no method, that will allow for the quantification of evil beyond the simple mathematical-counting corpses. But this, I take it, is not what is meant when the Holocaust is said to be more evil than other incidents, at least not when this formidable proposition is defended by competent authors and speakers possessed of even minimal philosophical sophistication. Moreover, on this measure, that is, numbers alone, the *Sho'ah*, as an empirical matter, is far from the 'most evil' event in history. In the absence of convincing criteria for making such absolute comparative judgements all such judgements become indefensible.[2]

Here I demur from Yehuda Bauer's contention that there:

> may be no difference between Holocaust and genocide for the victim of either. But there are gradations of evil, unfortunately. Holocaust was the policy of total, sacral Nazi act of mass murder of all Jews they could lay their hands on. Genocide was horrible enough, but it did not entail *total* murder.[3]

The categorical distinction that Bauer draws between *some* and *all*, between Holocaust and Genocide, is not best, or even properly, understood as a moral distinction but rather as a phenomenological and logical one. Seeking to kill all of a group is descriptively, even ontologically, different from seeking to kill part of a group, but it is not *necessarily*, morally worse. For example, the killing of some X may be a greater evil, assuming one could measure such things, than killing all Y, where there are more X than Y and the absolute number of X killed exceeds the total number Y even though the killing of X is not, using a form of Bauer's nomenclature, 'Holocaustal'. To repeat: This is not to deny that non-Holocaust X *is* different from Holocaust Y but, rather, to assert that the *nature* of this difference is logical and structural not moral. To impute less evil, for example, to Stalin than Hitler because of the categorical distinction between Holocaust and genocide (Stalin, on Bauer's definition being guilty of perpetrating the latter but not the former crime while Hitler perpetrated the former crime), appears unwarranted on its face and undecidable, except by stipulation, in both theory and practice. Again, to judge the young Turks or the Khmer Rouge less evil than Hitler because they failed to want to kill all Americans or Cambodians respectively is logically and ethically unconvincing.

Kenneth Seeskin, in commenting on an earlier and related argument of mine for what I called 'the intentionality of the Holocaust',[4] has given voice to the elementary confusion we wish to disclaim, as follows:

To his credit, Katz tries to avoid ethical or theological conclusions. He admits that numbers alone do not tell the full story. I his survey of mass murder, he refrains from judgements of better or worse. Unlike Maier and Aron, he does not get tangled in distinctions between an ideology and its interpretation. His thesis is simply that the uniqueness of the Holocaust consists in its 'genocidal intent against the Jewish people'. The question is whether he can employ a concept like genocidal intent without falling victim to moral comparisons he does not want to make. If the Nazi extermination of Jews os the first and only case of genocidal intent in history, how can we not conclude that it unleashed a new and previously unimagined form of evil? One cannot refer to a term like genocidal intent without expecting the audience to draw moral inferences for itself—particularly when writing on the Holocaust. So while Katz is anxious to stay clear of these inferences, his language gives him away. This is more than a verbal dispute. Even if Katz were to replace a charged word like intentionality with a neutral one like policy, the same problem would arise.[5]

But this criticism is unpersuasive for it rests on a logical error. There is no logical reason, that is, it is not a logical error, to maintain the distinction between G, the presence of genocidal intent, in event E, and G', the absence of genocidal intent, in event E_1, and again in every other event E_2 to E_n, while at the same time insisting that this phenomenological difference, between G and G', does not necessarily entail any hierarchy of immoral acts or events. It is true that the *Sho'ah* represents a 'new form of evil', but this is not logically or ontologically equivalent to the claim that the *Sho'ah* represents a 'new *and higher* level of evil'. The separable notions of form and degree, structure and quantity, intent and ethical valence, are not synonymous and should not be employed as if they were. Moreover, there is no incoherence or contradiction in entertaining the possibility that one could produce the same degree of evil through two alternate historic-systemic forms, assuming we could calibrate degrees of evil. *Contra* Seeskin, there does not appear to be any authentic reason why, given the careful disjunctive conditions here indicated, one cannot avoid 'falling victim to moral comparisons one does not want to make', indeed which one explicitly repudiates, and why intelligent readers, if requested to do so, cannot distinguish between different *forms* of evil 'without drawing [incorrect] moral inferences'.

In this connection it is also required, especially given the prominence of his work,[6] to reject the criticism of Irving Louis Horowitz. Horowitz writes: 'Those who take an exclusive position on the Holocaust [and argue for its uniqueness] are engaging in moral bookkeeping, in which only those who suffer very large numbers of deaths qualify'.[7] *Contra* Horowitz, however, it is an error to equate uniqueness with numbers. That is, the defense of singularity is unrelated to 'moral bookkeeping'. The two determinate categories that Horowitz erroneously equates, 'moral bookkeeping' and 'claims for exclusiveness', are in actuality distinct and can, and ought, to be separated. An admirable and supportable desire to empathize with all victims of oppression does not justify a fallacious argument.

(3) The phenomenological character properly associated with the notion of histor-ical incommensurability is to be wholly distinguished from more dramatic metaphys-ical claims sometimes associated with the concept of uniqueness. Though sympathetic to claims that 'The Holocaust has meant an otological redirecting of the course and fate of history'.[8] and agreeing with Emil Fackenheim that 'The Holocaust . . . was indeed a world, and it was dominated by the "logic of destruction" that left un-touched neither God nor man, neither hope nor will, neither faith nor thought',[9] no one, in my view, has produced *arguments* that demonstrate the transcendental unique-ness of the *Sho'ah*. A. Roy Eckardt is right to note that the murder of European Jewry 'raises the question of *Heilsgeschichte* ("salvation history"), perhaps even the total eclipse of 'salvation history', and again that 'if it is comparable at all, [it] can only be compared with a very small number of other "incomparable" events, such as the Exodus and the giving of the Torah or the Crucifixion and the Resurrection'.[10] However, it is just the unsettling accuracy of this observation that entails caution for the Exodus, the giving of the Torah, the Crucifixion and the Resurrection, insofar as one enters into and reclaims their theological or metaphysical meaning, are not givens whose singularity is *proven* and incontrovertible, but rather *realia* whose overpower-ing mysterious presence is assumed by the believer and affirmed by the transforming experience of faith. The immediate significance of this unremarkable observation in the present context, however, is exacting for it reminds us that, for example, Jews do not affirm the transhistorical reality of the Resurrection, the essential dogma of Chris-tianity, and no appeal seems able to convince them to abandon this skepticism. Though we must be open to the philosophical possibility that the *Sho'ah* is trans-cendentally unique, that it may transcend all inherited and established philosophical categories, categories that are unashamedly constructed to deny uniqueness by their categoricality, no one has so far made a convincing philosophical case for this position.

In particular, I would argue that the claim for the Holocaust's historical and phe-nomenological incomparability not be equated with Alice and A. Roy Eckardt's intriguing contention that among the various meanings of the term uniqueness there is one beyond others, 'transcending uniqueness',[11] that peculiarly applies to and indi-viduates the *Sho'ah*. This exceptional category they define as follows:

> The concept of transcending uniqueness refers to events that are held to be essentially dif-ferent from not only ordinary uniqueness but even unique uniqueness. With transcending uniqueness the quality of difference raises itself to the level of absoluteness.[12]

And they go on:

> One way to situate the qualitative shift to transcending uniqueness is to speak of a radical leap from objectness to subjectness, a total existential crisis and involvement for the party

who makes one or another affirmation of transcending uniqueness. This extraordinary about face is accompanied by a marked transformation in modes of language.[13]

One recognizes that in this odd language the Eckardts are wrestling with the limits of the sayable, are striving to identify a distinctive ontic circumstance whose conceptualization may point to something philosophically fertile, but given the ambiguities of their formulation, the notion of 'transcending uniqueness' is unendorsable. To the degree that I understand their meaning, the shifts and modifications they introduce, especially insofar as these involve highly subjective factors'—a total existential crisis' —apply to many collective tragedies and do not provide compelling grounds for historical and metaphysical individuation. The Eckardts are correct to note that:

> Antisemitism, as it has manifested itself within the entire history of the West, is itself a markedly unique phenomenon. This phenomenon is radically discontinuous with ordinary forms of 'prejudice', such as is race and religion, forms that have their occasions and their locales and then atrophy or are superseded. Antisemitism is the one perennial malady of its kind within the history of the Western World, and it is spread universally within the entire geography of the West. Distinctively, it is pervasive in time as in space. Thus is the peculiar generality of antisemitism wedded indissolubly to the peculiar peculiarity of the Holocaust.[14]

But this penetrating judgement, even while being unimpeachable, does not serve to make their larger historiosophical and hermeneutical claim convincing. The authentic anomalousness of antisemitism, as well as its disquieting endurance over place and time, entails no transcendental correlates. It is true that the antisemitism of the West is rooted primordially in Christian theology, that on Christian grounds Judaeophobia is generated and warranted by meta-historic oppositions, but this intra-Christian dogma is not to be misunderstood, and extrapolated, *per se*, into a genuine transcendental reality or analysis. Thus we remain satisfied with a more modest phenomenological, *contra* transcendental, definition of the historical *novum* that is the *Sho'ah*.

(4) In a recent work that attracted considerable scholarly notice, George Kren and Leon Rappaport attempt to define the uniqueness of the Holocaust in terms of the notion of 'historical crisis'. According to Kren and Rappaport an 'historical crisis' is to be understood as

> a crisis has occurred when events make such a profound impact on the way people think about themselves and the world around them that the apparent continuity of their history seems drastically and permanently changed. In the lives of individuals, such events are usually called life crisis; when they happen to whole societies or civilizations, they must be recognized as historical crisis. Moreover, like a personal life crisis, a historical crisis is compounded of events or situations which render accumulated past experiences or learning quite irrelevant. In many respects, the effect of historical crisis is to turn the world upside down, as Dwight MacDonald indicated when he suggested that in post-

Holocaust society, it was not those who break the law but those most obedient to the law who would be the greatest threat to humanity.

Societies facing historical crises are usually thrown into a period of chaos until they can replace their traditional but now ineffective modes of conduct with new, more appropriate modes. It is, therefore, possible to define a historical crisis as involving any new situation of sufficient impact or magnitude to require serious, wide, and comparatively rapid changes in the normative behavior of a society. If these normative changes are at least minimally effective, they tend to become institutionalized as relatively fixed patterns of thought and action which resist serious change until another crisis situation occurs.[15]

Now while this proposal does not lack suggestiveness it is finally unsatisfactory for rigorous purposes of definition. As Kren and Rappaport themselves note:

Applied to the Holocaust, the concept of historical crisis can as yet only be suggested rather than demonstrated, although the main thrust of the succeeding chapters is to show how the relevant cultural, historical, and psychosocial dimensions converge to require a crisis of the twentieth century—a crisis of human behavior and values. If this has not yet been widely acknowledged, it is because the consequences of such a crisis—unlike economic, political, and ecological crises—tend to be impalpable, especially when they are masked by a language that seems unable to express them and a public rhetoric that seems unwilling to try. But these are matters that must await discussion in the concluding chapter, after diverse substantive material has been exposed to critical examination.[16]

And again:

Yet the Holocaust may be hard to grasp as a historical crises because the breakdowns of consensus and culturally defined meaning consequent to it are not easily perceived. There were no great changes in ideas concerning government and political power, for example, because the Holocaust was not a revolution. Economic systems and practices were not influenced, for it was not a financial or economic collapse. Furthermore, the Holocaust itself led to no startling changes in national boundaries; it did not generate any sweeping new religious forms or views of human nature; and it had no discernible impact on modern science.[17]

That is, on their criterion for the *Sho'ah* is not, except as an article of faith and in contradiction to their own definition, an 'historical crisis'. As an empirical matter the world appears little changed morally or otherwise by Auschwitz. As Elie Wiesel has complained: 'Nothing has been learned: Auschwitz has not served as a warning. For details consult your daily newspaper',[18] viz. the tragedies of Ethiopia, Nigeria, Sudan, Cambodia, Vietnam, Botswana, Burundi, Indonesia and various parts of South America (to name only a few of the scores of deadly happenings that have occurred since the end of World War II).[19] Reflecting upon this abysmal aggregate historical evidence ought we not to conclude that the notion of 'historical crisis' is just a well-intentioned 'wish', a pious hope that the *Sho'ah*, given its monumental depravity, does mean something after all. And this recognized, the category of 'historical crisis'[20] appears to offer little, if any, genuine help in explicating and defending the claim for the Holocaust's uniqueness.

(5) Ismar Schorsch criticizes those who are 'obsessed' with uniqueness because such a claim 'impedes genuine dialogue', because it introduces an extraneous, contentious issues that alienates potential allies from among other victims of organized human depravity. Similarly, our fixation on uniqueness has prevented us from reaching out by universalizing the lessons of the Holocaust.[21] But such apologetics, however well intended, however ecumenical, are misplaced. The question 'Is the Holocaust Unique?' is a legitimate question, a meaningful question, and perhaps even an important question in a variety of ways. To rule it out because of some extraneous politics, or even ethical, agenda, no matter how virtuous, is to confuse scholarship and homiletics, the often lonely search for truth with the altogether different effort to build practical coalitions or to win popularity contests. Even if the claim of incommensurability makes enemies, which if properly understood it should not, this conclusion is neither to be avoided nor denied. One could keep silent on this cardinal issue, exercising strict self-censorship, or even lie abut one's hard-won conclusions to satisfy, at what high cost, those who object to the implications of the defense of uniqueness, but such behavior would hardly negate the truth of the claim. Moreover, and not inconsequentially, it would introduce undesirable elements of 'bad faith' into the serious, already difficult, discussion of the *Sho'ah* and its meaning, contravening thereby the very effort to create *genuine* dialogue between Jews and non-Jews that Schorsch advocates. Half truths and purposeful evasions are bad foundations for authentic cross-cultural, inter-communal, encounter. Then, too, the interpretive disjunction that Schorsch makes, the distinction that underwrites his entire polemic, between concluding for uniqueness and 'universalizing the lessons of the Holocaust' is neither necessary nor necessarily correct. There is no logical or normative reason why the maintenance of the notion of uniqueness I *must* 'prevent us from reaching out [to other victims]'. Knowing that X is not Y does not entail that those who know phenomenological U about X cannot empathize and be *practically* concerned with the victims of Y, even if Y lacks U. There is nothing in warranting phenomenological U that makes a universal care and sympathy, a trans-X activism and involvement, impossible. Conversely, knowing X may make one more, not less, concerned with others, if only so as to deny the possibility of the repetition of X.[22]

(6) In defining and defending uniqueness it is important that we repudiate the mystification of the *Sho'ah*, and this in at least four senses.

First, all efforts at *linguistic* mystification according to which the *Sho'ah* is said to transcend all language are said to be rejected. If any event 'X' is described as being 'unique' in this *absolute* sense, in the strict form that: 'for X no predicates apply', then 'X' effectively drops out of our language and with its departure any coherent discussion of our reference to 'X' becomes logically impossible. Entailed by such a self-sacrificing logical scenario os the elimination of the notion of 'uniqueness' for what is incomprehensible, 'that X to which no predicates apply', logically cannot be said to be 'unique'. The incomprehensible, the unintelligible, are not 'unique'—they are merely incomprehensible and unintelligible.

Though this apophatic status, this numinous being beyond language, would appear to be exactly what proponents of such a radical *via negativa* intend, even they, upon reflection, must reject this linguistic gambit. And this because it makes the Nazi terror unimaginable and unintelligible as well as irrelevant. Unimaginable and unintelligible because this is the logical consequence of such obliterative negations, irrelevant because what can post-Nazi generations understand of and learn from, not least in the arena of morality, an event that, by definition, transcends all language, all appraisals, all normative matrices, and is thus unavailable for transmission from one generation to the next. Apophatic claims deny efforts at both historical understanding and moral evaluation and, on these compelling grounds, are unacceptable.

In truth, rhetoric aside, no one *really* holds to the non-predicative form of the term 'uniqueness', because this sense of the term is actually meaningless. To summarize a highly complex philosophical argument, one could not even make sense to oneself regarding the concept of uniqueness or the reality of the Holocaust if one actually employed the concepts 'unique' and 'uniqueness' in accordance with the rule 'For any predicate Y, X is not Y'. This is because the present apophatic claim is another, if special, instance of what Wittgenstein labeled the search for 'the beetle in the box',[23]—the search for that elusive 'private language' that retains its intelligibility even though it is, by definition, uncommunicable.[24] But such a 'language' is self-devouring; the absence of public communicability negating private intelligibility.

Secondly, one must reject the metaphysical mystification of the *Sho'ah*. For this reason one should oppose, for example, the language (and approach) employed by the Eckardts that would draw an analogy between the *Sho'ah* and religious experience as such experience is described by Rudolf Otto:

> The response that finds in the Holocaust a transcendent, crushing mystery incarnates the dimension of the numinous, as described by Rudolf Otto in *Das Heilige*. The mental state called the numinous by Otto presents itself as *ganz andere*, wholly other, a condition absolutely *sui generis* and incomparable whereby the human being finds himself utterly abashed. There is a feeling of terror before and awe-inspiring mystery, but a mystery that also fascinates infinitely.[25]

But this is to confuse the issue not to clarify it. It must be shown, not merely asserted, that the *Sho'ah* is, in the mystical sense, *ganz andere*. Despite their well-intentioned efforts, the Eckardts have not been able to do this because the assumed analogy between the *Sho'ah* and God, the *ganz andere*, is misconceived. Whatever else the Holocaust is or is not, it is *not* beyond space-time nor does it stand in the same oblique relation to the categories of human understanding and meaning as dies the *Eyn Sof*,[26] the Ineffable One, of the mystics.

The *Sho'ah* is not an ontological reality that is necessarily incomprehensible, except when it is so defined, as it often is. But creating incomprehensibility by stipulation does no make for convincing philosophical argument. Conversely, this is not to claim that we who were no there can 'know' the *Sho'ah* like those who were,[27] but this salient epistemological disparity obtains with regard to all historical experiences, indeed it is inherent in the difference between first and third person experience as such. It is, of course, in its actuality, made far more complex when we are dealing with a multi-dimensional, many person, event like the *Sho'ah*, but the epistemological problem of how we may know that past of which we were not a part is in no way unique to the experience of the *Sho'ah*.

Thirdly, I reject the *psychological* mystification of the *Sho'ah* according to which the Holocaust was *irrational per se* and thus is beyond discussion and analysis—except by psychoanalysts or psychohistorians—and beyond morality 'by virtue of insanity'.

Whatever the real contribution of the irrational, the pathological, the insane, to the murder of European Jewry, these psychological elements have to be placed within the larger, encompassing, metaphysical, historical and socio-political context of the event itself lest the Holocaust be understood as little more than a Rorschach test. In so contextualizing the psychological one comes to recognize that Nazism had a logic of its own, its own way of organizing the world, that, once its premises were accepted, most especially its racial theory, made its program, however evil on alternative moral and ontological criteria, 'reasonable'. This is to acknowledge that *racial theory, per se*, is not inherently irrational, even if it is false, and even though its fallacious imperatives led to genocidal enactments. Similarly, Nazism's, romantic embrace of Volkisch 'feeling' is not deranged, but rather a rational, if unacceptable, theory of what is fundamental, decisive, in individual and group behavior. One may disagree or despair at this conclusion, but it does not violate any canon of reason *per se*.

Saul Friedlander, a sophisticated practitioner of the psychoanalytic analysis of Nazism, has made an important methodological remark about the balance that must exist between the psychoanalytical and other factors whose consideration is vital for understanding Nazism aright:

> during crises in which existing interests, norms and certainties collapsed or seemed threatened, the emotional regression experienced by masses of people, the weakening of rational controls, offered vast opportunities to the extreme antisemitic minority. In German society extreme antisemitism, including Hitler's own obsession, expanded against such a background after World War I. Yet while this very general analysis identifies conditions permitting the rise of Nazi anti-semitism, it leaves open the question of the specific relationship between the antisemitic obsessions of the Nazi leadership and the huge bureaucracy industriously implementing the Final Solution. Here our starting point should be, it seems to me, a re-examination of the myth of the Jew in the Nazi world view, and particularly in Hitler's world view.[28]

This embedding of the psychological in the larger historic and ideological context renders psychoanalytic mystification impossible. For it reminds us that to understand why the pathological was let loose cannot be explained by some recourse to the pathological. And here it must be remembered that Hitler and his circle were not 'insane' in any ordinary sense. They threaten us precisely because while *unique*, their uniqueness comes from their merciless willingness to pursue a logic, however unconventional, that is recognizably intelligible to others,[29] even though others dared not dream it before they made it real. Having been manifest, it is now conceivable. What makes Nazism dreadful is not its contended irrationality, but its unlimited rationality, a rationality that devoured all opposition, all morality, all values other than its own and which, because rational, can be replicated. It was a case in which the *Idea* was supreme and would brook no exceptions, no compromises, no limits as a consequence of existing social norms and inherited fellow-feelings. Given the incontrovertible assumption that Jews are bacilli, Auschwitz was the logical conclusion: if one's home is infected, one calls the exterminator.

Fourth, one must reject the historiographical mystifications of the *Sho'ah* according to which the confused and erroneous claim is made that because we cannot know everything about this event, or because we cannot know it like those who lived it knew it, we can know nothing at all about it. Post-Holocaust scholars can, despite their indirect relationship to the horrors, know about the *Sho'ah* even while acknowledging the real epistemological and existential limits and difficulties involved in their ability to know. Conversely, given their 'distance' from the event, such observers may actually be at an advantage at least as regards certain non-existential types of historical and philosophical knowledge.[30]

A similar, acute, epistemic sensitivity illuminates the discussion, the search, for *causes* in regard to the *Sho'ah*. Insofar as there were undoubtedly multiple casus at work in creating the *Sho'ah* their complete specification is difficult, in practice even impossible. However, this fact does not justify the argument that because we can only supply a partial and incomplete causal explanation we should resist offering any causal explanation whatsoever. The often-made presumption underpinning this false contention, that causal explanations must be complete explanations is merely a prejudice. That is, if we can offer partial and incremental explanations that cumulatively build a clearer and clearer account of the Holocaust we should not, on the grounds of some dubious *a priori* principle, reject these explanations or this approach to explanations. It may well be that the logical confusion that reigns in this area stems, at least in part, from the erroneous notion that a unique event E cannot be subjected to causal decipherment of the sort, 'Why is it the case that P?' without reducing its uniqueness. But this assumption, for it is only that, is indefensible and unwarranted.

The related misconception that insofar as the *Sho'ah* was not predictable[31] it transcends causal explanation is likewise to be rejected. Predictability and causal explanation are two distinct conceptual operations. So, for example, no one could predict the outbreak of AIDS but no biologist or physician would construe this as entailing that AIDS is not subject to causality and not open to causal explanation.

All these subtle ways of obscuring the study of the Holocaust, these multiple methods and forms of mystification, must be rejected. And they must by rejected precisely because we want to maintain, and retain, the singularity of the *Sho'ah* as a meaningful claim. The mystifiers by contrast, and contrary to their intentions, make this objective impossible.

The avoidance of the philosophical, methodological and logical errors here analyzed will not yet produce, in itself, a convincing argument for the incommensurability of the *Sho'ah*. However, if these confusions are not repeated it will at least make it possible to open up the conceptual space in which an explanation of uniqueness might reasonably take place-and even succeed.

Endnotes

[1]For further analysis of many of these recent Jewish theological views see my *Post-Holocaust Dialogues: Critical Studies in Contemporary Jewish Thought* (New York, 1983). I, however, do not discuss the argument of R. M. Schneerson, the Lubavitcher Rebbe, in this work.

[2]In light of this I want explicitly to distance my defense of the uniqueness of the *Sho'ah* from Pierre Papazian's charge that: 'To claim that the Holocaust was unique can only imply that attempts to annihilate other national or cultural groups are not to be considered genocide, thus diminishing the gravity and moral implications of any genocide anywhere, any time. It also implies that the Jews have a monopoly on genocide, that no matter what misfortune befalls another people, it cannot be as serious or even in the same category as the Holocaust' ('A Unique Uniqueness?' *Midstream* 30:4 [April, 1984] 18). Papazian commits the logical error we are here rejecting, if in an inverted way. He holds that Jews in denying the comparability of the Holocaust are advancing a moral claim and diminishing, if only by indirection, the 'misfortunes [that] befall another people'. That is, he too equates uniqueness with morality and again uniqueness with 'types' or 'degrees' of evil. Thus the Armenian tragedy can only be *as evil* as the Holocaust if the Holocaust is not unique. But if we do not commit the basic error of equating uniqeness with levels of moral evil then we can assert, without either logical contradiction or offensive moral chauvinism, the uniqueness of the Holocaust while at the same time resisting any comparison (or judgement) of the amount of evil represented by, in this case, the comparison of the Armenian massacres and the destruction of European Jewry. As Papazian employs the unsatisfactory and ambiguous notion of 'implication' ('implies') twice in the few lines quoted above I here state my position directly so no one will take it, erroneously, as 'implying' its converse.

[3]Yehuda Bauer, *The Holocaust in Historical Perspective* (Seattle, 1978) 36.

[4]He is referring to the essay entitled 'The Unique Intentionality of the Holocaust' (*Post-Holocaust Dialogues*) 287-317.

[5]K. Seeskin, 'What Philosophy Can and Cannot Say about Evil', in A. Rosenberg and G. Myers (eds.), *Echoes from the Holocaust* (Philadelphia, 1988) 98.

[6]See especially his *Taking Lives: Genocide and State Power* (3rd ed., New Brunswick, 1982).

[7]I. L. Horowitz, 'Many Genocides, One Holocaust? The Limits of the Rights of States and the Obligations of Individuals', *Modern Judaism* 1:1 (May, 1981) 75.

[8]A. Roy Eckardt, *Long Night's Journey into Day* (Detroit, 1982) 54.

[9]E. Fackenheim, *To Mend the World* (New York, 1982) 24.

[10]Eckardt, *Long Night's Jourcey into Day*, 54.

[11]Alice Eckardt and A. Roy Eckardt, 'The Holocaust and the Enigma of Uniqueness: A Philosophical Effort at Practical Clarification', *The Annals of the American Academy of Political and Social Sciences* 45 (1980) 168.

[12]Eckardt and Eckardt, 'The Holocaust and the Enigma of Uniqueness', 169.

[13]Eckardt and Eckardt, 'The Holocaust and the Enigma of Uniqueness', 168.

[14]Eckardt and Eckardt, 'The Holocaust and the Enigma of Uniqueness', 170-71.

[15]G. Kren and L. Rappaport, *The Holocaust and the Crisis of Human Behavior* (New York, 1980) 13.

[16]Kren and Rappaport, *The Holocaust and the Crisis of Human Behavior*, 15.

[17]Kren and Rappaport, *The Holocaust and the Crisis of Human Behavior*, 129.

[18]*One Generation After* (New York, 1970) 15.

[19]Over 100 wars have been fought worldwide since 1945.

[20]Kren and Rappaport's description, already quoted, of the Holocaust as an 'impalpable' crisis raises the elementary logical question: can a crisis that is *impalpable* be a crisis given the definition of the terms 'crisis' and 'impalpable'. *Webster's New World Dictionary of the American Language* (Cleveland, 1956) defines the latter term as : '1. not perceptible to the touch, that cannot be felt; 2. too slight or subtle to be grasped easily by the mind; inappreciable' (727).

[21]I. Schorsch, 'The Holocaust and Human Survival', *Midstream* 17/1 (January, 1981) 39.

[22]Note: On my definition of 'uniqueness' the notion means not that X cannot happen again but that to this point it has only happened once.

[23]L. Wittgenstein, *Philosophical Investigations* (ed. G. E. M. Anscombe and R. Rhees; Oxford, 1967) sec. 293.

[24]I have explored some of the peculiar and unintended consequences of this linguistic claim in the context of mystical reports and the study of mysticism in my essay, 'Language, Epistemology and Mysticism', in S. T. Katz (ed.), *Mysticism and Philosophical Analysis* (New York, 1978) 22-74; see also my 'Utterance and Ineffability in Jewish Neoplatonism', L. Goodman (ed.), *Jewish Neoplatonism* (Albany, 1991) 247-63.

[25] 'The Holocaust and the Enigma of Uniqueness', 169.

[26]The term applied by Kabbalists to God as He is in Himself and beyond all human comprehension.

[27]This epistemological dilemma is further complicated as a consequence of E. Fackenheim's salient methodological caution regarding survivor reports: 'It is normally assumed that, with all due allowance for bias of perception and memory, the eyewitness is the most reliable source of "what actually happened". When the eyewitness is caught in a scheme of things systematically calculated to deceive him, subsequent reflection is necessary if truth is to be given to his testimony' (*The Jewish Return to History*, 58). Fackenheim's remark is cited from A. Rosenberg, 'The Crisis in Knowing and Understanding the Holocaust', in A. Rosenberg and G. E. Myers (eds.), *Echoes from the Holocaust*, 388, where Rosenberg offers some pertinent glosses on this point.

[28]S. Friedlander, 'On the Possibility of the Holocaust', in Y. Bauer and N. Rotenstreich (eds.), *The Holocaust as Historical Experience*, 7.

[29]'The trouble with Eichmann', Hannah Arendt suggested in one of her few correct observations on the Eichmann trial, 'was precisely that so many were like him and that the many were neither perverted or sadistic, that they were and still are terribly and terrifyingly normal. . . . This normality was much more terrifying than all the atrocities put together' (*Eichmann in Jerusalem: A Report on the Banality of Evil* [New York, 1964] 276).

[30]Here the philosophical distinction between 'knowledge by acquaitance' and 'knowledge by description', that is, existential versus propositional knowing, should be recalled and applied.

[31]Jacob Katz has written very wisely on some of the historiographical and moral issues related to this difficult question, 'Was the Holocaust Predictable?' in Y. Bauer and N. Rotenstreich (eds.), *The Holocaust as Historical Experience*, 23-42.

Chapter 4

The Fall of Jerusalem and the Birth of Holocaust Theology*

Richard L. Rubenstein

One of the principal figures in Holocaust theology, Rubenstein here raises the challenge that classical Judaic theology must meet. He spells out in a clear way the theological issue that confronts normative Rabbinic theology. That theology found value in submission to God's will, but then left Israel, the eternal people, defenseless before an enemy not bound by God's word. The issue of the Holocaust therefore extends to the sound social policy and the wise politics to be followed by a minority, but the theological dimension of that issue transcends this world: How can God through the Torah have given eternal Israel such remarkably poor advice?

This essay is critical because of Rubenstein's insistence that Holocaust-theology begins not in 1945 (or as we shall see in a moment, in 1967) but in the aftermath of the destruction of the Temple in 70, so he says, "Holocaust theology is at least as old as the fall of Jerusalem."

***

The passing of time normally serves to diminish memory and personal involvement. Most of us are less agitated by unpleasant events that happened to us a decade ago than a week ago. Yet, there are exceptions. There is, for example, far more concern with the long-range implications of the Holocaust today than there was in the immediate aftermath of World War II. At the time, the trauma was simply too severe to permit disciplined reflection.

To the best of my knowledge, no book on Jewish theology published between 1945 and 1966 regarded the Holocaust as in any sense a challenge to Jewish religious belief. As we know, since 1966 there has been a fundamental change. It is now generally conceded that the Holocaust is *the* central issue for contemporary Jewish theology. Moreover, many who have devoted careers to disciplined reflection on the meaning of the Holocaust have long been convinced that it raises moral and religious issues that do not concern Jews alone but are, in fact, of the greatest significance for all of western religion and civilization.[1]

One obvious indication of the intensifying involvement of thoughtful men and women in the moral and religious question arising from the Holocaust has been the

*From *Go and Study: Essays and Studies in Honor of Alfred Jospe*, ed. Raphael Jospe and Samuel Z. Fishman. Copyright © 1980 by B'Nai B'rith Hillel Foundations. Reprinted by permission of B'Nai B'rith Hillel Foundations.

very wide interest in the literary achievement of Elie Wiesel. Although this writer has reservations about Wiesel's intellectual perspectives, as well sa the ways in which his work has been used, he nevertheless recognized its very great significance. It sometimes happens that literary exploration of a problem precedes and makes possible other modes of reflection. Wiesel's *Night* comes as close as any work to taking the mammoth, inhuman Kingdom of Death out of the realm of statistics and bringing it into the realm of individual experience. At his best, Wiesel is a witness of supreme importance to his time.   Nevertheless, there is a very important difference between the *individual* witness who offers the testimony of his own experience and disciplined reflection on the *structures* that created the Kingdom of Death. Because the witness focuses on personal experience, he is usually handicapped in comprehending the larger structures that entrapped and destroyed his world. If we recall that one of the strategies of those in command in wartime Germany was to manipulate the perceptions and indeed the modes of consciousness of the victims, it becomes apparent that, in addition to the indispensable testimony of witnesses, other types of reflection are also indispensable.

Regrettably, the conclusions of those who reflect on the structure which made genocide possible often arouse the anger of those who seek to comprehend what took place primarily from the perspective of individual experience. Thus, Wiesel has stated that, while the Holocaust is an appropriate subject for religious questions, he rejects the possibility that the questions can be given adequate answers.[2] He also vehemently rejects the appropriateness of the analysis of the phenomenon by historians, sociologists, political theorists, and theologians who did not share his experience.[3] This writer cannot concur in Wiesel's rejection of disciplined reflection on the Holocaust for reasons that will become apparent in this essay.

The most obvious challenge to accepted notions presented by the Holocaust is, of course, the theological issue. Unlike philosophy, which knows nothing of the doctrine of covenant and election, Holocaust theology begins by taking with the utmost seriousness the biblical-rabbinic belief in the God-who-chooses-Israel. Its starting point is not speculation about a philosophy defined First Cause, but careful reflection on what the Bible, the rabbis and, in the case of Christianity, the earliest Christians said about God and Israel. On the basis of such reflection, it would seem that only two conclusions are possible concerning the nature of God as understood within the biblical tradition. If such a sovereign Lord exists, the Holocaust must be seen as ultimately an expression of his purposes. Such a conclusion can only be justified within the biblical-rabbinic tradition, if like the Flood, Auschwitz is interpreted as punishment visited by a just and righteous God upon a sinful people.

Alternatively, one could conclude that no crime of fallible mortals could have justified so drastic a punishment of an entire people. Hence, the kind of God affirmed within the biblical-rabbinic system, one who is both just and faithful to his covenant with Israel, could not possibly exist. An infinitely sadistic or capricious God might exist; a less-than-omnipotent God might exist; a God who is indifferent to the actors in human history might exist, but the just, righteous, and all-powerful God as understood within Jewish tradition could not possibly exist. Thus, while the Holocaust would not serve as empirical disconfirmation of all belief in God, one would have to conclude that the experience of Auschwitz presents a most serious disconfirming challenge to the understanding of both God's nature and his relationship to Israel.

Nevertheless, while this writer is perhaps best known for having argued that it is impossible to maintain the normative-biblical-rabbinic belief in God in the light of Auschwitz, it is his conviction that the Holocaust presents a grave religious challenge to normative Jewish institutions for the reasons *other* than the question of God's involvement in that event.

As is well known, normative rabbinic Judaism did not become dominant within the Jewish world until after the Holocaust of ancient times, the fall of Jerusalem in 70 C.E. Before the Judeo-Roman War, the Pharisees, the party of rabbinic Judaism, were but one of a number of competing religious sects within the nation.[4]

Control of the officially sanctioned "media of redemption" was not in their hands but in the hands of the party of the priestly upper class in Jerusalem.[5] In the aftermath of the defeat of the Jews by the Romans, control of the media of redemption passed for the first time to the Yavnean Pharisees.

At Yavneh, Rabbi Yohanan ben Zakkai and his successors created new religious and communal institutions to take the place of the destroyed Jerusalem cult. As in our time, so too in the aftermath of the Holocaust of ancient times, the question of the theological meaning of the debacle was a matter of overwhelming concern to the Jewish religious community. Yohanan met the crisis of meaning by affirming that Israel's God had been the ultimate author of the catastrophe and that the event was truly a heaven-sent chastisement for Israel's sin.[6] He further specified that the most important offense for which Israel had been afflicted was her failure to obey God's commandments, *as they had been interpreted by the Pharisees*. It followed from Yohanan's interpretation of the catastrophe that Israel's sole hope for redemption lay in turning wholeheartedly to obedience to the Torah as taught and expounded by the Pharisees.

The achievement of Yohanan and his circle in meeting the new situation was extraordinary. These men were responsible for a sociological as well as a religious revolution which involved the rise to primacy of a new class of leaders, a new set of institutions, and a new hierarchy of values. We need not review that transformation here, but it is worthwhile to recall that the political and religious revolution that attended the shift of power from those whose power was based upon the Jerusalem Temple and its related institutions to the Yavnean institutions of the rabbinic party was more a consequence of deliberate Roman imperial policy than the power of the Pharisees.

According to Jacob Neusner, in the aftermath of 70 it was Roman policy "to re-constitute limited self-government among the Jewish population through loyal and non-seditious agents."[7] In plain language Rome initiated a political process which turned control of the Jewish people over to those who were her willing collaborators. Without Roman support, the religious opinions of the men of Yavneh and the successors would have been at best a sectarian curiosity. With Roman support, the rulings of the Pharisees came to possess the force of law Rabbinic Judaism is, thus, in large measure the sacrilized expression of political decision made by Imperial Rome as a means of controlling one of its most important ethnic minorities.

And, in choosing the Pharisee, Rome chose wisely. As Neusner has asserted, the Romans wanted to avoid an ethnic revolt.[8] The rabbis were eventually able to assure Rome that under their leadership the hitherto warlike Jews could be transformed into docile and submissive subjects. There were, of course, flare-ups under Trajan and under Hadrian, but after the Bar Kokhba War, neither the Romans nor their European successors ever again had to fear a Jewish rebellion until the Warsaw Ghetto uprising of 1943. Every Diaspora rabbi for almost two thousand years has been the heir of Yohanan and his bargain with the Romans. More important, every rabbi has encouraged his people to develop those traits of inner discipline that would enable them to foreswear acts of aggression in their dealings with overlords, no matter how grave the provocation.

In effect, Yohanan gambled that the only remaining defense available to his community was the credibility of its utter defenselessness. It was, of course, a good gamble. Any other course of action could easily have resulted in the annihilation of the community and its traditions. Nevertheless, the gamble did have profound risks which were clearly understood by both Yohanan and his Jewish contemporaries. It is doubtful that Josephus had any way of knowing exactly what Eleazar ben Yair said to his followers on Masada before they took their own lives rather than surrender to the Romans in 73 C.E., but the speech ascribed to Eleazar by Josephus does present accurately the issue at stake in the decision of the men of Masada:

> Let us take pity on ourselves, our children, and our wives while it is still in our power to show pity. For we were born to die . . . and this even the fortunate cannot escape. But insult and servitude and the sight of our wives being led to infamy with their children, these among men are not natural or necessary evils, though *those who do not prefer death, when death is in their power, must suffer even these because of their cowardice.*[9]

The words ascribed to Eleazar by Josephus make it clear why Eleazar could have accepted neither the authority nor the institutions of Yohanan ben Zakkai. Both Eleazar and Yohanan understood the risks of powerlessness, but Eleazar was not prepared to take them. The conditions Yohanan accepted and upon which he built a religious civilization made the question of Jewish survival totally dependent upon the good will of the conqueror and his heirs. Eleazar was not prepared to place his trust in the good will of Caesar.

In the language of contemporary sociology and political theory, Eleazar understood intuitively that Yohanan's program involved the transformation of Jews into a people of servile consciousness, in the technical philosophical sense that such a consciousness has been understood in the thought of both Hegel and Nietzsche. As Hegel observed, while the slave submits, he nevertheless works for the day when the power relationships will be reversed.[10] As Nietzsche understood, the slave's act of submission is an expression of his will to power.[11] Above all, the servile consciousness is only tenable as long as it is sustained by a hopeful vision of the future, by the conviction that the day will surely come when the present degradation will be reversed. Diaspora period messianism must thus be seen as an expression of a servile consciousness. Only the slave, never the master, yearns for the day when *a* messiah will redeem him.[12] When in need of redemption, the lordly consciousness redeems itself.

Yohanan felt the risks of defenselessness had to be taken, and that it be conceded that the survival of both the people and the religion were thereby assured. There was no other viable choice at the time. Nevertheless, the bargain struck by those who surrendered and the conqueror, as well as its religious legitimation, only made sense as long as the conqueror and his heirs kept their part of the bargain, namely in allowing the Jewish people sufficient cultural and religious autonomy to maintain a dignified existence. When the conqueror sought seriously to tamper with the spiritual integrity of the community, as happened in the time of the Bar Kokhba War of 132–135, even the heirs of Yohanan thought that the bargain was not worth keeping.

The bargain between the Caesars and the Pharisees was more often kept by every European ruler until Adolf Hitler. Even those European rulers who expelled the Jews from their realms were acting within the limits of Vespasian's bargain. When rulers such as Ferdinand and Isabella of Spain decided that they could no longer permit a religiously autonomous Jewish enclave within their realm, they gave their Jewish subjects the option of conversion or forced emigration. Harsh as they were, these options were predicated upon the humanity of the Jews. The Jews had some choice in their future. By contrast, the Nazi Final Solution was predicated upon a total rejection of Jewish humanity.

Thus until the twentieth century, the strategies adopted by the rabbis for Jewish survival were both adaptive and functional. *The naturalized culture of submission made sense as long as the bargain with Vespasian's political heirs retained its credibility.* However, as soon as the successor of Vespasian determined to take advantage of Jewish powerlessness for the purpose of a policy of unremitting extermination, the culture of submission no longer made sense. This was understood by the Nazis long before it was understood by their victims.

It was for that reason that the Nazis consistently sought to disguise their real intentions in their dealings with European Jewish communities, even in the midst of the war. For their part, the *Judenräte* that cooperated with the Nazis reacted according to characteristic patterns of response the rabbis had fostered for two millennia. These patterns of response had become a predominant element in their pre-theoretical consciousness as a result of two thousand years of religio-cultural conditioning. Regrettably but understandably, in their dealings with their oppressors, the *Judenräte* were less dependent upon realistic perceptions concerning the enemy's intentions than upon inherited assumptions concerning what Jews might expect in their dealings with a gentile ruler. Admittedly, Jews were not alone in responding according to predetermined patterns, but such responses proved to be a luxury the Jews could ill afford. It was not until the Warsaw Ghetto uprising that there was a large-scale transformation in Jewish patterns of response. By that time, all that was available was a choice between and Auschwitz and a Masada-type death. The Warsaw rebels chose Masada as their model.

As soon as World War II was over, the vast majority of the Holocaust's survivors attempted to flee the European continent. Understandably, they could no longer trust their neighbors and had no desire to attempt to start life again in a graveyard. As we know, a goodly part of the survivors made their way to Palestine, where it was by no means certain that they would gain their safety. That, however, was not the fundamental issue. It was clear that the patterns of response fostered by rabbinic tradition could no longer meet the needs of Europe's Jews. The survivors rejected them in the most dramatic way they could, by a primordial movement of return to their nation's place of origin, where survival depended upon a very different pattern of response.

Yohanan had counselled submission and a strategy of non-violence. He had built his religious culture on that basis. Without reflection the survivors understood that once a ruler used his power over the Jews as had Hitler, Europe's Jews had little choice but to gather themselves at a location and under circumstances in which Jewish survival was no longer solely dependent upon the unilateral decision of strangers. As was the case with Yohanan's bargain, so with the return to Israel after Auschwitz, a gamble was taken, but this time the gamble involved the rejection of the strategies and the culture of the rabbis and a partial return to the strategies of the men and women of the ancient Jewish resistance against Rome. Such a gamble might someday result in another Masada; it could never result in a second Auschwitz.

As we know, the Holocaust was followed by the birth of the state of Israel after a hiatus of almost two thousand years. It is possible that the significance of this revolutionary transformation was understood with least ambiguity by that sector of the extreme Orthodox wing of contemporary Judaism which refused to give the State of Israel wholehearted allegiance and which minimized the spiritual, as contrasted with the political and social, significance of the Holocaust. The extreme Orthodox understood instinctively that the kind of men and women the new state would bring forth would be moved by a radically different people than those who had been loyal to the traditions of rabbinic Judaism.

It is interesting to note the convergence between the views of the extreme Ortho-dox and that of the French sociologist Georges Friedmann, who sees the establish-ment of the state of Israel as marking the "end of the Jewish people."[13] To the extent that it survives as a predominant religious and cultural force within the Jewish com-munity, rabbinic Judaism survives with greatest vitality not in Israel but the United States. (By "rabbinic Judaism," I mean all variants of Judaism which receive their fun-damental perspectives from the religious world of the Pharisees. I include all three branches of mainstream American Judaism.) Rabbinic Judaism is fundamentally a diaspora phenomenon. It survives best where Yohanan's bargain remains socially and politically relevant, as it does in North America.

Rabbinic Judaism was not the only modern religion that was formed in response to the fall of Jerusalem, the Holocaust of ancient times. In addition to its reflections on the religious situation of contemporary Jewry, Holocaust theology lends its own distinctive perspectives to our understanding of the birth of Christianity. Christianity was born at a time when the Jewish people were rapidly approaching the most over-whelming disaster they were to experience until the Nazi Holocaust. If the Gospel accounts are accurate, not only did Jesus foretell the destruction of the Temple and Jerusalem's ancient Holocaust, he also proclaimed the catastrophe to be a fitting expression of God's righteous judgment against the Jews.[14] Today, many critical New Testament scholars question whether Jesus actually pronounced the prophecies of Is-rael's doom is the form ascribed to him.[15] It is the consensus of many, though by no means all, critical scholars that the four Gospels were written in the aftermath of the fall of Jerusalem.

It is also the opinion of many critical scholars, an opinion I share, that the Gos-pels contain extensive evidence of the Christian response to that event.[16] Even those scholars who date Mark before 70 seldom date it before the outbreak of the war in 66. All four Gospels are at one in their interpretation of the Holocaust of ancient times, but none expresses it with the bitter emotional intensity of the most Jewish of the Gospels, Matthew. The classical Christian response to the fall of Jerusalem is ex-pressed in the parable of the Wicked Tenants, the tale of the householder who planted a vineyard and "let it out to tenants and went into another country" (Mark 12:1). When the land rents fell due, the landlord sent three servants, one after another, to collect from the tenants. The wicked tenants assaulted the first and murdered the sec-ond and third servants. Finally, the landowner sent his own son to collect the rents. Matthew records what is then said to have transpired:

> But when the tenants saw the son, they said to themselves, "This is the heir; come, let us kill him and have his inheritance." And they took and cast him out of the vineyard, and killed him. (Matthew 21:38, 39)

Matthew then depicts Jesus as describing the householder's angry response:

> When therefore the owner of the vineyard comes, what will he do to those tenants? . . .
> He will put those miserable wretches to death and let out the vineyard to other tenants.
> (Matthew 21:40, 41)

In their version of the parable, Mark and Luke depict Jesus as saying that the land-lord will destroy "the tenants." Matthew adds an element of emotional intensity by substituting "miserable wretches" (Greek, *kakous kakos*) for the older, more original reading.

In Matthew the parable of the Wicked Tenants is immediately followed by the parable of the Marriage Feast. In this parable Jesus is depicted as likening the king-dom of heaven to a marriage feast given by a king for his son. Twice the king sent forth his servants to invite the guests. On both occasions those invited refuse to come. Some even dared to abuse and kill the messengers. Jesus is then depicted as saying:

> The king was angry and he sent his troops and destroyed those murderers and burned
> their city. (Matthew 22:7)

According to Bultmann and other critics, this is a clear reference to the fall of Jerusa-lem and was composed, not as a prophecy of, but as a response to that event.[17]

The most savage expression of Matthew's response to the fall of Jerusalem oc-curs in the terrible scene found only in his Gospel in which Pontius Pilate, finding no fault in Jesus, nevertheless condemns him to appease the Jewish mob, washes his hands before the crowd, and proclaims,

> And *all* the people answered, "His blood be upon us and our children." (Matthew 27:25,
> italics added)

The moral is clear. It is constantly reiterated. no difference of opinion on the issue separates the Jewish Christianity of Matthew from the Gentile Christianity of Mark and Luke. *The Temple was destroyed, Jerusalem ruined, and the Jewish nation slaughtered, not by the profane strength of the Roman empire, but by a just, all-pow-erful, avenging God who was determined to teach the Jews the true cost of rejecting his Son.*

It is sometimes said that Holocaust theology was born in the nineteen sixties when, after a generation of silence, theologians finally turned to the extermination of Europe's Jews and began to seek for religious meaning in the most devastating catas-trophe to befall the Jewish people since the fall of Jerusalem. In actuality, Holocaust theology was by no means solely a product of the sixties. *Holocaust theology is at least as old as the fall of Jerusalem. Moreover, the four Gospels are the oldest clas-sical expression of Christian Holocaust theology.*

In the aftermath of the Judeo-Roman war, Christians had no doubt that Jesus himself had pronounced the dire judgement against Jerusalem ascribed to him in the Gospels. The fall of the city was taken by Christians to be the fulfillment of his prophecies and the confirmation of his divinity. Whoever may have been the actual author of the prophecies-and it is impossible to work out Jesus-all that was sacred to Christians moved them to interpret the Jewish catastrophe as incontrovertible evidence of God's rejection of the Hews and their religious institutions. This view was reinforced by the fact that the misery of the defeated Jews seemed to confirm the Church's claim to be the successor of Judaism.

Consider the situation of thoughtful Gentile Christians in Rome about the year 75. Even those who did not have direct contact with the Jews knew that they actively rejected such distinctively Christian beliefs as Jesus' messianic status, his atoning death, his resurrection, and his heavenly lordship. Christians regarded these beliefs as decisive for their eternal salvation. Jewish opposition was no small matter because it came from the people who were of the same nation as Jesus and shared with Christians a common faith in the authority of Scripture.

Moreover, because of their superior numbers, Jews could and often did express their rejection with harsh and undiplomatic arguments, as well as with outright persecution of those Christians who had not broken completely with the Jewish community. Such conduct was bound to anger believing Christians. Today, as a result of the work of social psychologists in the field of cognitive dissonance, we are able to understand the way a group is likely to respond to those who present disconfirming evidence or who seek to discredit beliefs in which the group has a very strong emotional investment.[18] One of the most frequent responses is to discredit the integrity and even the humanity of those who question the group's beliefs. Apart from all considerations of class, ethnic, or economic conflict, there has always been a built-in element making for mutual hostility between believing Jews and Christians in the profound challenge the faith of each poses for some of the most deeply held beliefs of the other.

Since both traditions affirm the existence of the God-who-acts-in history, it was inevitable that Christians living in the year 75 would regard the fall of Jerusalem as an expression of divine judgement. If events had demonstrated that the unbelieving Jews had been rejected by God, there was no reason to be concerned with Jewish arguments against Christian faith. Thus, *the supreme Jewish disaster of ancient times was quire logically seen as a confirmation of the truth of the very faith the Jews had rejected.*

The more one studies the history of the first Christian century, the more one realizes how important the ancient Holocaust was for the development of early Christianity.[19] Furthermore, if one enters the thought-world of both Christianity and biblical Judaism with their shared belief in God's purposeful intervention in Israel's history, it becomes apparent that the Christian interpretation of the significance of the fall of

Jerusalem is altogether plausible from a theological perspective. Jesus is portrayed as having predicted the catastrophe; his prophecies appeared to have been speedily fulfilled. When the Pharisees offered their own equally plausibly explanation of the reasons why Jerusalem fell, they did not deny that the event was an expression of God's punishment of Israel. The Pharisees only differed with the Christians concerning the nature of the sins that had moved God to act.

Moreover, if one applies the categories of the Christian thought-world to the Nazi Holocaust, that event can be interpreted as further punishment of the Jews for having rejected Jesus. As a matter of fact, no other interpretation of the Holocaust is consistent with the classical Christian theology of history as it is expressed in the Gospels.[20] Yet, when one turns to the writings of Christian theologians and New Testament scholars writing between 1945 and 1965, one finds that the Nazi Holocaust is passed over in almost total silence, as if there were no connection between the disaster Jesus is said to have predicted and the Jewish misfortunes of the twentieth century.[21] This does not mean that Christian scholars are necessarily indifferent to the Nazi Holocaust. Some are; many are not.

One evidence of Christian concern is to be found in some, though by no means all, of the more recent Christian commentaries on the books of the New Testament. Post-war commentaries often attempt to mitigate the harshness of the anti-Jewish prophecies ascribed to Jesus.[22] The tendency is by no means uniform or consistent even in the same work, but when Jesus' dire predictions about the fate that awaits the Jews begins to resemble descriptions of the Nazi Holocaust, some recent commentators tend to argue that Jesus' words were not meant to be taken as a blank condemnation of all Jews. Nevertheless, when Christianity is understood on its own terms, as a religion that proclaims the deeds of the God-who-acts-in-history, no Christian interpretation of Jewish disaster is theologically more plausible than that which is ascribed in Gospels to Jesus.

Furthermore, no group of scholars has contributed more to the study of the Bible in modern times than the Germans. Taken as a group, German scholars have been the world's most innovative and authoritative interpreters of the New Testament for generations. Most of the senior professors of New Testament in German universities today were adults during the Second World War. Many served in the German armed forces on the Eastern Front where the slaughter of the Jews took place. As citizens of the Third Reich, the professors could not avoid some measure of involvement on the most violent assault on Jews since the birth of Christianity. Yet, we find a studied silence in their works on the theological significance of the Holocaust and their own personal involvement in it.

No matter how much a German might have been privately opposed to Nazism, it was impossible for any adult living in the Third Reich not to have been *structurally* involved in the destruction of Europe's Jews. The Holocaust was not carried out by a band of criminal adventurers but by the legally constituted government of Germany, a government which commanded the loyalty of the overwhelming majority of its citizens until almost the very end of the war. In 1942, for example, to be a patriotic adult German male meant to serve in the war effort. Every victory of *any* branch of the German armed forces, the Wehrmacht as well as the SS, sealed the doom of yet more communities of Jews. Even if one were a member of one of the church groups opposed to the Nazis, as were a number of New Testament scholars, to be a German Christian at the time meant to be objectively involved in the massacre of Europe's Jews.[23] Those who had been trained in the world's foremost institutions for the study of the Bible had a more informed conception of what Jesus was depicted as having said about the Jews than any other group within Germany, if not the rest of the world. They also knew how important the physical destruction of ancient Israel had been for the rise of Christianity. Yet when we turn to their writings, we look in vain for any indication that the assault, which took place often before their very eyes, has any relevance to their theological enterprise.

This writer cannot pretend to fathom the motives for their silence. Perhaps they are silent because, like the first Christians, they see the Holocaust of their era as a further chastisement visited by God against the Jews for their unbelief but find it inexpedient to say so explicitly. Immediately after World War II, some very respectable German theologians were less reticent. They assembled at a nation-wide conference, bade the Jews to learn well the lesson of the death camps, repent, and confess Jesus Christ as their Savior.[24] In so doing, of course, the Germans were no different than those Christian theologians elsewhere who interpret the Holocaust in triumphalistic categories.

Perhaps some scholars find such a theology humanly unacceptable but know of no acceptable alternative within their own tradition. perhaps they simply regard the fate of the Jews as of too little relevance to their religious and scientific concerns to warrant special attention. They may regard the years of the Third Reich as a parenthetical moment during which they were involuntarily distracted from their real concerns. Still, the silence is puzzling in view of the Gospel's accounts of Jesus' prophecies and the extraordinary importance the fall of Jerusalem is known to have had for the emerging Christian Church. Whatever the motives for the silence, it is this writer's conviction that no one can ignore the contemporary Holocaust and arrive at an understanding of Jesus of Nazareth or the birth of Christianity that is relevant to our time. If nothing else, can there be any doubt concerning Jesus' fate had been quietly reappeared and rejoined his people in wartime Europe?

In conclusion, it is this writer's conviction that the theological issues raised by the Holocaust are of decisive significance for both contemporary Judaism and Christianity. The normative forms of both faiths, Rabbinic Judaism and emergent Gentile Christianity, were born in the aftermath of and were very largely responses to the Holocaust of ancient times. Before the Judeo-Roman War, it is likely that none of the Gospel had been written, and Christianity was a Jewish movement in leadership if not in total membership. Before the war the Jewish-Christian Mother Church enjoyed unchallenged prestige and authority among the churches of Christendom. Afterwards, Christianity ceased to be a movement within Judaism and became instead a predominantly Gentile rival over against it. In all likelihood, it was to foster the irreversibility of this development that the earliest Gospel, Mark, was written.

In all likelihood the Pharisees were one of several competing Jewish sects, including the Jewish Christians and the Essenes at Qumran, each of which claimed that theirs was the true religion of the Jewish people. By 75 the Pharisees were well on their way to becoming the unquestioned spiritual masters of the household of Israel. In both Judaism and Christianity, those who enjoyed the greatest prestige and authority before 70 did so no longer afterward. Both Rabbinic Judaism and Christianity as we know them were born in the wake of the greatest catastrophe experienced by the Jewish people until the Holocaust of the twentieth century. Both the Judaism and the Christianity that arose in the aftermath of the fall of Jerusalem utilized a theology of history which when applied to the Nazi Holocaust, must interpret that event as God's chastisement of a sinful Israel.

Admittedly, there is little public evidence of satisfaction with such an interpretation by either religious Jews or Christians. Yet, it must by admitted that the Nazi Holocaust can be utilized to confirm the plausibility of an uncompromising Christian theology of history. Only one crime could conceivably justify God to act so drastically against an entire people and that crime would be deicide: a deicidal people would by definition be a satanic people, and, as such, deserving of no mercy whatsoever. Such enemies of God could only be dealt with by being exterminated root and branch. This kind of legitimation of uncompromising violence against Israel is implicit in the following remarks the author of the Fourth Gospel depicts Jesus as having said to the Jews:

> If God were your Father you would love me, for I proceeded forth from God; I came not of my own accord but he sent me. Why do you not understand what I say? It is because you cannot bear to hear my word. You are of your father the devil, and you will is to do your father's desire. He was a murderer from the beginning and has nothing to do with the truth because there is no truth in him. When he lies, he speaks according to his own nature, for he is a liar and the father of lies. But because I tell the truth you do not believe me. (John 8:42-45)

The ascription of a satanic nature to Jews had the effect of legitimating even the basest violence perpetrated against them. Furthermore, this condemnation was not uttered by man, but, from a Christian perspective, by God himself. It is therefore far more resistant to critical scrutiny than a condemnation uttered by even a saintly human being would have been.

Thus, a literal reading of the gospels presents us with a perfectly plausible theological legitimation of the Holocaust, a fact that was clearly understood by the Nazi leaders who claimed that, in elimination the Jews, they were doing the Lord's work.[25] The literal reading becomes entirely consistent with faith in an all-righteous God who acts in history, if, as in the Gospels, a satanic identity is ascribed to the Jews. More than any event since the bight of Christianity, the Holocaust can be used as confirming evidence that Jesus was the Messiah whom Israel rejected and crucified and for which they were rightly and justly punished.

Yet, we seldom hear this kind of argument publicly expressed even among conservative, believing Christians, although one wonders what is sometimes stated in private. Nevertheless, few Christians want to draw the obvious parallel between the way their faith interpreted the fall of Jerusalem and the way their faith logically might interpret the Holocaust today. Perhaps this reticence is not without a measure of wisdom, for no matter what the alleged offense, decent people shrink from associating the just and righteous God, to whom they have committed their ultimate fate and destiny, with anything so pervasively obscene as Auschwitz. Perhaps that is why one Christian thinker, Professor John Rosh of Claremont College, has argued that the Holocaust is a time bomb ticking away in the midst of Christianity.[26] Christian faith can no more reject God who acts in history nor deny the special concern of that God for Israel's fate than can rabbinic Judaism. Yet, there is no way it can affirm such a God without regarding Auschwitz as one of his most decisive historical acts. This issue is yet to be dealt with openly and frankly by theologians of the two faiths that emerged out of the Jewish Holocaust of ancient times.

Endnotes

[1]This view is expressed by John T. Rosh in his *A Consuming Fire: Encounters with Elie Wiesel and the Holocaust* (Atlanta: 1979) 37-57. See also Alan T. Davies, *Anti-Semitism and the Christian Mind: The Crisis of Conscience After Auschwitz* (New York: 1969) 35ff.

[2]See Elie Wiesel, "Trivializing the Holocaust: Semi-Fact and Semi-Fiction," *New York Times*, Sunday April 17, 1970, Arts and Leisure Section.

[3]Wiesel, *loc. cit.*

[4]See Morton Smith, "Palestinian Judaism in the First Century" in *Israel: Its Role in Civilization*, ed. Moshe Davis (New York: 1956) 67-81.

[5]See Shelly Isenberg, "Millenarism in Greco-Roman Palestine" in *Religion*, 4:26-30, Spring 1974; Shelly Isenberg, "Power Through Temple and Torah in Greco-Roman Palestine" in *Morton Smith Festchrift*, ed. Jacob Neusner (Leiden: 1975) 25-52. On the conception of "media of redemption", see Kennelm Buridge, *New Heaven New Earth Study of Mellenarian Activities* (New York: 1969) 6-7.

[6]See *Mekhilta de R. Ishmael*, trans. Jacob Z. Lauterbach (Philadelphia: 1933), *Bahodesh I*, Vol. II, 193-94; *The Fathers According to R. Nathan*, ed. Judah Goldi (New Haven: 1955), Chapter 4, esp.p. 34, and Chapter 17, 88-89. for a succinct discussion of R. Yohanan ben Zakkai's theological and religious response to the Fall of Jerusalem see Jacob Neusner, *First Century Judaism in Crisis* (Nashville: 1975) 156-75.

[7]Jacob Neusner, *From Politics to Piety: The Emergence of Pharisaic Judaism* (Englewood Cliffs, N.J.: 1973) 148.

[8]Neusner, *op. cit.,* 147.

[9]Josephus, *The Jewish War*, trans. H. St. J. Thackeray (London: 1928), Vol VI 381-83, 613.

[10]It should, however, be understood that Hegel sees the Slave as transcending his situation through *labor* rather than through a renewal of the original combat. See G. W. Hegel, *Phenomenology of Spirit*, trans. A. V. Miller (Oxford: 1977) 117ff. This interpretation is dependent upon alexandre Kojeve's reading of the *Phenomenology*. See Kojeve, *Introduction to the Reading of Hegel*, ed. Allan Bloom, trans. James H. Nichols Jr. (New York: 1969) 42-70.

[11]Friedrich Nietzsche, *Genealogy of Morals*, trans. Walter Kaufmann and R.J. Hollingdale (New York: 1967) First Essay, Sections 10 and 14.

[12]It is surely no accident that Nietzsche's aristocratic ethic is linked with his doctrine of eternal recurrence. Eternal recurrence is the polar opposite of the idea of a messianic redemption at the end of history. For an informed discussion of eternal recurrence see Ivan Soll, "Reflections on Recurrence: A Reexamination of Nietzsche's Doctrine *Die Ewige Wieder-Kehr des Gleichens*" in *Nietzsche*, ed. Robert Soloman, (Garden City: 1973) 322-42.

[13]See Georges Friedmann, *The End of the Jewish People?*, trans. Eric Mosbacher (Garden City: 1967).

[14]Matthew 22:7.

[15]See S. G. F. Brandon, *The Fall of Jerusalem and the Christian Church* (London: 1968) 231; W. D. Davies, *The Setting of the Sermon on the Mount* (Cambridge: 1966) 298 ff.

[16]Davies, *loc. cit.;* Brandon, *loc. cit.;* see Norman Perrin, *The New Testament: An Introduction; Proclamation and Paraneses, Myth and History* (New York: 1974) 40-41.

[17]See Norman Perrin, *Rediscovering the Teaching of Jesus* (New York: 1976) 110ff.

[18]See Leon Festinger, Henry W. Rieken, and Stanley Schachter, *When Prophecy Fails* (Minneapolis: 1956); Elliot Aronson and Herdner Lindzey, eds., *The Handbook of Social Psychology* (Reading, Mass.: 1968-70); Elliot Aronson, *The Social Animal* (New York: 1972), Elliot Aronson, "The Rationalizing Animal" in *Psychology Today*, May, 1973.

[19]"The destruction of Jerusalem and the Temple by the Gentiles sent a shock wave through the Judaeo-Christian workd whose importance it is impossible to exaggerate. Indeed, much of the subsequent literature both of Judaism and Christianity took the form it did precisely in an attempt to come to terms with the catastrophe of 70 A.D." Norman Perrin, *op. cit.,* 40-41.

[20]See Richard L. Rubenstein, "The Dean and the Chosen People" in *After Auschwitz* (Indianapolis: 1966) 47-60. In that essay the author relates an incident that took place in Berlin in 1961 in which Dean Heinrich Gruber's statement was that it was *not* uttered out of malice but was consistent with the classical Christian theology of history.

[21]One important exception is Jurgen Moltmann who is a theologian rather than a New Testament scholar. However, Jewish readers may come away from Moltmann's discussion with the feeling that they have been exposed to an expression of Christian triuphalism. Moltmann contends that "God in Auschwitz and Aushswitz in the crucified God . . . is the basis for a real hope which both embraces and overcomes the world and the ground for a love which is stronger thatn death and can sustain death." Jurgen Moltmann, *The Crucified God* (New York: 1978) 278.

[22]Commenting on the Parable ot the Vineyard (Matt 21:33-46) in which the wicked tenants kill the owner's "son" and in which Jesus is depicted as saying that the owner will "put these wretches to death" and on the Parable of the Wedding Feast (Matt 22:1-10), W. F. Albright observes, "It is necessary here to add that nothing which has been said above is meant to imply a permanent

rejection by God of his ancient people. Still less that the judgments pronounced by Jesus . . . are to be taken as they have unhappily in the past as valid judgments against the entire institution of Judaism." W. F. Albright in *Matthew: A New Translation and Commentary by W. F. Albright and C. S. Mann* (Garden City 1971) cxxxiii. For yet another example of the tendency to mitigate the harshness see Raymond Brown's comments on John 8:31-59 in *The Gospel According to John,* Introduction, translation and notes by Raymond Brown, S.S. (Garden City: 1966) 361-68. For a commentary which is unmitigated in its harshness after the Holocaust, see John Marsh's comments on John 8:31-59 in John Marsh, *The Pelican Gospel Commentaries Saint John,* (Harmondsworth, Middlesex: 1968) 365-66. For Marsh nothing has changed.

[23] Among the New Testament scholars who were at least passively anti-Nazi was Hans von Soden, Heinrich Schlier, Julius Schniewind, Günter Bornkamm, and Rudolf Bultmann. I am indebted to Professor David Levenson of Florida State Universtiy and Professor Dieter Georgi of Harvard for this information.

[24] "Ein Wort zur Judenfrage" Der Reichsbruderrat der Evangelischen im Deutschland, Darmstadt, April 8, 1948 in *Der Ungekundigte Bund: Neue Begegnung aus Juden und christlicher Gemeinde,* Hrsg. von Dietrich Goldschmidt und Hans-Joachim Kraus, Stuttgart, Berlin 2. Auflage (1963) 251-54.

[25] See Raul Hilberg, *The Destruction of the European Jews* (Chicago: 1961) xxx.

[26] See John K. Roth, *op. cit.,* 37-57.

Part Three
Bearing Witness

Chapter 5

Faith after the Holocaust*

Eliezer Berkovits

The first of the two principal Holocaust theologians portrayed here, Berkovits meets head-on every challenge to faith, morality, and theological anthropology raised by Holocaust theology. The very long selections presented here allow him full voice, since he exemplifies and typifies the Judaic religious affirmation—the renewal of faith in the aftermath of Auschwitz—that these five volumes portray in detail.

Berkovits comes to the heart of matters: the meaning of eternal Israel, the mystery of Israel. He speaks, moreover, not concerning abstractions but about concrete persons and events. At the same time, he frames his thought within the received structure of Judaic theology. This he does, first, by asking about the meaning of Galut, or exile, meaning, the Jews' living outside of the Holy Land and under alien governments until the coming of the Messiah and the in-gathering of the exiles at the end of time.

Second, he invokes the doctrine of Israel as the suffering servant of God, a profound account indeed of who and what eternal Israel is in God's sight.

Then, and only then, he comes back to the issue of theodicy: How are we to understand God in light of the Holocaust, and the Holocaust under the aspect of God? He then reframes the issue: "whether after Auschwitz the Jewish people may still be witnesses to God's . . . presence in history . . . ?

In many ways, Rubenstein's question finds its full response in Berkovits's thinking abut precisely the same questions, but in precisely the opposite way. That is what makes all the more compelling Berkovits's sustained essay on the meaning of authenticity of being, which I regard as the single most important theological consequence of the Holocaust.

***

God's unconvincing presence in history is testified to through the survival of Israel. All God's miracles occur outside of history. When God acts with manifest power, history is at a standstill. The only exception to the rule is the historic reality of Israel. That faith history has not been erased from the face of the earth by power history, notwithstanding the incalculable material superiority of the forces arrayed against it all through history, is the ultimate miracle. Since, however, it has been accomplished without manifest divine intervention, it remains within history, the only miracle that is a historic event, the miracle of the viability of faith history. It is for this reason that Isaiah could say of Israel on behalf of God: "Therefore ye are My witnesses, saith the Eternal, and I am God."[1] Rightly do the rabbis add the comment: If you are my witnesses, I am God; if you do not witness, I am—as it were—no God.[2] There is no other witness that God is present in history but the history of the Jewish people. God's own destiny in history is joined to the history of Israel. Great empires do not testify to divine presence in history. Whatever they are and accomplish is fully explicable in terms of their material resources. They have their self-explanatory place in power history. Half a billion Christians all over the world prove nothing about God's presence in history. They are too many, too influential, too pervasive. They are a this-worldly power in the context of power history. The same is true of any other of the great world religions. They have too many followers, control too much territory, too many resources of influence and power to prove anything. God is a mere adjunct to their position in history. Their religious affirmatives are incidental to their position in history. They all function in power history. Only a small people whose very existence is forever assailed by the forces of power history and yet survives and has an impact on world history, completely out of proportion to its numbers and its material power, proves the validity of another dimension of reality and testifies to God's "powerless" guidance in the affairs of men. God's own destiny in history is linked to the history of Israel. Only by means of Israel may His, of necessity, unconvincing presence in history be surmised.

   This is the ultimate significance of the idea of the chosen people. God needs a small and relatively weak people in order to introduce another dimension into history —human life—not by might nor by power but by His spirit. "The Eternal did not love you nor choose you because you were more numerous than any other people";[3] He could not associate his cause with the mighty and the numerous. It is not through them that a God who renders himself "powerless" in history, for the sake of man, can advance his purpose for man. Only a nation whose presence in and impact on history testify to God's presence may be God's people. God's relation to human history is such that he needs a chosen people. The chosen people satisfied a need for divine concern for all men. Why the Jews? No matter whom he would have chosen, they would have to become Jews. This idea of the divine need comes to expression in the passage in Isaiah to which we had occasion previously to refer. The concept of the witness is also stated in the following manner:

> Ye are My witnesses, saith the Eternal,
> And my servant whom I have chosen;
> That ye may know and believe Me, and understand
> That I am He;
> Before Me there was no God formed,
> Neither shall any be after Me.[4]

A careful reading of the text will show that Israel does not witness, nor was it chosen, because it knows, believes, and understands. On the contrary, it has been made the witness and has been chosen, so that it may know, believe, and understand. Out of his chosenness, from his own history he should learn to know, to believe, and to understand. He is the witness, whether he knows it or not, whether he consciously testifies or refuses to testify. His very existence, his survival, his impact, testifies to God's existence. That he is here, that he is present, bears witness to God's presence in history. He has been chosen for this purpose and he should have the moral courage to draw the consequences from his own function in history. Then he will know and he will learn to believe, and through faith will learn to understand.

2.

Jewish survival has confounded Israel's enemies and opponents and has been a source of disquieting puzzlement in the affairs of men. It is the great mystery of world history. The survival of a people that has lived without power is inexplicable in a world that lives essentially by reliance on power. A people without a country, without an organized government, without any of those resources of material power that alone seem to count in human history—whence its staying power, whence its stamina to preserve its identity? In the Christian dark and Middle Ages the mystery of Israel's survival was explained as the work of the devil: The Jew was in alliance with the Adversary, the Jew was satanic or Satan himself. Given the Christian premise, this was in a sense "logical." The Jew lived and endured by a strength unrecognized in Christendom. It was a strength unknown in Christian lands and therefore hidden and mysterious. If it was not of God, surely it must come from the Adversary. Given the Christian premise, there was some truth in the argument. Israel endured in the midst of Christendom in a manner that defied all the "Christian" requirements for survival in history. To discern in the features of the Jew the face of Satan was a Christian necessity of the dark and Middle Ages. It was the tragic recognition of God's people by the medieval Christian psyche. In more modern times, the "explanation" was not readily acceptable. The Satan of Christendom was replaced by the secret international conspiracy of the elders of Zion. This idea, however fantastic, also has a certain logic of its own. It acknowledges the fact that Israel's survival is not explicable in terms of the historical dimensions within which people normally live. It rightly surmises that there is a secret to which the mysterious survival power of this powerless nation is due. It is wrong in the identification of that secret. That, too, is understandable. For the secret is God's hidden presence in history. There is indeed a "secret world government" at work in history. It consists of God's power-divested guidance in history. Because it is "powerless" it is hidden; yet its reality is intimated in the inexplicable survival of God's people.

The most tragic testimony to this presence-in-absence is provided by the Nazi crime of Germany against Israel. The ferocity with which this crime was perpetrated represents the ultimate of irrationality. The conscious and radical removal of every vestige of moral restraint on subhuman passions, the limitless inhumanity, the calculated reversal of all human values and the extirpation of all human feelings, the ideology of hate and the religion of brutality pursued and practiced by the Germans was not "of this world." It had a quality of the transcendental about it; it was metaphysical barbarism. It was not just inhuman; it was satanic. Many millions perished at the hand of the Germans, but the satanic hatred of Nazi Germany was reserved for the Jews exclusively. In terms of "this world" the hatred is inexplicable. Nazi Germany was, indeed, afraid of Israel. The fear was utterly unjustified in terms of material or political power. Nothing could be more ridiculous than to imagine that there was any rational foundation for one of the great military powers of history to be afraid of the might of "world Jewry." Nothing could be further from the truth than the mad suspicion of a Jewish conspiracy against Germany. Yet the fear was real; more real than any fear human beings may have of superior material or political forces that may be arrayed against them. It was a metaphysical fear of the true mystery of God's "powerless" presence in history as "revealed" in the continued survival of Israel. It was a well-justified fear. For the presence of the "powerless" God in history indeed spelled the doom of the Nazi-German rebellion against all universal human values from the very beginning. The rebellion had to be satanic because it was to dethrone God. The "hiding" God of history was a repudiation of everything Nazi Germany stood for. He was to be eliminated for all times. There lies the origin of the satanic idea of the Final Solution. If the symbol of this presence-in-absence were eliminated, if the witness were destroyed, God himself would be dead. The metaphysical quality of the Nazi-German hatred of the Jew as well as the truly diabolical, superhuman quality of the Nazi-German criminality against the Jew are themselves testimonies to the dark knowledge with which a nazified Germany sensed the presence in history of the hiding God. God is revealed in the midst of the hiddenness in the suffering of his people. At times, his enemies sense his hidden presence more acutely than those who are of his people.

No wonder that communist Russia is so much more anti-Jewish than it is anti-Christian. If it were only a matter of the antagonism of an atheistic society to religion, there should be no difference between communism's rejection of Christianity and that of Judaism. There is, of course, the ingrained traditional Christian antisemitism that the new Russia inherited from its czarist past. But this by itself is hardly sufficient to explain the ruthless oppression of Jewish religious and cultural life and the systematic closing of all avenues that might serve to preserve Jewish identity. Nor can it explain the revival of the Nazi-like antisemitic propaganda in the authentic style of Streicher's *Stürmer* that is sweeping Soviet Russia these days. The key to the understanding of Soviet antisemitism may be provided by the case of Karl Marx, a man of Jewish parentage yet a venomous antisemite. The case of Marx cannot be explained by quoting the intellectual conflict between atheism and religion; it reaches much deeper. The whole materialistic interpretation of history stumbles over the reality of the Jew. The Jew as the witness to God's presence in history is a refutation of dialectical materialism. His existence, his survival, is not a theoretical refutation—that would be of little concern to the presently mighty communist empire—but a factual one. As long as the Jew is around he is a witness that God is around. And as long as God is around any purely materialistic civilization can only be a passing phase in history. The reality of the witness arouses the venom of those whose avowed purpose it is to build against God.

The case of Christianity, for instance, is rather different. Since the days that Christianity sold its soul to the sword of Constantine, its progress has been explainable in this-worldly terms. Its influence is due to its numbers. It is fully understandable within the power-political frame of reference; there is nothing mysterious, nothing strange about it. Power one can meet with greater power. But the Jew, he is the mystery. His survival capacity, his influence, his impact, are unrelated to his material strength. In terms of the world, as the Gentiles know it and dominate it, he is inexplicable. He is the mysterious stranger in world history. Yet, he is—exists and survives—and thus witnesses to another power, to another meaning, to another plan for man—to God.

The fear that so many different civilizations have of the Jew, the suspicion with which he is met, is utterly irrational, yet it has its justification. It is utterly irrational because it has no basis in the behavior of the Jew or in his character. It is a form of international madness when it is founded on a belief in Jewish power and Jewish intention to hurt, to harm, or to rule. Yet it has its justification as a metaphysical fear of the staying power of Jewish powerlessness. The very existence of the Jewish people is suggestive of another dimension of reality and meaning in which the main preoccupations of the man of power history are adjudged futile and futureless in the long run. Israel's survival has a corollary in the judgement that is, sooner or later, executed in history notwithstanding God's silence. While God is long-suffering, he is not so forever. That would not be divine mercy, but divine indifference. Were there no judgement in history over power history, faith history would have no chance of survival. Israel has survived because of the world judgement that is also found in world history.

According to Jewish tradition, God originally planned to create the world according to his attribute of justice. But he saw that a world ruled by a just God could not exist. He, therefore, let his attribute of mercy precede and, thus, he associated mercy with justice and created the world.[5] What is not stated in the teaching but is implied, is the equally true thought that although it is sure that the world will not stand by divine justice, it is at least extremely doubtful that it could survive by unlimited divine mercy. For it is God's love and mercy that gives men the opportunity for satanic self-assertion and rebellion against God himself. Because of God's long-suffering, man may indulge in hubris and get away with it. But hubris too, if it remains unchecked, will destroy man. A world ruled by divine justice would perish because of God's justice; a world ruled by divine mercy would perish because of human hubris. A world of justice could not endure the divine wrath; a world of pure divine long-suffering could not endure man's wrath. There is judgement, but mercy precedes it. Judgement is delayed by divine mercy and forbearance. Because mercy delays judgement, man may indulge in rebellion and become guilty of hubris. Because God is forebearing, man may get away with it for a while. But judgement is only delayed. The man of hubris does not escape nemesis. There is judgement and there is a Judge in world history. The manner of Israel's survival testifies to the long-suffering Judge of history.

Galut

Galut, exile, seems to be the dominant feature of Jewish history. The Jewish people have lived longer in exile than in their homeland in Eretz Yisrael, yet *Galut* is considered an abnormal condition both politically and spiritually. The Jew in the *Galut* is fenced in on all sides, politically, socially, economically; his very life is continually in jeopardy. The area, too, in which Judaism may grow and live is narrowly circumscribed—it is largely limited to the synagogue and the home. How did Jews understand their exile? How did they explain it to themselves? They looked upon it as part of the great dialogue between God and Israel. In the Books of Moses, and later on by the prophets, they already were warned that if they did not keep their covenant with God, the land would "spew" them out and they would be scattered among the nations. Indeed there exists a deep-rooted tradition that *Galut* is a punishment for sins. It is the old *Mipnei Hataeinu* (because of our sins) idea that we discussed earlier. It was not easy to maintain such an idea. Exile had gone on much too long; the suffering was often too heavy to bear. The questions were unavoidable: Are we so much worse than the others? Are our transgressions so much more grievous? A great deal of ingenuity was spent in order to justify the idea of punishment. If one would wish not to lose faith in the mercies of the Almighty, one could take recourse in the talmudic teaching that God is exacting of the righteous "up to a hair-breadth." The righteous are judged much more strictly, because they ought to know better. One could also take refuge from the searching questions of threatening disbelief by recalling the words of Amos (3:2):

> You only have I known of all the families of the earth;
> Therefore I will visit upon you all your iniquities.[6]

Although, as we saw earlier, even in the Bible and the Talmud it was not accepted as the only satisfactory explanation, Jews through the ages clung to it stubbornly. It is understandable; there was solace in it. One could preserve one's self-respect and also retain one's faith in God's justice. Israel's very closeness to God explained Israel's destiny in exile.

Such ideas were supported by another trend in Jewish thought—the positive value of suffering. Rightly endured, suffering purifies and deepens the human personality. It induces man to turn inward; to foreswear the superficial pleasures of the passing moment and to concentrate on the enduring values of human existence, perhaps to seek ultimate meaning where alone it may be found—in a realm beyond time and space. The ideas were often helpful in the darkest hours of the *Galut*. They enabled the Jew to carry on, to move from catastrophe to catastrophe without surrendering either faith or hope. Indeed, after each catastrophe his spirit revived in faith, sure that suffering was the necessary phase preceding the coming of the Messiah. Jews could believe it because through suffering they had atoned for their sins, they were purified, they were tested and stood the test. Because of suffering they were ready for the Messiah, worthy of him. The periods of great crisis and persecution were usually the hour of the false Messiah. If the Messiah did not come, there was always an explanation. Somehow, Jews failed again. The explanation was not always convincing. The *Galut* had gone on too long, it was too cruel. In the numerous penitential prayers of the synagogue, the *S'lihot*, the question for the reason of it all, is recurring continually. It was summed up in a famous passage: "All exiles come to an end, only mine increases; all questions are answered, but my question returns ever to the place from which it came."[7]

Is there nothing but punishment, purification, and waiting only to be disappointed? Needless to say, in the light of all that has been said earlier in this essay there is also another approach to the problem, more valid and equally well rooted in the teaching. Exile as a single event may well be punishment. But exile as an enduring condition, and entailing survival in spite of it, belongs to a fundamentally different category. Usually, exile is understood as a sequence, an abnormal phase following upon a normal one. *Galut*, the specifically Jewish form of exile, is rather different: it does not follow; it is at the beginning. Jewish history begins with God's words to Abraham: "Get thee out of thy country, and from thy kindred, and from thy father's house, unto the land which I will show thee."[8] The history of Judaism commences with *Galut*. If exile is at the very start then there must be something in the nature of Judaism, in God's plan for the Jewish people, which is inseparable from it. Abraham, in order to become the patriarch of Israel, had to leave his father's house and the land of his birth. He embraced his destiny in a world which was alien to him, to his faith, to his values, to his truth. He went into exile, because in the world as it existed then, Abraham could not find a home. He had the choice: either to be true to himself and become a stranger, or wanderer, or to become one with his surroundings and remain at home. He chose himself, his own personal destiny; but in order to do that he had to go into exile. Even before they were born, it was decreed concerning his descendants that they would be strangers in a land that was not theirs, where they would be oppressed and afflicted for four hundred years.[9] Obviously this could not have been a punishment. The children of Israel, whom the natural course of events had taken to Egypt, could have merged with the Egyptian people and have been completely absorbed by Egypt's civilization. But if they were to remain Jews and loyal to the obligations of their descent, they had to remain apart. Again, like their father Abraham, they had a choice: to surrender their identity and submerge in the majority or to remain true to themselves and become strangers and live in exile.

What is the significance of *Galut* as a starting point? One might generalize and say: There are certain ideals that are not easily absorbed by the order of the world; there are values that are repulsed by the laws of power history; ideas and values that are strangers among men and are of tragic necessity forced into exile. Such a stranger in history is the idea represented by the Jewish people in the history of mankind. The history of a people of God, a people that enters on the scene of history on the strength of a covenant with God, that sees its responsibility as a people to obey God's word and to do His will, must begin in a condition of *Galut*. As Abraham did not fit into the local world of his birthplace so do his children not fit into the universal world of the nations to the extent that it is dominated by materialistic self-interest and ambitions of power. We say in our prayers, "Because of our sins we have been exiled from our land," but the truth is that during the period of the Second Temple the Jewish people had already completely given up every form of idolatry. It was the period of the great teachers of the Mishnah. During that time Israel was probably closer to God than in any previous phase in its history. Yet, this generation was overtaken by the catastrophe of the *hurban*, the destruction of the Temple and the state and the scattering of the people into the four corners of the world. There was no metaphysical reason for this. What happened was quite natural. For in the world as it existed then, a world ruled by the Roman Empire, there was indeed no room for the people of the prophets, the people of a Hillel and a Rabban Gamliel.

There are many passages in the Talmud and Midrash that describe God as weeping over the exile of his children.[10] This is in keeping with our earlier analysis that God, having created man, rendered himself "powerless" in a sense. Why should exile involve the kind of suffering Israel had to endure? It is taken for granted that a minority scattered all over the world that attempts to retain its identity will be oppressed and persecuted. But this can only be taken for granted because there is something very wrong with man and with the world. Whenever a minority is persecuted, justice, humanity, decency are all in a state of exile from the affairs of men. The case of the Jew is, of course, aggravated by the fact that, not by what he does, but by what he is, indeed by the fact that he is, represents a challenge to the principle by which nations "normally" live. And God himself is "powerless." He could crush man and destroy man's world. But if he desires man, he must take the risk with him and wait for him until man becomes what he ought to be. This, of course, means that exile is a cosmic condition. God himself is a refugee in the world. This is the final meaning of the Jewish concept of *sh'khinta b'Galuta*, the Divine Presence in exile in the world. The *Galut* of the Jewish people is a specific cause of this cosmic condition and a necessary outcome of it.

In spite of the suffering involved there is also majesty in exile, the majestic loyalty of a people that in an unprecedented and unparalleled manner has kept faith with an ideal. Even Jews are often inclined to look upon their *Galut* as a phase of passivity in which the Jewish people are a mere object for the butt end of history. The truth is that their condition was a matter of choice. But for the Nazi period, Jews could always escape persecution through apostasy, by conversion, through assimilation and complete surrender of identity. The arms of Christianity, especially, were always spread out invitingly toward the Jew. Because of the daily pressures and persecutions, everyday that the Jew endured and remained loyal to his God or to his identity was a day of choice and decision. To accept the day-by-day challenge and not to surrender, no matter what the consequences, has been a deed of the spirit that for intensity, duration, and willingness for self-sacrifice remains unique in the history of mankind.

The Suffering Servant of God

If God is "powerless," God's people, too, will be powerless. To be God's people is more than acknowledging God; it means accepting God's world in all its consequences for those who acknowledge Him. God's people may cry out in their agony: How long still, O God! but will put up with God's long-suffering, with His questionable experiment, man. To be chosen by God is to be chosen for bearing the burden of God's long-suffering silences and absences in history. It is for this reason that at the beginning of Israel's history stands the *Akedah*, the binding of Isaac. Abraham was not guilty, nor was the sacrifice desired of him, punishment. It was initiation into the sacrificial way of the Chosen Ones. What was revealed to the patriarch was repeated as his children were led onto the path that they were to take through history: "Know of a surety that thy seed shall be a stranger in a land that is not theirs, and shall serve them, and they shall afflict them four hundred years."[11] It was all decided before the child, destined to become father to the nation, was even born. It was repeated innumerable times later. God's chosen ones suffer guiltlessly. It is what is called in Hebrew terminology *gezeira*, an inscrutable divine decree. The decree is not that there be human suffering; the decree is that there be divine long-suffering with man in spite of man's criminal turpitude; indeed, the decree is that there be this world of man which could not stand without divine forbearance. Suffering of the guiltless is the indirect result of the decree of creation. The thought finds its moving expression in the awesome solemnity of the liturgy of the "Ten Martyrs," which is recited on the Day of Atonement. The very angels in heaven cried out bitterly: "Is this then the Torah? And this its reward?" Whereupon a heavenly voice was heard: "If I hear another sound, I shall turn the world back to water and my throne's footstool (i.e., the earth[12]) to *tohu v*ᵉ*bohu*. This is a decree (*gezeira*) from before me. Accept it ye who find your pleasure in the Law, which precedes the creation." Why did they not utter that one sound, that protesting No to the abomination, euphemistically called "the footstool of his throne"? If such is the footstool, by all means let it go crushing down into its primordial *tohu v*ᵉ*bohu!* The martyrs, Rabbi Akiba and his saintly friends, did not speak that condemning No. They knew that the real issue was not their suffering; at stake was God's act of creation, his freedom and authority to say, "Let there be!" The chosen ones know that the choice is between *tohu v*ᵉ*bohu* of non-existence and their acceptance of the yoke of the divine experiment of creation. Without their acceptance, the world would indeed have to be turned back into nothingness. Only when the chosen ones choose to accept "the decree" does the world acquire the moral right to continue to exist. As they accept the yoke, God may go on being long-suffering with the rest of mankind. The world is sustained by the suffering of the guiltless.

God's chosen people is the suffering servant of God. The majestic fifty-third chapter of Isaiah is the description of Israel's martyrology through the centuries. The Christian attempt to rob Israel of the dignity of Isaiah's suffering servant of God has been one of the saddest spiritual embezzlements in human history. At the same time, the way Christianity treated Israel through the ages only made Isaiah's description fit Israel all the more tragically and truly. Generation after generation, Christians poured out their iniquities and inhumanity over the head of Israel, yet they "esteemed him, stricken, smitten of God, and afflicted." At the same time, they misunderstood the true metaphysical dignity of the suffering of God's servant. What is the weight of one sacrifice compared to the myriads of sacrifices of Israel? What is one crucifixion beside a whole people crucified through centuries? But, it is maintained, the one crucified was a god, whereas the untold millions of Jewish men, women, and children were only human beings. Human beings only! As if the murder of an innocent human being were a lesser crime than the killing of a god. A god, after all, does not have to die. If he is killed, it is because he offers himself freely as a sacrifice. A god chooses to be killed; he knows what he is doing and why he is doing it. And when he dies, he does not suffer as a god. As a "very man" he suffers the agony of a single man. But the little boy who at the door of the gas chamber says to his mother: "But, Mama, I was a good boy!"[13] that is something quite different. That is crucifixion! Or the little boy of eleven pressed into the indignity of a cattle truck on its way to Treblinka. The endless journey in the heat of a burning summer. There is hardly any room to stand. Occasionally, one steps on a corpse who only moments ago was a neighbor, a friend, a loved one. There is no air, no water, no sanitary facilities; ultimate darkness and doom! The father beside him. "My little boy, whom I was holding by the hand was almost suffocating from lack of air and thirst. His legs were giving way under him; he was sagging to the floor. I had to support him. He spoke in his fever: Daddy! We are going to Mama. Aren't we? I do see her. Hie! Open the doors! Shoot us! An end! Let there be an end to it!" This too is something quite different. This is what I call crucifixion. Or the eight-year-old in the refugee center in the Warsaw Ghetto. The child is by now mad and runs around screaming: "I want to steal, I want to rob, I want to eat, I want to be a German." Such is crucifixion. And it has been suffered not by gods, but by human beings, endured again and again on innumerable occasions all through Jewish history in Christian lands. That deicide is the greatest of human crimes is among the most dangerous fallacies ever taught to man. The truth is that the capital crime of man is not deicide, but homicide. To torture and to kill one innocent child is a crime infinitely more abominable than the killing of any god. Had Christianity, instead of being preoccupied with what it believed to have been a deicide, concentrated its educative attention on the human crime of homicide, mankind would have been spared much horror and tragedy. There would have been much less suffering and much less sorrow among all men; nor could there have been either Auschwitz or Treblinka. Unfortunately, the teaching of deicide became an excuse, and often a license, for homicide. Pity any god thus caricatured by his devotees!

God suffers not on account of what man does to him. What could man do to God? He suffers because of what man does to himself and to his brother. He suffers the suffering of his servant, the agony of the guiltless. In all their affliction, he is afflicted.[14] In the liturgy of the High Holy Days, God is referred to as the one who suffers, as he averts his eyes from the rebellious. He is long-suffering with man and suffers with the victims of man who carry the burden of his long-suffering patience and mercy. How he must love those who suffer innocently because he cannot but bear even with those of his creatures who have failed him! God's servant carries upon his shoulders God's dilemma with man through history. God's people share in all the fortunes of God's dilemma as man is bungling his way through toward messianic realization. The status of the dilemma at any one moment in history is revealed by the condition of Israel at that moment. God's people is God's challenge to man. God, who leads man "without might and without power" sent his people into the world without the might of power. This is the essence of the confrontation between Israel and the world. It was in this confrontation that Western man had to prove himself. God has pushed Israel right across the path of Christianity. Israel was God's question of destiny to Christendom. In its answer, the Christian world failed him tragically. Through Israel, God tested Western man and found him wanting. This gruesome failure of Christianity has led the Western world to the greatest moral debacle of any civilization—the holocaust.

The Witness after the Holocaust

1.

Does all this justify God's silence during the European holocaust of the Jewish people or does it even explain it? As we have already stated it is not our intention to explain it, and certainly not to justify it. We have tried to show what is implied in Judaism's faith in the God of history independently of our contemporary experience. The question is, of course, well-grounded: Can such faith still be maintained in the face of the destruction of European Jewry? People of our day are often apt to give quick and mainly emotional answers to the question. This is understandable. We have been too close to the catastrophe, too deeply and personally involved. However, notwithstanding our deep emotional involvement, it is essential first of all to gain a clear intellectual grasp of the problem.

The Jewish, radical theologian of our day—and the numerous less sophisticated people whose preoccupation with the problem of Auschwitz does not let them reach any other solution but the negative one—do not understand the true nature of the quandary of faith that confronts us. The problem of faith here is a problem of theology in the broadest sense of the word. What becomes questionable is the manner in which God relates himself to the world and to man. Strictly speaking, the questioning of God's justice in his relation to history has little to do with the quantity of undeserved suffering. The enormity of the number of martyrs of our generation—six million—is not essential to the doubt. As far as our faith in an absolutely just and merciful God is concerned, the suffering of a single innocent child poses no less a problem to faith than the undeserved suffering of millions. As far as one's faith in a personal God is concerned, there is no difference between six, five, four million victims or one million. Nahmanides expressed the thought clearly in his *Sha'ar Ha'gmul* in the following words: "Our quest [regarding theodicy] is a specific one, about [the plight of] this particular man. . . . This problem is not reduced if those who fall are few in number; nor does it become more serious if their number increases. For we are not discussing [the ways of] man. . . . Our arguments concern the Rock, whose work is perfect and all His ways just; there is nothing perverse or crooked in them."[15] Nothing is easier than to miss, for emotional reasons, the decisive importance of such a statement. How can one compare the suffering of a few to that of a multitude? How dare one raise the problem over the death of one innocent child as one must over that of a million and a half innocent Jewish children slaughtered by the Germans! One cannot and one dare not—as long as one judges man. There is a vast difference between less injustice and more injustice, between less human suffering and more. One human tragedy is not as heartbreaking as the same tragedy multiplied a millionfold. A man who murders one person is not as guilty as a mass murderer. The German crime of the ghettos and concentration camps stands out in all human history as the most abominable, the most sickening, and the most inhuman. But justice and injustice, guilt and innocence are matters of degree only for man. When one questions the acts of an Absolute God, whose every attribute, too, is absolute by definition, the innocent suffering of a single person is as incomprehensible as that of millions, not because the sufferings of millions matters as little as those of one human being, but because with Him the suffering of the one ought to be as scandalous as that of multitudes. An absolute just God cannot be a tiny bit unjust. The least injustice in the Absolute is absolute injustice. An infinitely merciful God cannot be just a little bit unconcerned about innocent suffering. The least amount of indifference in the Infinite is infinite indifference. With Elisha ben Abuyah, to have witnessed one case of undeserved suffering of the innocent was sufficient to raise the problem and cause him to lose faith. Such was also the insight of Camus. One compares the two sermons of the priest in *The Plague*. The first is a fire-and-brimstone preachment about the divine judgement that descended upon the sinful city; the second one is the mild acknowledgement of an impenetrable mystery. What happened between the two preachings? The priest had to witness the agony of a single child dying of the plague. One case was sufficient to change the man, who ultimately dies of the sickness of the incomprehensible.

Once the problem of evil is understood in its valid dimensions, the specific case of the holocaust is not seen to be essentially different from the old problem of theodicy.

It is still the old problem of Epicurus that confronts us. If God desires to prevent evil but is unable, he is not omnipotent. If he is able to prevent evil, but does not desire to do so, he is malevolent. If he is able and desires to prevent it, whence evil? The problem has been discussed by all thinking and believing people through the ages. It is one of the themes in Plato's *Statesman*. Already in those days there were those who from the presence of evil in the world concluded that God must be absent from history. He had to be far removed from the earthly scene; he could have no knowledge of man. If he did, how could he tolerate the evil that was done under the sun! This consideration was also one of the reasons for the assertion in later Aristotelianism that God had no knowledge of "singulars" and thus, divine providence was in no way concerned with the plight of the individual being or creature. These were the early forms of what in our day likes to call itself radical theology.

Once the questioning of God over the holocaust is motivated by the vastness of the catastrophe, the questioning itself becomes ethically questionable. It is of course more human to query God about the suffering of the many rather than the few, but it is certainly not more humane. On the contrary, it is more ethical, and intellectually more honest and to the point, to question God about the life and happiness of which even a single soul is being cheated on this earth than to base one's doubts and quest on the sacrificial abandonment of millions. With God, the quantity of injustice must be immaterial. To think otherwise is itself a sign of callous indifference toward injustice and human suffering. To suggest that one could put up with less evil and less injustice, but not with so much, is cruelly unethical. Indeed, the holocaust was only possible because mankind was quite willing to tolerate less than the holocaust. This was the decisive aspect in the guilt of man in our times. It is important to understand the true nature of the problem if one involves God in it, questioning his ways with man and the world. It is the precondition for developing the attitude that may enable us to live meaningfully with the problem, even though its ultimate solution may forever escape us. Understood in its vastest intellectual dimension and its radical ethical relevance, the question is not why the holocaust, but why a world in which any amount of undeserved suffering is extant. This, of course, means that the question is tantamount to, why man? Why a world of man? For, indeed, if man is to be as a being striving for value-realization, God must tolerate and endure him as a failure and an accusation.

How long is he to be tolerated as a failure, how long to be endured by God as an accusation of God? Who is to say! In order to answer the question, one ought to know the heart of God. How long God is willing to endure his creation even as a failure is the secret of creation itself. God's dominion over the world is not a dominion of justice.[16] In terms of justice, he is guilty. He is guilty of creation. But is he guilty of indifference or is he guilty of too much long-suffering? How vast is the infinitude of his mercy, his patience with man? When is it the moment for his justice to intervene and to call a halt to misused human freedom? Can we gauge the reach of his love even for the wicked, be they even those of his creatures who choose to become his failures? According to midrashic teaching, at the time of the drowning of the hosts of Pharaoh in the Red Sea, the angels in heaven, as is their wont, were preparing to chant the daily hymn in praise of the Almighty. But God silenced them with the words: "The works of my hands are drowning in the sea and you sing my praises!"[17] It is not an easy matter for God to execute judgement over the guilty. Even "his failures" are the works of his hands.

2.

The question after the holocaust ought not to be, how could God tolerate so much evil? The proper question is whether, after Auschwitz, the Jewish people may still be witnesses to God's elusive presence in history as we understand the concept. What of the nemesis of history and what of Jewish survival?

The Nazi crime of the German people attempted to eradicate the last vestiges of a possible innate sense of humanity; it sought the conscious extirpation from human nature of the last reminder of the fear of God in any form. It was the ultimate rebellion of nihilism against all moral emotion and all ethical values. However, this up to now mightiest and most morbid manifestation of human hubris too was overtaken by its complete and inescapable nemesis. In every field the very opposite of its goals has been accomplished. "Das Tausendjahrige Reich," the empire for a millennium, was in ashes after twelve terrible years. Instead of the much heralded "Gross Deutschland" there is a divided Germany with greatly reduced frontiers. The nemesis is not limited to Nazi Germany alone, it has overtaken Western civilization itself. The holocaust is not exclusively the guilt of Germany; the entire West has a goodly share in it. One of the most tragic aspects of the world catastrophe of nazism is to be seen in the fact that it was able to assume its vast dimensions of calamity mainly because of the tolerance and "understanding" that it enjoyed in the world community of nations for many years. During the period of favorable international climate, nazified Germany was able to create one of the most powerful war machines in all history, to poison the minds of vast sections of the world's population, and to corrupt governments and public officials in many lands. This was possible partly because, with the help of the antisemitic heritage of the West, Nazi Germany was able to bring about the moral disintegration of many peoples with diabolical efficiency and speed and partly—and not altogether independently of it—because of the cynical calculations of worldwide power politics. Germany was meant to become the bulwark of the West against the threat of Russian communism. To this end many were willing to ignore the German-Nazi challenge to elementary justice and humanity. After all, its worst venom was directed against the Jews only. Even after the second World War had already pursued its horrifying course in Europe for several years, there were still influential forces in the high seats of power, and even on the throne of so-called "spiritual grandeur," that hoped for a rapprochement between Nazi Germany and the Western powers. They thought it politically wise to go slow on Nazi-Germany criminality, piously hoping to bring off the brotherly alliance that would enable them to launch the greatest of all crusades, that against Soviet communism. Thus they became accomplices in the criminality of Auschwitz and the gas chambers. Nothing of what they had hoped for has been achieved. Instead of a curbing of communism, for which Germany and her sympathizers hoped, communism has reached its widest penetration the world over. This is not stated with any partiality for communism, but solely from the point of view of an observer who tries to detect the functioning of nemesis in history. Nazi Germany could have been stopped early in its track had there been less indifference toward the plight of the Jews and a better understanding of the demoralizing power of antisemitism. But antisemitism had long been a respectable trait in Western civilization. Thus, the Second World War became inevitable, as a result of which all the formerly great powers of Europe had been reduced to second and third rank. And even Russia and the United States, who came out of the war as superpowers dwarfing all others, what have they gained if, as a result of their overwhelming might, they render each other's future, as well as that of all mankind, rather questionable? It is no mere coincidence that having countenanced the Final Solution to the Jewish problem, partly with glee and partly with equanimity, the world is now confronted with the serious possibility of a Final Solution to the entire problematic existence of man on this planet. Every one of the ambitions that the forces of power history have been pursuing have been weighed and found wanting. Had the nations and their churches not been silent and indifferent to what was recognizably afoot in the early days of nazism, world history would have taken an entirely different course and mankind would not now be balancing on the very edge of the thermonuclear abyss. This post-holocaust era is charged with the nemesis of history. This is the ignoble twilight hour of a disintegrating civilization.

It is true the Jewish people had to pay a terrible price for the crimes of mankind and today, too, as part of mankind, they are themselves deeply involved in the crisis of the human race, yet the Final Solution intended for it is far from being final. Though truncated, Israel survived this vilest of all degradations of the human race. Not only has it survived, but rising from one of its most calamitous defeats, it has emerged to new dignity and historic vindication in the state of Israel.

The most significant aspect of the establishment of the state of Israel is the fact that Jews through the ages knew that it was to come. They were waiting for it during their wanderings for long and dark centuries. There was little rational basis for their faith in the eventual return to the land of their fathers. Yet they knew that one day the faith would be translated into historical reality. They lived with that faith in the sure knowledge of divine concern. For the Jew, for whom Jewish history neither begins with Auschwitz nor ends with it, Jewish survival through the ages and the ingathering of the exiles into the land of their fathers after the holocaust proclaim God's holy presence at the very heart of his inscrutable hiddenness. We recognized in it the hand of divine providence because it was exactly what, after the holocaust, the Jewish people needed in order to survive. Broken and shattered in spirit even more than in body, we could not have been able to continue on our Jewish way through history without some vindication of our faith that the "Guardian of Israel neither slumbers nor sleeps." The state of Israel came at a moment in history when nothing else could have saved Israel from extinction through hopelessness. It is our lifeline to the future.

3.

Confronting the holocaust, the relevant consideration is the full realization that it does not preempt the entire course of Jewish history. One dare not struggle with the problem of faith as if the holocaust were all we knew about the Jew and his relation to God. There is a pre-holocaust past, a post-holocaust present, and there is also a future, which is, to a large extent, Israel's own responsibility. Auschwitz does not contain the entire history of Israel; it is not the all-comprehensive Jewish experience. As to the past, we should also bear in mind that the Jew, who has known so much of the "Hiding of the Face," has also seen the divine countenance revealed to him. Notwithstanding Auschwitz, the life of the patriarchs is still with him; the Exodus did not turn into a mirage; Sinai has not come tumbling down; the prophets have not become charlatans; the return from Babylon has not proved to be a fairy tale. It is, of course, possible for people to secularize the history of Israel and deny the manifestation of a divine presence in it. However, such secularization is independent of the holocaust. It is not very meaningful to interpret the entire course of Jewish history exclusively on the basis of the death-camp experience of European Jewry. If the believer's faith in Israel's "encounters" with God in history is false, it must be so not on account of Auschwitz, but because the "encounters" just did not happen. On the other hand, if these manifestations of the divine presence did occur, then they are true events and will not become lies because of the holocaust.

For the person who does not recognize the presence of God in the Exodus, at Sinai, in the words of the prophets, in innumerable events of Jewish history, Auschwitz presents no problem of faith. For him God is forever absent. Only the Jew who has known of the presence of God is baffled and confounded by Auschwitz. What conclusions is he to draw from this terrifying absence of divine concern? Is God indifferent to human destiny? But the Jew knows otherwise. He knows of the most intimate divine concern. Has God, perhaps, died? Is it possible that once upon a time there was a God who was not indifferent toward Israel, but that now something has happened to him, he has gone away, he is no longer? This is plain silly. It is possible for a human being to lose faith in God. But it is not possible for God to die. He either is and therefore, will ever be; or he is not and, therefore never was. But if God who was, is, and will ever be, is it possible that at Auschwitz he rejected Israel, he turned away from Israel as a punishment for its sins? To believe this would be a desecration of the Divine Name. No matter what the sins of European Jewry might have been, they were human failings. If the holocaust was a punishment, it was a thousandfold inhuman. The only crime of man for which such punishment might be conceivable would be the Nazi crime of Germany, and even there, one would hesitate to impose it.

The Jew of faith is thus left with the perplexing duality of his knowledge of God. He knows of the numerous revelations of the divine presence as he knows of the overlong phases of God's absence. Auschwitz does not stand by itself. Notwithstanding its unique position as perhaps the most horrifying manifestation of divine silence, it has its place in Jewish history beside the other silences of God together with the utterances of his concern. The Jew was called into being by the revelation of the divine in history. It is because God allowed his countenance to shine upon man that he is what he is. Only because of that does he know of the absence of God. But thanks to that, he also knows that God's absence, even at Auschwitz, is not absolute. Because of that it was possible for many to know God even along the path to the gas chambers. There were many who found him even in his hiding. Because of the knowledge of God's presence, the Jew can find God even in his absence.

No, the Holocaust is not all of Jewish history, nor is it its final chapter. That it did not become the Final Solution as was planned by the powers of darkness enables the Jew who has known of the divine presence to discern intimations of familiar divine concern in the very midst of his abandonment. This, too, is essentially an old Jewish insight.

Yet all this does not exonerate God for all the suffering of the innocent in history. God is responsible for having created a world in which man is free to make history. There must be a dimension beyond history in which all suffering finds its redemption through God. This is essential to the faith of a Jew. The Jew does not doubt God's presence, though he is unable to set limits to the duration and intensity of his absence. This is no justification for the ways of providence, but its acceptance. It is not a willingness to forgive the unheard cries of millions, but a trust that in God the tragedy of man may find its transformation. Within time and history that cry is unforgivable. One of the teachers of the Talmud notes that when God asks Abraham to offer him his son Isaac as a sacrifice, the exact rendering of the biblical words reads: "Take, I pray thee, my son."[18] In the view of this teacher the "binding of Isaac" was not a command of God, but a request that Abraham take upon himself this most exacting of all God's impositions. In a sense, we see in this a recognition that the sacrificial way of the innocent through history is not to be vindicated or justified! It remains unforgivable. God himself has to ask an Abraham to favor him by accepting the imposition of such a sacrifice. The divine request accompanies all those through history who suffer for the only reason that God creates man, whom God himself has to endure. Within time and history God remains indebted to his people; he may be long-suffering only at their expense. It was hardly ever as true as in our own days, after the holocaust. It is perhaps what God desires—a people, to whom he owes so much, who yet acknowledge him? Children, who have every reason to condemn his creation, yet accept the creator in the faith that in the fullness of time the divine indebtedness will be redeemed and the divine adventure with man will be approved even by its martyred victims?

The Nemesis of Power History

We realize that after all is said the question might be asked: Agreeing that the survival of the Jew and the emergence of the state of Israel are in intimation of God's hidden presence in history, how much has really been accomplished by either or both events? Looking at the world today, what impresses one most at a first glance is the emergence of vast power blocks, like the United States, the Soviet Union, and the People's Republic of China. States and countries like the British Empire, France, and Germany, which only a few decades ago were mighty and influential on a universal scale, have been reduced to second- and third-rate powers. Today, Jews may well ask themselves the question: What is the significance of Israel, the people and the state, on the world scene in the context of present-day world history? History has become the battleground of giants. What does a small people like the Jews amount to in a world dominated by a few colossi of overwhelming might and power?

The question is induced, in particular, by the rise of the state of Israel. Through the ages Jews longed for it and hoped for it. When the state was finally created, it was the culminating triumph of Jewish survival through the darkest experiences of human history. Yet, one cannot help pondering the question: Coming, as it did, in the atomic age, did not—perhaps—the state of Israel come too late? What a difference it would have made to millions of Jews, who perished in pogroms and concentration camps, what a difference to the entire position of the Jewish people in the world today, had the establishment of the state of Israel come one or two centuries sooner! In earlier days, the Jewish Problem held a major position in the Zionist analysis of the Jewish situation. The problem was seen as the homelessness of the Jewish people. It was believed that national sovereignty in the ancient homeland was the solution. However, in this age of the colossi, how much security is to be derived even from national sovereignty in a small state like Israel? We realize today that a state of this kind, notwithstanding its remarkable achievements and the industry and bravery of its citizens, may not be more secure than was the individual Jew during his long exile. In the world of giants, a state, too, may be "homeless."

The question as to the significance of the Jew in the context of present-day world history may of course be raised even more poignantly as regards the position of the Jew in the rest of the world. From the ancient lands of Jewish history on the European continent, Jews have been eliminated as a source of any kind of influence. In Soviet Russia, Jewry and Judaism lie prostrate under the heavy yoke of communism. Only on the American continent, and chiefly in the United States, does a large Jewish center exist whose members, enjoying the freedom of citizenship in a great democracy, take their place—and may make their mark—in every field of human endeavor. But notwithstanding the Jewish position on the American continent, it is extremely doubtful that any significant role may be ascribed to the Jew in the broader context of present-day human history. As the result of the radical transformations that have taken place the world over in our generation, all the major issues of human existence, issues of politics, economics, technology, human welfare, and progress have become more and more universally comprehensive. They are dominated by the Universal powers: the power blocks of the atomic giants and the explosive energy of the vast population blocks like China and the African and South American continents.

The world is being organized in global terms. What is the significance of the Jew in this global phase of human history? About a generation ago, the German historian Theodor Mommsen called the Jews and Judaism the ferment of history. Has the Jew now become a *quantité négligeable*, a negligible quantity on the world scene?

So it would seem, at first glance, if we evaluate the world transformation in quantitative terms only. However, looked at from the angle of a qualitative interpretation, there is yet another view which presents itself to the observer. The emergence of the colossi also illustrates the futility of power as an arbiter of history. In our days it has become commonplace to state that man, having amassed so much power that he is able to destroy life and civilization on a global scale, must learn to renounce power as a means of ordering or controlling relations between people and nations. It is true that at the moment the potential of sheer physical force is used as a deterrent and peace is preserved by a balance of terror. Quite clearly, however, such a situation cannot continue indefinitely. The colossi's fear of each other is a very shaky foundation on which to erect a lasting peace. If that is all on which man may base his hope for the future, there is little ground for optimism. In such a situation, the delicate balance of terror is bound to break down sooner or later and bring in its wake the dreaded universal conflagration. The inescapable demand of the historic moment requires the honest renunciation of material force in the dealings of the nations and power blocks with each other. But the honest and wholehearted renunciation of the use of power and might implies a genuine embracing of ethical and moral principles for the ordering of the life of all mankind. This is no longer mere sermonizing; it has become the "iron law" in this new phase of global history. Be decent or perish!

From the point of view of a philosophy of history the present phase offers an intriguing phenomenon. Man has known for a long time that the use of force against man was evil. But how was force to be defeated in history? By the use of greater force. Thus, mankind was caught in a vicious circle. Every defeat of power led to the rise of more power. And more power only intensified the power competition between the nations. In our days, history teaches us the solution to the problem: force is being weeded out of history by its own surfeit. Whereas in former times what nations could do with power induced them to use it, today the very immensity of power gathered in human hands compels man to surrender its use against his fellow man. Power has overreached itself and, thus, it has defeated itself. Philosophically speaking, this is a rather amusing phase in the dialectic of history. For some time now Marxists have been declaiming about the iron laws of dialectical materialism. One phase follows upon another in an inescapable sequence of necessity: slavery, feudalism, capitalism, and the ultimate culmination, communism. Each phase carries within itself the seeds of its own disintegration; each phase perishes of its own surfeit. In a sense, this was a rejection of the Jewish concept, as formulated by the prophet: "Not by might, nor by power, but by My Spirit, saith the Lord." Dialectical materialism denied any influence to the spirit, to ideas and ideals. Today, the dialectics of history is carrying mankind into a phase in which, "but by My Spirit" is no longer an ideal, but practical politics, the basic requirement for human survival. Dialectical materialism has suffered its own dialectical defeat. The scientific and technological transformation of the human situation demands the spiritual reformation of man and nations. It is the irony of history that, when materialism has reached one of its greatest triumphs—in world-embracing capitalist and communist power blocks—it has been outmaneuvered by a higher dialectics of the spirit.

It is, of course, true that mankind as a whole is psychologically not yet prepared for the dialectical need of survival by the might of the spirit. The present moment follows upon an age of materialism of the capitalist as well as the communist brand, of disenchantment, of the surrendering of ideals, of "the death of God," of cynicism and despair. For quite some time yet man will have to survive by the balance of terror, if he is to survive at all. However, the significance of our age as the dialectical self-defeat of physical force remains unaffected by the lack of human understanding.

The meaning of the world transformation, as it has taken place in this generation, is to be recognized as the task, imposed upon mankind today, to render the Spirit effective as a history-making force. Only because such is the nature of the challenge that confronts man in this hour is there any point in inquiring into the role destined for the Jew in this new phase of human history. One should have thought that the Jew was ideally suited, both by temperament and historical experience, for the task that faces mankind. Has he not survived because of the truth of the words, "but by My Spirit"? Has he not proved by his very survival that "My Spirit" is indeed a determining factor in history? Has he not proved it long before the present dialectical self-defeat of might and power in this atomic age? In his *The Meaning of History* Nicolas Berdyaev wrote the following about the meaning of Jewish history:

> I remember how the materialist interpretation of history, when I attempted in my youth to verify it by applying it to the destinies of peoples, broke down in the case of the Jews, where destiny seemed absolutely inexplicable from the materialistic standpoint. And, indeed, according to the materialistic and positivistic criterion, this people ought long ago to have perished. . . .[19]

One might say that the new historical situation requires of mankind what God demanded of the Jew from the beginning. Mankind is entering upon its "Jewish era" or else upon an era of self-immolation. As in the past so today, we are a nation without power. But how strange are the ways of the God of history who has led mankind to a juncture where it too will survive as Jews have survived to this day—by the renunciation of force as the arbiter of human destiny! How mysterious are His ways that have turned the specific Jewish stance in history into an inescapable universal necessity! How wondrous the plans of God with Israel that this vindication has come about immediately after the historical position of Israel had received its most shattering blow! Auschwitz has tragically dramatized the meaning of the new era that has broken in upon mankind. In our days, man has concentrated in his own hand adequate physical force to bring about the final solution to all of man's problems in one apocalyptic world conflagration. The holocaust has shown that man's lack of moral force is sufficient to bring about such a "final solution." For what was proved by the holocaust is not what man was capable of doing to the Jew, but what man is capable of doing to his fellow. The bomb has rendered the final solution on a universal scale a practical possibility; Auschwitz has demonstrated it to be morally feasible. The holocaust has presented man with the issue of all issues that looms on the horizon as mankind enters upon this new era. Not only has nazism been discarded upon the rubbish heap of history, but so has any system of society or government that seeks to triumph by force on a worldwide scale. The global powers are like men deified in terms of might. They are omnipotent. Yet, from now on they will have to function in history not unlike God's own functioning as we see it described in the traditional terms of the Talmud: "Such indeed is His mightiness that He subdues his omnipotence and grants long-suffering to the wicked. And such is the proof of His awesomeness; for were it not for the fear of Him, how could one people survive among the nations!"[20] Now that mankind as a whole has entered upon the perilous destiny that till now has been reserved for Israel, the global powers, our earthly gods of history, will have to act in a manner following the example of the Divine Ruler—hiding their omnipotence, subduing it, and treating each other and the smaller nations with "long-suffering," even though "the other" may seem to each of them to be "the wicked one." When man himself reaches the goal of quasi omnipotence, true might consists in the self-control of such omnipotence, in the renunciation of its use. From now on mankind will survive by the same critical minimum of what in religious language we call "the fear of God" by which the Jewish people were able to survive to this day. From now on, *imitatio dei* is no longer a mere religious idea, but the practical requirement of human survival. The quasi-omnipotent man must, as if, absent himself from history, as the omnipotent God is wont to do.

The universal significance of both Jewish survival and the return of the Jewish people to their ancestral land should be understood in the context of the new era which mankind has reached. Jews have survived as a homeless people through the long centuries, without political might and significant material power, while mankind pursued the illusion that human destiny is to be determined by exactly those factors which the Jewish people were lacking. They have survived, witnessing again and again the nemesis of mere material power, into the world era when the Jewish affirmation has become a necessity for universal survival. Similarly, the return of the Jewish people to its ancient homeland should be seen in a historical context. This hour, in which man has ascended to the pinnacle of material power, is also the hour of his deepest moral and spiritual exhaustion. Because of the surfeit of power and the exhaustion of the spirit, everything is in jeopardy. Quite clearly, the wave of the future is with neither of the power colossi of the moment. If either of them should insist on forcing the future of man in its own likeness, the world will be left only with the shambles of an inglorious past.

The immensity of the possibilities for "the works of peace" which is inherent in this great power and which, in the present world situation, is also wrought with ultimate peril, has already rendered archaic both giants, capitalism and communism, as modes of coping with the challenges that confront man. The foundations on which they arose have sunk away into the depths of past time. The historic moment calls for a civilization that surpasses both. The universal significance of Israel's return to the land of the fathers we see in the fact that it has taken place after the holocaust, i.e., in this hour of universal spiritual exhaustion and universal need for a spiritual rebirth of man. The restoration of Jewish sovereignty in Zion is not a goal in itself. What could be the political significance of a little Jewish state in the world of today! Political sovereignty is only the framework within which this remarkable people of history may lead its life according to its own vision and create a culture whose essential resources can only be of the spirit. That the relevance of that creation for mankind need not be proportionate to the political and material size of Israel has been sufficiently proven by the past history of the Jewish people and of the world.

Endnotes

[1]Isaiah 43:12.

[2]Sifrei.

[3]Deuteronomy 7:7.

[4]Isaiah 43:10.

[5]Cf. Rashi's commentary on Genesis 1:1.

[6]Amos 3:2.

[7]Quoted from *Galut* by Yitzhak F. Baer, New York: Schocken Library, 12, 1947, 26.

[8]Genesis 12:1.

[9]Ibid., 15:13.

[10]Cf. f.i., *Talmud Babli, B'rakhot*, 59a.

[11]Genesis 15:13.

[12]Cf., Isaiah 66:1.

[13]This is a quote from Andre Schwarz-Bart's, *The Last of the Just*. The next episode is described in a letter by the father of the child, published in *Kiddush Hashem*, ed. S. Niger, N.Y., 5707 A.M. The last episode referred to is recorded in *Notes from the Warsaw Ghetto*, the Journal of Emanuel Ringelblum.

[14]Cf. Isaiah, 63:9.

[15]*Shaar Ha'gmul* in *Hiddushei Ha'Ramban*, Part I., 193, ed. B'nei Brak, 5719 A.M.

[16]We are not unaware of the biblical verse that asserts that "all His ways are justice." (Deut 32:4) Obviously, the midrashic statement we have quoted in our text about the creation of the world by mercy and justice is not in keeping with such a reading. However, the Hebrew Bible does not have: "all His ways are justice." But, "all His ways are *Mishpat*." I have shown in a recent work how misleading it is to translate the biblical *Mishpat* as "justice" in the sense of Western civilization. See the chapter, "The Biblical Meaning of Justice," in my *Man and God, Studies in Biblical Theology*, Detroit: Wayne State University Press, 1969.

[17]*Talmud Babli, Sanhedrin,* 39b.

[18]Ibid., 89b.

[19]Nicholas Berdyaev, *The Meanning of History*, Cleveland, World Publishing Co., 1962.

[20]*Talmud Babli, Yoma,* 69b.

Chapter 6

Authenticity of Being*

Eliezer Berkovits

The concept of authenticity of being was introduced into modern existentialist philosophy by Martin Heidegger. He meant by this the form of human existence that is not determined by external conditions and whose values do not derive from "them," from the standard bearers of the established social order in the midst of which a human being may find himself. Jean-Paul Sartre developed the thought further when he spoke of freedom as a condition to which man is "condemned," meaning that no matter in what situation a person may find himself, he is always free to make his choices and, indeed, he always does choose between different possibilities of behavior. The decision is always his. When the Gestapo tortured a member of the Maquis to get him to betray his comrades, he was still free to choose to die or to reveal. His betrayal might be understandable; it is not a matter of condemning him. But in all circumstances the decision is his.

Sartre's position is no mere theory. His understanding of human freedom is based on his actual experiences in the French underground. Similarly Frankl, basing himself on his observations in the concentration camps, affirms the reality of human freedom even in extreme conditions. He writes: "The experiences of camp life show that man does have a choice of action. . . . Man can preserve a vestige of spiritual freedom, of independence of mind, even in such terrible conditions of psychic and physical stress." There were always choices to make, and it was your decision that "determined whether you would or would not submit to those powers which threaten to rob you of your very self, your inner freedom. . . ."[1]

For the Jew there is no surprise in these discoveries of Sartre and Frankl. He has made his choices all through history and the Jewish people have survived to this day because there were always Jews who knew that no matter what the conditions and circumstances, it was always up to them to make the decision. We are not only thinking of the untold martyrs who made their choice, in the supreme freedom of the spirit, to die rather than to surrender, but also—and perhaps chiefly—of the ordinary daily life of the Jewish masses through the ages. They lived in confrontation with cultures and civilizations whose values they often rejected and whose lifestyles they mostly did not share. The Jew has been the nonconformist of history and has lived in authenticity of selfhood through many centuries.

Though living through a persecution radically more severe than anything experienced previously, the Jews who suffered under the Nazis in essence continued the historic lifestyle of the Jewish people. To be sure, this lifestyle, as embodied in the *halakhah,* is a style of living. It does not consider physical existence unworthy of its concern. On the contrary, it is concerned with existence in its entirety. But human life is not limited to physical or biological existence; its physical and biological components are not a bit more "real" than its spiritual, value-oriented and meaning-seeking aspects. In the same sense, external reality, whose determination has been the preoccupation of modern philosophy for generations, is no more real than the internal life of the person. A thought, an idea, a concept, is no less of this world than a cell, a molecule, or a biological drive. The human being, as a potentiality, and the world that he encounters, are the raw material out of which selfhood emerges. The reality of man is never given; he has to shape it for himself out of what is given to him. How he does it, that alone determines the quality of his humanity.

The significance of what we have called authentic Jewish behavior is that even in the ghettos and the death camps there were numerous Jews who determined their own lifestyles. In the midst of the filth of the SS kingdom they established their own realm of Jewish continuity, giving structure to the wilderness into which they were cast. What did this mean in terms of the actual, daily camp situation?

In a moving passage, Frankl describes one of his personal experiences that could have occurred on any ordinary day:

> "Almost in tears from pain (I had terrible sores on my feet from wearing torn shoes), I limped a few kilometers with our long column of men from the camp to our work site. Very cold, bitter winds struck. I kept thinking of the endless little problems of our miserable life. What should there be to eat tonight? If a piece of sausage came as extra ration, should I exchange it for a piece of bread? Should I trade my last cigarette, which was left from a bonus I received a fortnight age, for a bowl of soup? How could I get a piece of wire to replace the fragment which served as one of my shoelaces? Would I get to our work site in time to join my usual working party or would I have to join another, which might have a brutal foreman. . . ?"

Unlike the mass of prisoners, Frankl, having been able to safeguard a high measure of personal dignity, became disgusted with a situation that compelled him to think "daily and hourly . . . of only such trivial things." Fighting off the onslaught of the trivia, he found relief in falling back on his professional interest. Suddenly, as if in a vision, he saw himself standing "on the platform of a well-lit, warm and pleasant lecture room." In from of him sat "an attractive audience on comfortable upholstered seats," to whom Frankl lectured on the psychology of the concentration camp. Thus the daily camp experience became objectified as a phenomenon for scientific examination. Frankl then explains: "By this method I succeeded somehow in rising above the situation, above the sufferings of the moment, and I observed them as if they were already of the past."[2] Needless to say, matters which in normal conditions would be considered mere trivial received extraordinary importance in the camps Hosts of prisoners found themselves in the predicament of having to limp many kilometers from the camp to their work site and back in pain because of their sore feet. What would authentic Jews be thinking of during such a march? Probably of the very same trivial needs that so occupied Frankl. But they would not be thinking of these things "daily and hourly," and their concern was not only with "such trivial things." They would be no less deeply involved with problems of an entirely different nature: would they be able to find a corner in their barracks where they might be able to pray *Ma'ariv* (the evening service) with the prescribed quorum of at least ten men? How could they get their hands on a pair of *tefillin*? How many rations of bread would it cost? Or, if *Purim* was approaching, where could they get a *megillah* (the Scroll of Esther)? Would it be another *Pesah* without *matzah*? How could they minimize the need for eating the hot soup of the camp, which was *terefah*? How could they make a *menorah* for Hanukkah and smuggle it into the camp? And once it was there, how could they light it without it being discovered? Innumerable problems of this nature, and the devising of possible solutions for them, were among the foremost of their "daily and hourly" concerns. Victor Frankl had the strength of character to create his scientific vision and thus to escape the degrading misery of the death camps. These Jews, however, were not escaping. They imposed another rhythm on that raw reality to which they were subjected and thus drew out its dehumanizing poison. They lived their lives as Jews.

Trying to understand, trying to empathize with the suffering of Frankl, his feet covered with sores, limping along with his fellow prisoners from the hill of the camp to the hell of the work site and back, I see in my mind's eye another long column of men, marching perhaps along the same road, in all kinds of chafing footwear, their torn rags exposing them to the elements, many of them limping along supported by their comrades; and the same long column returning exhausted in the evening, usually dragging along a few lifeless bodies with them. But somewhere there, intentionally lost in that same columns, is a group of Jews, keeping close together. In their midst there walks one, a *Talmid Hakham*, who knows large sections of the Talmud by heart. He teaches Talmud, he teaches Torah. The others are listening; they interrupt with questions or to make their own contribution to the discussion. And of course there are other roads, other threadbare marchers, and other intense groups of Jews studying Talmud, or perhaps Mishnah, or reciting chapters from the Psalms by memory.

The camps had their own geographic pattern, designed to serve the goals of the extermination squads. But for these Jews, some of the roads were not paths of SS-prescribed misery, but were transformed by them into paths of daily renewal. The authentic Jewish lifestyle superimposed a space-structure of meaningfulness on the camp geography of humiliation and degradation. Similarly, the occupants of the *Tahara Bretter* (the boards of purity) at Buchenwald changed the space structure of the camp in their immediate area, establishing a focal point of direction for the Jews all around them, and not only for those who were still practicing Judaism. In that section, the map of the camp received the impact of a humanizing purpose. Or think of the deathpit turned into the *Bet Medreshel*, a place of prayer and study; the various spots in the Holocaust kingdom where *sukkot* were built secretly; the hiding places for *tefillin*, for a *Hanukkah menorah*, for a *shofar* to blow on *Rosh haShanah*-all points of a conspiratorial changing of space structure, a reorientation of directions in the camps.

Nowhere did this autonomous restructuring of camp reality achieve a more penetrating influence than in the dimension of time. Using the example of Bernard Malamud's *The Fixer*, Terrence Des Pres effectively discusses the trying experience of unstructured time that was the lot of the prisoners in the concentration camps. He writes: ". . . in extremity the forms of time dissolve, the rhythms of change and motion are lost. Days pass, seasons, years pass and the fixer has no idea how long his ordeal will go on." There is "an emptiness complete in itself, a suspension in the sameness of identical days which could last a year or a lifetime."[3] What was true for the fixer was even more oppressive and demoralizing for those in the German death camps.[4] However, for the Jews whose lifestyle we are examining, the "suspension in the sameness of identical days," the complete emptiness of endless duration, did not exist. Their time was not the SS-imposed structureless sameness; their time was structured by the Jewish calendar. Calendars were handwritten in the ghettos and camps, and even where they were not available, there were always Jews who could calculate and compute the necessary dates on the basis of the scanty information that was available. Thus, for the Jews, time was divided into days, weeks, months, seasons, and years. The division represented an experienced rhythm of sequence, each part of which carried its remembered and observed meaning and significance.

According to Frankl, the most ghastly moment of the day was "the awakening, when, at a still nocturnal hour, the three shrill blows of a whistle tore us pitilessly from our exhausted sleep and from the longings of our dreams." He tells the story of how a comrade beside him was having a nightmare. At first, instinctively, he meant to wake him; but then he decided not to disturb him, for no matter how frightening his nightmare might have been, the awakening would have been even worse. To Frankl, it was a wonder that prisoners got up at all. What was awaiting them? An endless day or torture, humiliation, exhaustion, and hunger. "Prisoners were driven awake by fear, by anxiety, and often by the blows of a whip or club."[5] But what was each new day in the structured time of the Jewish calendar? Needless to say the tortures, the humiliation, the fatigue were all there in it. But for those Jews who rose one or two hours before the general *appell* in order to put on *tefillin* for a few moments, and for the thousands who had no access to *tefillin* but who nevertheless rose before the other prisoners, without the three shrill blows of the whistle, in order to say their morning prayers, it was a day given by God, on which one praised him as the Creator of light. One got up, because one had to, not because of the whip and the club, but because the morning is the time for *Shaharit*, the daily morning service. The day of the camp was indeed endless misery, yet another daily order was superimposed on it. With the sun about to set, one had to find an inconspicuous spot for a quick *Minha* prayer. And at night, one did not drop with senseless exhaustion into one's bunk. One collected oneself. The order of the day called for its conclusion with *Ma'ariv*, the evening service. The week: for those who live in unstructred time there is no such thing as a week, but empty duration stretching infinitely. Only he who knows of the Sabbath knows of the week. Of course, the Sabbath could not be observed traditionally. One *had* to work; yet, one could, and did, celebrate the Sabbath even in the most extreme circumstances. This is how one survivor describes it:

> Come Sabbath we feel the *Neshama Yeterah*, the enrichment of our souls.[6] She sings in the depth of our being. How we love the Sabbath! We draw from her strength for all the days of the week. In the dim light of the descending evening we sing quietly . . . God is with us. *Imo Anokhi beZarah.* "I am with him is his trouble". . . *Shekhinta beGaluta*, yes, the Divine Presence itself is in exile with us.[7] We are not so lonely. A High Guest is staying with us. He, too, is now homeless, lonely without His people, suffering through our suffering. As the day is passing, in a darkening world we hold on to her, to our Sabbath. It is hard to take leave of her. We shall be alone again for such a long gray frightening week. Beginning with the first day of the week we start counting the days in our hearts till *Erev Shabbat*, till the sixth day. . . .[8]

A long week indeed, full of hardship and suffering. But on Monday it would be only five days till the next Sabbath; on Tuesday, only four; by Thursday they would have almost made it. And what is true of the day and the week in that calendar is also true for the months, the seasons, and the year. All along the road there are station; one moves toward them, one prepared oneself for them. The time spent in the evenings studying, usually by heart, the talmudic tractate *Megillah* in anticipation of *Purim*, or going over the laws of *Pesah* as that festival approached, or on studying the relevant Talmud passages in mental preparation for *Hanukkah*—all this was not the time suspended in empty repetition of the same eternal misery; it was the ordered time of a lifestyle imposed on chaos.

Frankl makes the point that a human being must have a future to live for. But since in the camps one could not see an end to the incarceration, one could not aim at a future. Therefore, he saw his life as "provisional existence of unknown limit." This is one of the causes of so many losing their hold on life. Everything became pointless for them.[9] Future for them meant time beyond camp existence. But in the structured time sequence of the authentic Jew the future was also the next moment, wit its demands and promises, waiting to be lived through as a Jew. His future was the continuous anticipation of the meaning and purpose of the next date in his calendar—*Pesah*, the festival of liberation; *Shavu'ot*, the festival of the revelation at Sinai; *Rosh haShanah* and *Yom Kippur* were waiting for him.

One is deeply stirred by Frankl's words as he describes what the futureless existence in empty time meant for a sensitive prisoner who told him that as he marched in that long column of new inmates from the station the camp he felt

> as though he were marching at his own funeral. His life seemed to him absolutely without future. He regarded it as over and done, as if he had already died. . . . The outside life, that is, as much as he could see of it, appeared to him almost as if it might have to a dead man who looked at the world from another planet.[10]

Now the authentic Jew never had his roots in that "outside life." In fact, at all times he would look at it with a measure of reservation. Living in a different dimension of the spirit, he indeed looked at that world as if from another planet. The concentration camp was hell on earth. But even in such a hell one lives, in the embracing context of historic Judaism in the presence of God.

Frankl has a counterpart to the story of the man who felt as if her were walking at his own funeral. It is the story of the human greatness of a sick young woman who knew that she had only a few more days to live. Yet, cheerful in spite of her knowledge, she told Frankl that she was grateful for her fate. "In my former life," she said, "I was spoiled and did not take spiritual accomplishments seriously." Then, pointing with her finger through the window of the hut, she continued: "This tree here is the only friend I have in my loneliness." All that could be seen through the window was a single branch of a chestnut tree with two blossoms on it. "I often talk to this tree," she confessed. At first Frankl was startled, imagining that the woman might be delirious or that she suffered from occasional hallucinations. But when he anxiously asked her whether the tree replied, she said: "Yes! It said to me, 'I am here-I am here-I am life, eternal life.' "[11] The woman's answer is very reminiscent of Martin Buber's I-Thou relationship. According to Buber, it is possible to establish such a dialogically personal relationship even with a tree. Through the finite Thou of that tree one might gain a glimpse of the Eternal Thou. Quite clearly, this young woman did not feel that she was seeing an outside world of unreality, as if she were dead or on another planet. In fact, never previously had she been so much alive to the reality of the world, never before so intimately close to it. Such are, of course, the unique experiences of unique people. But it is remarkable to what extent the authentic Jews remained in touch with reality of the world. Even though separated from the world of men, these Jews were not alienated from God's creation. This resulted, in a way, directly from their continued observance of the seasonal festivals. *Pesah* does not only commemorate the Exodus, it is also *Hag haAviv*, the Spring festival; *Shavu'ot*, when the Torah was given, is also remembered as *Has haBikurim*, the festival of the first fruits of the land that used to be offered in the Temple of Jerusalem; and *Sukkot*, the "season of our joy," is also the season of the harvest. They were not only memories of the past; the Jews knew very well that no matter what their personal fate might turn out to be, *Pesah, Shavu'ot,* and *Sukkot,* as well as the other significant dates in the Jewish calendar, would outlast Nazi Germany. The structured time of the Jewish calendar preserved their contact with the world that brought to them the message of the eternal life of its source.

In the ghetto of Lodz a few young men were in hiding on order to be able to do nothing else but study *Torah*. We know the address. The place was in Radogshaz Street. We know their names: Moishe Podembizer, Leibel Rosenblat, Moishe Liss, and two Bornstein brothers, Naftoli and Falk. When the Gestapo discovered their hiding place they were accused of spying and sabotage and taken to a prison. There they were tortured in order to get them to reveal the "secrets of the underground." After one of these bloody "examinations," when the boys met for a short moment in the prison corridor, Moishe Liss called to the others: "Remember to start saying *Tal uMatar*, tomorrow evening," referring to a two-word seasonal change which is introduced into the *Shemoneh Esrei* (Eighteen Benedictions) prayer early in December each year. The exact date of this change varies between December 4 and 5, but since Jewish calendars were no longer printed in the ghetto, Moishe Liss mush have know the calendar of that year by heart and thus could remind his friends not to forget to insert the change in their prayers the next evening.[12] Who cared about the Nazis! In the midst of the inferno, these young Jews, bruised and bleeding from German barbarism, could focus on such a small nuance of their prayers, reflecting the change in season.

If the festivals are chiefly seasonal, the Sabbath has its place in the cosmos. For God created the world in six days and He rested on the seventh. "And God blessed the seventh day and sanctified it."[13] The same survivor, whose words about the Sabbath in his bunker we quoted earlier, experiences the holy day in its cosmic context:

> At the time of sunset on the eve of the Sabbath it would seem as if the fields were being covered with plush carpets in honor of Queen Sabbath. The lights in the far-away little windows flicker as if they were Sabbath candles lit in universal space. Our saintly mothers who kindled those lights hover above in the distant blue. They cover their faces with their hands . . . they put their hands on our hands and bless us. The stars across the sky twinkle . . . twinkling Sabbath candles. Soon they will fade and be extinguished. A Sabbath song is in the air, floating in from somewhere behind the woods. Oh, how we wish to sit at the hole of the bunker and let the song filter into us till the rise of the sun.[14]

A partisan. The battle has subsided. Quiet. His head fills with confusing thoughts. A maddening desire overcomes him: to smoke, to smoke. To take a piece of paper, to roll a cigarette and to forget. To forget everything.

> Suddenly, a thought passes over my mind, cutting as if with a knife's edge. Shabbat! Shabbat?

Behind him a red sun ignites flames of fire at the end of the horizon and floods with purple some scattered and lonely grayish clouds. Far, far away, other clouds rise thickeningly above the trees, hastening to extinguish the conflagration. Roll that cigarette! The sun . . . Shabbat!

> Raise your head and look at the sky-spoke a voice within me-it is already dark. The Sabbath has descended.

His fingers clasped the tobacco in his pocket as if it were some precious and desired treasure that one did not have the courage to bring out into the light of the day. Just to touch it gave him a pleasurable feeling.

> I looked at the sky. As if there were something there before which I was ashamed, . . . nor did I have the strength to pull my hand out of my pocket.

The partisan struggled against that voice on behalf of his consuming desire.

> Gradually the dark cloud covered the last tongues of fire that were still spreading from the horizon. The sun was emitting some of its last weakening sparks. Then it disappeared as if it had never been. Shabbat! Shabbat!

His head sunk onto the soft earth. He closed his eyes and his thoughts took him away from the still unfinished battle and from everything around him.

> I did not sleep, nor did I see any visions in a dream. Only my eyes were closed. Suddenly, well-known faces of long ago, forgotten under the burden of time, were flowing towards me. Sabbath evening! The *Shtiebel* is filled from one end to the other with Jews in black 'kapotes' of silk, and velvet hats on their heads . . . long tables covered with white tablecloths . . . red-cheeked little children with long descending curly sidelocks squeeze themselves through the crowd. Heart-warming tunes are heard as some study the *Zohar* and others recite *Sir haShirim*.[15] The wax candles are dripping from the warm atmosphere of the *Shtiebel*.
> "L'kha Dodi . . . Come, my beloved to meet the Bride
> Let us welcome the Shabbat."[16]
> It is the voice of my father who has been honored with *Kabbalat Shabbat*, to welcome the Shabbat. And I am assisting him . . . with a tune that inspires and caresses at the same time.

The Germans interrupt the silence; the tear apart the web of the dream. Bullets, flying like stars, erred in their paths and were whistling over his head. Quickly he emptied his pocket. Temptation had been conquered. The tobacco was swallowed up in the mud. He felt better; he breathed restfully, as if a heavy burden had been taken from off him.

I felt light, refreshed; as if born anew. I sat on the trunk of a rotting tree. I looked up into the star-studded sky; I knew that the night was a Shabbat night. My lips were whispering . . . I did not know what . . . I thanked God for the loving kindness that he rendered unto me on that day.[17]

For this survivor the experience brought back the memory of a far-away, wondrous world, a world that had disappeared and no longer existed. And yet, it was speaking to him with the cosmic voice of a Shabbat night in the universe.

The authenticity of being reached its deepest validation when the Jew was confronted with the ultimate, when powers beyond his physical strength were about to put an end to his physical existence. The prototype of this autonomous Jew has been Rabbi Akiva, the story of whose death, as told in the Talmud, is well known. When the Romans were leading him to be executed it became time to recite the morning *Shema*. As he was being tortured, he said the *Shema*, taking upon himself the "yoke of the Heavens."[18]

Struggling intellectually with the nightmarish bequest of the destruction of European Jewry makes one think with awe of the majestic simplicity of the words in this story "it was time to recite the morning *Shema*." It has been customary for many generations that when a Jew's life is threatened, or, on his sickbed when he feels that his end is approaching, he would use his last moments on earth to recite the first verse of the *Shema*. With a last effort and fervor he would call out the words: "Hear, O Israel. . . ." There is a drama in this call that surpasses the mundane and is sounded in a transcendental realm at the border line between two worlds. It was, however, not like this that Rabbi Akiva said the *Shema*. There was nothing of drama in his words, nothing of the sublime that one might notice in the voice of a man who with his last breath affirms the meaning of his whole life. Rabbi Akiva did not say the *Shema* because they were taking him to his execution, not because the ultimate test was approaching. On the contrary, there was nothing extraordinary about his *Shema*. The reason he said it was very simple; "it was time to recite the morning *Shema*." He said it just as on any other day, because that hour of the day had arrived when one was supposed to say it. It was totally irrelevant to what the Romans were about to do to his body. The soldiers of Rome, all the might and glory of the empire-Rabbi Akiva ignored them. They were of no consequence; he was busy with something else. It was time to recite the *Shema* and according to the law one should not delay in saying it.

To be unconcerned with what others may do to you, even when your life is at stake, because you are committed to the truth of your own life, is the supreme act of personal autonomy. In the spirit of Rabbi Akiva such acts of autonomous being occurred not infrequently in the ghettos and the death camps. We are not thinking here of the tens of thousands who went to the gas chambers with the *Shema* or some other form of affirmation of faith on their lips, though this, too, was a majestic deed of devotion to the truth of one's life. We are thinking of those who showed that radical indifference to the external reality that had been imposed on them. Such for instance, was the behavior of a group of fifty *bahurim* (young yeshiva students) who stood at the door to the gas chambers in Auschwitz on *Simhat Torah* (the festival of the Rejoicing of the Law): "It is *Simhat Torah* today. There are no scrolls of the Torah here; but surely God is here. Let us celebrate with Him." It was the same indifference, the same contempt for all the might of the oppressor that Rabbi Akiva showed so many centuries earlier to the Roman Empire.

There were many similar situations in which others acted no differently. One Friday, the Germans took Rabbi Hayyim Yehiel Rubin of Dambrowe to the cemetery, together with twenty other Hews of the city. There they ordered them to dig their graves. As so often on such occasions, the Germans were in no hurry. Standing in their graves, the Hews were able to welcome the Sabbath Queen with the traditional prayers. After the prayers, the Rebbe greeted the little congregation, as well as the regular Jewish grave diggers who were there, with the traditional "Good Shabbes" and started singing, as on every other Friday night, *Shalom Aleikhem,* "Peace unto you, angels of peace." He recited *Kiddush,* sanctified the Sabbath over two *hallot,* two Sabbath loaves which the Jewish grave diggers had smuggled in to them, and taught Torah, interpreting the twenty-two letters with which the contents of the Torah are written. In the midst of his teaching, he was overcome with religious fervor and began to sing. Influenced by Rabbi Rubin, the other Jews joined in with him and, singing and dancing, celebrated the Sabbath, completely ignoring the Germans who, their machine-guns at the ready, were surrounding the grave.[19]

In Baranowicz, Rabbi Nissan Scheinberg was a *Dayyan,* a member of the rabbinical court. On *Shusham Purim,* in 1942, the Germans prepared a blood bath in the town at which thousands of Jews were murdered. Dr. Nehemia Kroschinsky, a surviving eyewitness, tells this story:

> A group of Slonim hasidim, who were caught in the 'selection,' stood together, preparing themselves for the moment of *Kiddush Hashem,* 'the sanctification of the Divine Name' in death. In the midst of the group stood the Dayyan, Rabbi Nissan, who called to the others: 'Jews! Let us not forget that today is Purim. Let us drink *L'hayyim,* to life.' He pourd out a cupful and said again: '*L'kayyim!*' He got hold of a few other Jews and started dancing. His face was shining as he sang the traditional Purim song, *Shoshanat Ya'akov,* 'Rose of Jacob,' and he shouted with joy until a German bullet silenced him.[20]

This kind of contemptuous indifference to the enemy is the ultimate of human autonomy. Dov Sadan called it *haEmunah haAharonah,* the ultimate faith. He rightly said that it is superior to all the might of the enemy, for while this might is considered by the foe the essential substance of reality, for men of ultimate faith this reality does not exist at all. Only such faith enables the human soul to rise to its highest exaltation, an experience so well-known to the Jew through his wanderings because of the truth that he represents in the history of man.[21] Many a survivor of the ghettos and camps speaks of such joyous exaltation. One of the survivors of the Lodz ghetto recalls the past in these words:

> The truth is that often I am ashamed of myself. How I have fallen from *igra rama*, from the lofty heights of those days to the life of comforts and smallness of today. Woe is me! How far removed I am today even from the mere perception of the sublime of that time. . . .What are our concepts of the ghetto today? *Gehinnom*, hell, graveyard! Dark and black abyss! Yet for us, for our group the ghetto was the furnace in which our unlimited commitment (*mesirut nefesh*) was purified and where one reached a purity of attachment to the divine than which nothing higher is conceivable.[22]

Another survivor, explaining how the Torah teachings of his father and other pious Jews helped him cope with continually mounting suffering in the ghetto, summed up his memories by observing: "Perhaps now some will believe me when I say in full truth and seriousness that to this day I have not tasted life as I did in those days of trouble."[23]

In one of the huts in a certain concentration camp some Jews were celebration the Passover *seder*. Suddenly the door was opened with force. They all expected the worst. But the "guests" were Nohumze and a few other young Jews. They all acted as if they were somewhat drunk, although it was clear that not one of them had touched a drop of alcohol. "What is the matter, Reb Itsche?" Nohumze demanded. "Is this how one conducts a *sedar*! Is this how one serves God with joy? And if there is no wine for the 'Four Cups' a Jew cannot get inebriated . . . that God has helped us to celebrate the *seder* even in a camp?" After that they started singing with fervor the traditional *seder* songs.[24]

Many a Jew understood that the way they met the tribulations had itself to be a form of divine service and one has to serve God with joy. Leib Brikman, a survivor of Dachau, tells of a hard winter in a camp he was in near Landsberg. Cold and hunger was gnawing at the prisoners and wearing down what remained of their strength. These are Brikman's words:

> I felt like a candle about to go out. All along the way . . . the snow was piled high. I skidded often and fell. The little will that was still left in the dying body whispered to me: "Lie down on this soft pile of snow and don't get up again."

At this moment his friend, Notte Eibschitz, a young man of eighteen, stepped up to him and said:

> What is the matter, my friend? True, we are walking to hell. (*Gehinnom*). But does not a Jew accept even suffering with love! Even to *Gehinnom* one has to walk in joy.

"It was then that I rose and stood on my feet," concludes Leib Brikman.[25]

Endnotes

[1]*Op.cit.,* 65-66.

[2]*Ibid.,* 73-74.

[3]*Op.cit.,* 12.

[4]Cf. also what Frankl has to say on the crushing burden of unstructured time, *op.cit.,*70.

[5]*Op.cit.,*75.

[6]According to a mystical tradition, the Jew receives an "additional soul" on the Sabbath which leaves him at the Sabbath's conclusion.

[7]Cf. Psalms 91:15; T. B. *Ta'amit* 16a; also T.B. *Sukkah* 45a and *Tosafot s.v. Ani veHoo.*

[8]Eliav, p.141; from Leib Rochman, *BeDamayikh Hayyee,* Jerusalem, 1961.

[9]*Op.cit.,* 69-70.

[10]*Ibid.,* 71.

[11]*Ibid.,* 68-69.

[12]Prager, I, 82.

[13]Genesis 2:2.

[14]Prager, I, p.82.

[15]The *Zohar,* the Book of Light, is the classic work of Jewish mysticism. *Shir haShirim,* the biblical *Song of Songs,* is often read in the synagogue by individuals prior to the communal Sabbath eve services.

[16]A refrain from the Sabbath eve liturgy.

[17]Eliav, 75-76.

[18]T. B. *Berakhot* 61b.

[19]Unger,135.

[20]*Eleh Ezkerah,* VII, 196.

[21]Dov Sadan in *Mahanayim Hanukkah* 5720 (1959).

[22]Prager, II, 100.

[23]*Ibid.,* 93.

[24]Unger, 322.

[25]Prager, II, 136.

Chapter 7

Confrontation—The Ultimate Issue*

Eliezer Berkovits

Psychiatrists who study concentration camp behavior examine it as a response to concentration camp condition. The lifestyle of the authentic Jew that we have described and analyzed thus far was behavior in concentration camp, but cannot be characterized in the same way as concentration camp behavior, for it was not prompted by concentration camp conditions. The Jews who refrained from eating cooked food, or who rose earlier than the others in order to put on *tefillin*, or who did not eat bread for the eight days of *Pesah*, did these things in spite of concentration camp conditions, not because of them. Various writers on the subject of behavior in the camps emphasize the humanizing and comforting aspect of the spiritual life, but strangely enough they usually refer to it as an escape from the tragic reality.[1]

The authentic Jew did not escape into spirituality but simply lived the life of the Jew in the circumstances in which he found himself. Nevertheless, most Jews fully realize that this was a confrontation unto death between the Jewish people and what it represents in world history and Nazified Germany and its spirit. While it is true that the Nazis killed not only Jews, but also Poles, Russians, Norwegians, and Gypsies, they did not plan a "Final Solution" for these peoples except for the poor gypsies, who fell victim to the Teutonic madness for ideological consistency. The diabolical hatred and venom of the Germans were reserved for the Jews, not as individual saboteurs, dissidents, political adversaries, war prisoners, or potential underground fighters, but as people. The Gypsies were exterminated as an "inferior race"; the Jewish people and Judaism were to disappear from the earth as salvation for mankind.

There are two kinds of people who cannot acknowledge that the Jewish people was singled out for ultimate destruction: the assimilationist Jew and the dogmatic ideologist of the Left. The assimilationist Jew usually does not recognize the existence of a Jewish people. How, then, could the Jews be singled out as a people? The assimilationist Jew has an uncertain position in the world. If the Jews are a people, he, too, might be rejected He is unsure of himself. If he *does* recognize the existence of a Jewish national entity, it is one with which he refuses to identify. In a sense he finds himself in a most uncomfortable psychological proximity to the Nazis themselves. He, too, considers this people unworthy of existence. To maintain his self-respect, he has to assert that the Jews were not really treated much differently from other nationalities, nor did they behave differently from other prisoners. On the one hand, there is really nothing special about Jews. On the other hand, in his estimation, they were

*From "Confrontation—The Ultimate Issue," *With God in Hell: Judaism in the Ghettos and Death-camps.* Copyright © 1979 by Eliezer Berkovits. Reprinted by permission of Mrs. Sali Berkovits

the only ones who went like sheep to the slaughter. Strange! If they were the only ones who were led like sheep to the slaughter, then they were singled out; and if they were the only ones who walked like sheep to the slaughter, then, somehow, they *did* behave differently form other prisoners. The assimilationist does not see the contradictions. For him, it is reassuring to know that the people of his ancestors, whom he had forsaken, did not really deserve much better. Those ghetto Jews had no courage to act, did not move, although it was quite clear to any enlightened, visionary assimilationist what was in store for them. Even later, when the "Final Solution" was already being implemented, the inferior ghetto Jews were unable to see the wide-open doors that were still available for them to escape.[2] The assimilationist Jew needs all this. On the one hand, there is no such thing as a Jewish people, therefore—unlike the Nazis—he does not reject them. On the other hand, there used to be a people of ghetto Jews who deserved nothing better than to be rejected. They got what they had asked for. Thus, the assimilationist Jew saves his self-respect and soothes his conscience.

Neither can the dogmatic ideologists of the Left recognize that the Jewish people and Judaism were a target of Germany, specifically selected for annihilation. According to them, the struggle was essentially a political one between Fascism and the progressive forces of freedom. This battle was chiefly fought by these forces and had very little to do with Jews *qua* Jews. Were they to acknowledge that the Jewish people as such were the target, it would mean only one of two things: either that the Jews were in the forefront in the political struggle for freedom, or that the battle was not a political one fought in accordance with the textbook rules on class struggle. The leftist ideology permits neither of these possibilities. Furthermore, the Jewish question itself is a body, since it is going to disappear in the classless society of universal brotherhood. There is, therefore, no such thing as a Jewish people. As for Judaism, there could be no point in making an issue of it. It has no influence on the course of human history, which proceeds in accordance with the laws of dialectical materialism. Very few, if any, have had the intellectual honesty of a Berdyaev, who foresaw dialectical materialism because he could not deny the reality of the history of the Jewish people.

The truth, of course, is that there was a direct confrontation between Hitler's Germany and the people of Judaism because the Nazi ideology was essentially not a political one, but a nihilistic rebellion against all human values and a satanic defacing of the divine image of which man is the bearer on earth. Ernst Junger, whom Camus, in *The Rebel*, calls "the only man of superior culture who gave Nazism even an appearance of being a philosophy," formulated the essence of this German nihilism by saying: "The best answer to the betrayal of the body of life by the spirit is the betrayal of the spirit by the spirit, and one of the great and cruel pleasures of our times is to participate in the work of destruction."[3] In order to understand what the issue at stake was, it is worth pondering this statement. What is the betrayal of life by the spirit? In this context the very existence of the spirit is ajudged to be a betrayal of life. Spirit, with its affirmation of freedom as an instrument of responsibility, with its demands of discipline, with its value affirmations that originate in a realm of transcendence reaching out toward the Divine, is seen as the enemy of life, a life limited to its purely biological needs, drives, and appetites. This, in itself, is nothing more than the negation of the spirit, not its betrayal. It cannot serve as the dynamic of a nihilistic state organization. The betrayal of the spirit by the spirit is an ideology; it is the conscious elevation of the satisfaction of primitive biological needs and dark demonic drives to the level of a cult. It is the "sanctification" of the satanic in human nature. It is the planned desecration of the spirit that demands the dehumanization of man. Nazism was not a political movement but, in its betrayal of the spirit, a spiritual one, and the battle against it should have been a spiritual one. it is this struggle that the nations refused to join, understandably, since Nazism itself was only a manifestation of a spiritually bankrupt civilization. This explains the world's indifference toward the plight of the Jewish people.

The natural adversary of this kind of a rebellion is always the Jew, not on account of what he does, but on account of what he represents in history. It is neither the Ten Commandments, nor the "Thou shalt love thy neighbor as thyself" of the Torah, nor the belief in God that is responsible for the singling out of the Jew by the nihilistic rebels against the domain of the spirit. Indeed, other religions may affirm the same principles and believe in the same kind of divinity. But it has been the spiritual misfortunes of the other world religions that they have been too successful in the domain of Caesar. In the history of the human race, half a billion believers in a God prove nothing about the presence and power of that God in history. The believers and their affirmations may have their psychological significance for the individual; ultimately the hundreds of millions of human beings, in possession of vast territories, natural resources, and vast military establishments, only prove the power of the material forced that they represent. The nihilistic rebellion has to aim at defeating the material power bases of such adversaries and this was the aim of Germany with regard to the other nations. There was no need for a "Final Solution" against the peoples themselves. But the Jew and Judaism represent in human history the affirmation of values that have survived without the physical power base that has otherwise been the sole guarantee of a permanent place on the world scene. That the Jewish people has withstood all the barbarous attacks upon it, that it has been able to maintain itself in the midst of deadly enemies, bespeaks the presence of another kind of power, invisibly playing its part in the history of men. The survival of the Jew, his capacity for revival after catastrophes such as had eliminated mighty nations and empires, indicate the mysterious intrusion of a spiritual dimension into the history of man. The more radical the rebellion against the world of the spirit, the greater the hatred against the Jew. The Final Solution was not only to eliminate the Jewish people form history, but through the destruction of Israel it was meant to finalize the defeat of that mysterious spiritual force against which the rebellion was directed. The Nazis were quite correct in believing that if they did not succeed in the elimination of the "Jewish influence" upon world history, they would also fail in their plans for world conquest. no matter what they said in their official propaganda, they sensed the mysterious nature of that influence, the presence of a hiding God in history. It was, indeed, a course of nihilistic violence that meant not only to conquer the earth, but also to poison the soul of man by successfully trampling on all human values and on all human feeling.

Jews understood instinctively the nature of the confrontation. However, nowhere did the meaning of the confrontation call for a more heroic opposition than among the underground groups of young *hasidim*, as expressed in the words of one of them:

> I shall not go to slave labor; I shall not join any workers' group! The intention of the Nazi Satan is not only to enslave the body; his main goal is to subjugate the soul. We shall not submit. We give up the food rations. We shall starve, but will not be moved. We shall find somehow some way of getting something to eat. . . . We shall oppose the decrees of the Satan.[4]

Who were these young Jews? In certain circles of the ghetto and camp survivors, legends are told abut a widespread association of young Gerer *hasidim* known as the *Mottesovzes*. They were numbers of a group organized by one Motte (Mattiyahu) Gelman. He was born in Vienna into a well-to-do, completely assimilated Jewish family. A highly gifted young boy, he distinguished himself in his studies at school. One day in 1933, after the Nazis had come to power in Germany, one of his classmates called him "a dirty Jew." Motte spat in his face. Since he knew nothing of Judaism—he did not even know how to read Hebrew and had never held a prayerbook in his hand—he decided, instead of going home, to cross over the bridge above the Danube into the *Zweiter Bezirk*, "the Second District," which was known for its Jewish population, many of whom were of Eastern European origin. He wanted to find out about Jews. It chanced that he encountered there the distinguished Rabbi Schapiro of Lublin, the founder of the world-renowned Yeshiva of *Hakhmei Lublin*. He approached the venerable rabbi. He wanted to find out why he was called "a dirty Jew." He had been insulted. The others had laughed; not one had come to his defense. "They are the ones who are crude and vulgar; who use dirty language; who often act immorally. And they call me dirty?" The rabbi told him: "Don't get excited about it. The prophet already warned about the same thing: 'Woe unto them that call evil good and good evil; that change darkness into light and light into darkness. . . .' "[5]

There it was, the classical summation of the betrayal of the spirit by the spirit. In this short encounter, Motte became a changed person and with the help of a religious youth organization he started to learn about Judaism. During his next summer vacation, with funds from a prize he had won for an essay on modern Austrian poetry, he joined a ten-day antiquities study tour of Poland. But his real purpose was to run away to Lublin and to learn in the yeshiva of Rabbi Schapiro. He was only fifteen years of age at the time, but all the efforts of his father to bring him back to Vienna were of no avail. Soon, Motte joined the Gerer *hasidim* and by the time he was seventeen he was already an outstanding Talmud student and a fervent *hasid*, an inspiration to numerous other young Jews. When the German armies shattered Poland and spread havoc, murder, and destruction among Polish Jewry, Motte became a tower of strength in the midst of the chaos. In numerous ghettos he organized secret groups who refused to obey the laws of the Germans and went into hiding to study Torah, to pray, sing, and dance. These groups, which then became known as *Mottesovzes*, "men of Motte," existed in Cracow, Warsaw, Szydlowiec, Radom and other cities. Strict voluntary discipline was the rule in their hiding places. Winter and summer, the members of the group had to be present in their bunkers at 6 A.M. In all the ghettos they lived together in communes sharing everything. Although their main purpose was the study of Torah, *biKedushah uveTohorah*, in holiness and in purity, they were also deeply engaged in charitable work. They took into their midst lonely children, remnants of families that were expelled from the ghetto, and helped children who had run away from places outside the ghetto, a capital crime is the eyes of the Germans. Motte, the moving spirit of this conspiratorial organization, traveling in his hasidic garb on all kinds of secret roads from ghetto to ghetto, from labor camp to labor camp, appearing and disappearing mysteriously, collecting donations, assembling help for his secret Torah communes. Although still in his early twenties, he became a legend in the ghettos.[6]

People who remember him would say, this is what Motte was like: he taught us to shatter the conditions around us and no to be shattered by them; to deny them, but not to deny ourselves. And he would sing: "Whatever is beauty in the world out there, see it in its defiling ugliness."

One of the survivors who knew Motte in the Szydlowiec ghetto writes about him:

> The personality of Mattityahu stands before my eyes as if alive. A great deal passed over me during the years of bereavement and destruction. But I was also privileged to witness many manifestations of spiritual exaltation in the midst of the valley of the shadow of death. However, the appearance of Mattiyahu was unique in its class. As I considered him, it became clear to me that here was a Jew; and that was his armour. . . . Though I, too, lived in the same ghetto I did not get to see him there too often because most of the time he was travelling. People ceased already to wonder how Mattityahu managed to escape the numerous armed guards that were watching the roads. They simply considered him a man of miracles.

One day he went on one of his errands and was never seen again. It was then that Yankel Gefen, another young Gerer *hasid* who had been Motte's deputy, became the central guiding personality of the *Mottesovzes* groups. Originally, he had been known as a *batlan*, a world-strange, impractical young man, but he suddenly revealed himself to be a Jew of great courage and fearlessness. He would hasten to join in every risky venture, and again and again he escaped from the deadly grip of the enemy. He jumped from the death train that was speeding him towards the extermination camp of Belzec. He succeeded in getting out of the prison of the *Juden Lager* (the Jewish camp) in the slave labor camp at Plaszow. But in the height of his heroism was thought to be his stealing himself across the Polish-Czech border to try to make his way on foot to the Gerer Rebbe in Jerusalem.

Two other incidents reveal something of his understanding of the nature of the confrontation, as well as his personal courage and strength of character in meeting it. Soon after the German conquest of Poland, a group of German soldiers was celebrating the victory by mocking and humiliating Jews in the streets of Warsaw. They happened to come upon a group of *hasidim* and fell upon them with derisive laughter. One of the officers pulled out a knife and turned to the Jews: "Moses! Give me your beard." The Jews were speechless as the Germans went ahead with their joke of pulling and cutting some of their beards. There was nothing they could do and they were glad to escape with their lives. Then the Nazis got hold of Yankel. "Shoot me; kill me; but I will not let you cut by beard," he shouted. The heroic Germans started cursing and threatening him. Finally, at the urging of some older *hasidim* who warned him that the Germans might avenge his resistance on all of them, Yankel agreed to let the officer cut off the edges of his beard. After the event, when he was asked how he dared endanger his life by inciting the murders, Yankel answered with complete composure: "I did it intentionally, I did not want these *resha'im* (wicked, evil men) to think that the world belongs altogether to them."[7]

The second incident occurred in Cracow, the seat of the German occupation authorities, where clandestine activity was much more difficult than in other places. Motte had moved to the Szydlowiec ghetto and the situation of the *Mottesovzes* in Cracow became critical. The large group disintegrated and the members were scattered in private homes where they studied in twos and threes. Then Yankel Gefen arrived in the ghetto, immediately filling the place that became vacant when Motte left. He reorganized the *havurah* (the Gerer fraternity), established a secret *shtiebel*, and became the organizer, the teacher, and the guide of a group of over thirty young *bahurim* who often studied Torah deep into the night. Their *shtiebel* was high up in the attic. One night their study was interrupted by loud banging at the gate of the building. There were wild shouts outside and the tension within was great. The danger was imminent, the Germans were at the gate.

> We held our breath. We all sensed what was bound to happen here within a few minutes. However, no one moved from his place. Yankel Gefen was standing . . . completely composed, completely quiet and at peace, altogether strength and trust.

Our witness thought of running away. There were possibilities of escape; it was a large building with many corridors, and secret nooks and niches. But he did not budge; nor did anyone else.

> Yankel Gefen looked at us with eyes free of fear. His glance removed our fear and sparked audacity in us. Let there be what may. We shall not be alarmed. We shall not run from them.

The shouting grew louder and wilder. The gate was shattered. Knocking and banging; curses and screaming. "They are here!" shouted one of the youngest members of the group. With a gesture of his hand, Yankel ordered the boy to be quiet and to remain seated in his place.

> We were all silent; sitting in our places. The pages of the Talmud were open. Our hearts were beating fast, but the determination was formed: "We shall not budge!" Many long minutes passed. Gradually our minds were once again engaged in the talmudic theme. We did not raise our voices, but quietly started to hum again the tune to which the *Gemara* is studied.

There was some more drunken shouting downstairs, cries and shrieking whistles. Then, silence! The Germans had left. It turned out that they had come for plunder and departed. When the danger was over, Yankel Gefen gave his students a lesson in the "virtue of indifference." Turning to the boy who had shouted out, he said:

> You lost yourself. So, what did you discover? Didn't we all now that they were here? Didn't we hear them? But what? Whom does it concern at all! That is exactly what they want; that we abolish ourselves before them. It is because of it that they make the noise and cause the terror—in order to break and subdue us. They cling to their own—and we stay with our own. Therefore, we shall not run nor withdraw before them. That is why it is written: "Blessed is the man who trusts in God; God is his safety."[8]

Yankel Gefen had no disrespect for life. But in his philosophy it was more important to ignore the enemy and retain the independence of one's being than to run in order to escape, to lose one's self-respect and submit in the spirit to threats and fear. The *Mottesovzes* were a fairly widespread conspiratorial organization. But they were no saboteurs in the normal usage of the term; nor were they partisans (though many of their survivors joined the ghetto fighters in the end). Yet, when the Germans would discover their hiding places, they would accuse them of sabotage and rightly so. From the point of view of a nihilistic faith, rooted in the betrayal of the spirit by the spirit, the manifestation of the authenticity of the life of the spirit is a much more dangerous threat than the blowing up of railway tracks by ordinary saboteurs. The emergence of a Motte Gelman from the apparently barren womb of a completely de-Judaized home of assimilated Vienese Jews symbolizes the mysterious capability of the Jewish people for eternal recovery and renewal. Motte Gelman, who appeared over the dark skies of the ghettos like a brilliantly shining meteor, demonstrated that the betrayal of the spirit by the spirit was doomed in the history of man, and proved the irrepressible mightiness of the spirit.

We know of at least one other group of young *hasidim* who saw the confrontation with the Germans very much like the *Mottesovzes*. Overcoming the tyranny of fear in the ghetto of Lodz, this *havrutah* trained itself to remember each day three fundamental principles:

(1) The German is Amalek (the traditional enemy of the Jewish people). Whatever he says, one has to do the opposite.

(2) Because he is indeed Amalek, one need not by surprised by his behavior and actions and one must not be afraid because of them.

(3) This is the method of Amalek: to confuse the sense and to prove in every possible way that all is lost; that there is no escape and that the only choice is—to submit.[9]

The meaning of this formulation was not intended as a call to arms, which—in their situation—was beyond them. It was similar to Yankel Gefen's "We shall not budge"; part of the battle in the realm of the spirit, the retention of the authenticity of one's own being, defying the force of the dehumanizing conditions, and, in the style of Motte Gelman, to break and not to be broken. In the terminology of these Jews, the battle was with Satan.

It is doubtful that anyone was able to offer a clearer understanding of the significance of the confrontation than Rabbi Mendele Alter of Pabianice, brother of the Gerer Rebbe. The account of his walk to the has chambers in Treblinka at the head of a large group of Jews has become a legend. As he was taken to the gas chamber, he pleaded with one of the Kapos for some water. To everyone's surprise, the man, who was one of the most sadistic among the German lackeys, brought the water. However, Reb Mendele did not drink it, but used it to wash his hands preparing himself for the last prayer on earth, the saying of the *Viddui* (the customary confession of sins before death). Along the way, a badly wounded child was thrown across Reb Mendele's path. He picked up the bleeding baby whose little body was quivering in his hands. There was still time; the Germans dragged out the death march for their entertainment. Reb Mendele, holding the child, turned to the others and said:

[T]his is holiness, purer than all purity, a Jewish child. This little Jewish child is sick, weak like a fly . . . how come that the Satan, in possession of the most advanced weapons of war and destruction, has to wage war and vent his cruelty on little children? These 'defiled ones,' when they see a Jewish child in the arms of his mother are immediately filled with the urge to murder . . . the forces of *tumah*, demonic defilement, cannot endure the sight of holiness, the spirit of purity that hovers over the face of a Jewish child.

Then he told them of a personal experience. When the Nazis first came to his home to beat and torture him, it hurt very much and he was in great pain. But suddenly his eyes were opened with understanding. The Germans discovered a scroll of the Torah in his room. At once they let him go and threw themselves with "cruel anger and mad murderous desire" upon the *Sefer Torah*. They trod on it with their feet and tore the parchment with fanatical hatred, as if sensing that the letters on them contained the life blood of the Jewish people. (Witnesses tell of similar events in other places. On at least one occasion know to us a German officer, upon discovering a Torah scroll in a secret *shtiebel*, pulled out his bayonet and stabbed the scroll several times in his fury.[10] Reb Mendele concluded his remarks by saying:

> When I saw this I regained my composure. I understood the meaning of the words in the Psalms: "You make me wise through my enemies."[11] It is not my body that the enemy means to crush. When he fights against the source of holiness, he slaughters the children of Israel; and when he wants to destroy the strength of the Jew, he treads underfoot the parchment of the Torah.[12]

It is doubtful if anyone had a deeper understanding of the nature of Nazi Germany than these Jews. The struggle was not a political one. It even transcended the realm of morality and ethics. It had to be fought against the consciously planned defilement of the very sources of man's humanity. Nazi Germany was the deification of the diabolical; the religious befouling of all purity and innocence. Jews rightly saw in it the rebellion of *Kohot haTumah* (a phrase well understood in the context of Judaism, which can only be weakly rendered in English as "the forces of impurity"), the satanic relishers of destruction. It was against all this that the authentic Jew was fighting. In the words of Yankel Gefen, he was holding on to his own, to himself. Even if his body was destroyed, in his own life the rebellion of *Kohot haTumah* was defeated. This truth found its dramatic affirmation in the final hour of the Chencziner Rebe. When a German soldier was trying to cut his beard, he shouted at him: "Don't touch me with your defiled hands." He was shot.[13] The incident recalls a passage from Paul Ricoeur's *Thy Symbolism of Evil*, which defines the "dread of the impure." It is a reaction to "a threat which, beyond the threat of suffering and death, aims at a diminution of existence, a loss of the personal core of one's being."[14] It was this that the Chencziner Rebbe dreaded more than death itself, the diminution of his existence, the loss of the personal core of his Jewish being.

Because of their conscious, and often unconscious, understanding of the nature of the confrontation, no matter what their personal fate might be, Jews did not doubt the ultimate defeat of Germany and the survival of the Jewish people. The two were inseparable from each other as the following story, from the early days of the German conquest of Poland, shows. The Germans came to Lublin to set up a "Jewish area" and ordered the chairman of the *Judenrat* to assemble the Jewish population in an open field outside the city for a "general parade." As the Jews presented themselves at the appointed time, the German commander ordered them to sing a gay and happy hasidic tune. The crowd was fearful and confused, but one hesitant voice started singing the moving song: *Lomir sich iberbeiten, Avinu shebaShamayim,* "Let us be friends again, our Father in Heaven." The crown remained unresponsive. The German soldiers threw themselves with murderous blows upon the Jews who would not obey their command. Suddenly, a voice broke from among the crowd singing the same tune with might and joy, but the words now changed to: *Mir wellen sei iberleben, Avinu shebaShamayim,* "We shall outlive them, our Father in Heaven." The song gripped the crowd. They sang it with enthusiasm and danced to it ecstatically. It became for them the hymn of Jewish eternity. The Germans, bewildered and at a loss, started shouting: "Stop it! Stop it!"[15] Did they sense that it was the song of their doom?

Endnotes

[1]C.f. Cohen, *Human Behavior in the Concentration Camp,* 162; see also Frankl, *From Death-camp to Existentialism,* 38.

[2]See, for example, Bruno Bettelheim, "Freedom from Ghetto Thinking," in *Midstream* (Spring 1962).

[3]*The Rebel,* Penguin Modern Classics 1971 edition, 147.

[4]Prager, I, 48.

[5]Isaiah 5:20.

[6]Cf. Unger, 102; Prager, I, the opening pages which discuss him, and also 43-44.

[7]Prager, I, 74-75.

[8]Jeremiah 17:7; Prager, I, 76-79.

[9]Prager, II, 84-85.

[10]*Ibid.,* 140.

[11]Psalms 119:28.

[12]Prager, I, 160-62.

[13]Schindler, 220; also M. Unger, *Admorim sheNispu baSho'ah,* Jerusalem, 1969, 103.

[14]Quoted by Terrence Des Pres in *The Survivor,* 68.

[15]M. Prager, *Nizuzei haGevurah,* Tel-Aviv, 1952, 10-11.

Part Four
The Commanding
Voice of Auschwitz

Chapter 8

The Commanding
Voice of Auschwitz*

Emil L. Fackenheim

The Madman's Prayer

The writer Elie Wiesel tells the story of a small group of Jews who were gathered to pray in a little synagogue in Nazi-occupied Europe. As the service went on, suddenly a pious Jew who was slightly mad—for all pious Jews were by then slightly mad—burst in through the door. Silently he listened for a moment as the prayers ascended. Slowly he said: "Shh, Jews! Do not pray so loud! God will hear you. Then He will know that there are still some Jews left alive in Europe."

This tale calls to mind another tale referred to earlier in this discourse. Friedrich Nietzsche, too, tells a story of a madman bursting in on a group of men, uttering dreadful words about God. There, however, all similarity ends. For in the one tale there is horror because God is dead; in the other, because He is alive. One madman addresses God's murderers; the other, His victims. The first hopes that tomorrow some men will be free; the second fears that tomorrow all Jews will be dead. An abyss yawns between the prophecy of a dead God and a prayer addressed to a living God, but spoken softly lest it be heard.

Yet all these contrasts, however stark, pale in comparison to another. The Nietzschean event of the death of God may have its ambiguities. Thus it signifies the loss of old and also the gain of new treasures, and it inspires a mixture of mourning and celebration. In one crucial respect, however, it lacks all ambiguity; and this is true of Nietzsche's own version of the event, as well as of those of his present-day Christian followers. The death of God occurs in the inward realm of the spirit alone, and nowhere else. Such catastrophes as it includes are internal catastrophes only; and even

*From *God's Presence in History: Jewish Affirmations and Philosophical Reflections*. Copyright © 1970 by Emil L. Fackenheim. Reprinted by permission of Georges Borchardt, Inc. for the author.

the vast contemporary external catastrophes, such as Auschwitz and Hiroshima, appear only, as it were, by accident. In Wiesel's story, however, Auschwitz is not an accident. It is and remains the center of the event, and this despite and because of the fact that God is part of it. Wiesel's is a Jewish story, for it refuses to spiritualize history.[1] Nietzsche's is a Christian, pseudo-Christian, or post-Christian[2] story, for in it spiritualization of history is of the essence. And yet in the story in which Auschwitz is accidental, God is dead, and in the story in which it is essential, He is alive.

The two madmen, therefore, suffer two wholly different kinds of madness. As we have seen, Nietzsche's madman comes too late to have gods for company and too soon to be able to bear the new solitude;[3] his present madness is therefore of the spirit alone, and so are the two sanities—the old, past sanity, which was companionship with the gods, and the new, future one, which will be human solitude. In the sharpest possible contrast, Wiesel's madman has all along held fast to a God who is Lord of actual history, its external events included. His was a sanity which held fast to God and to the world and was unable to disconnect the two. Hence it now turns into an unheard-of madness. For if sanity is not of the spirit only, but rather contact with the world (and with God *in* and *through* the world), then such sanity, when the world is Auschwitz, is destroyed by madness. And if insanity consists of flight from the world (and to gods who have themselves fled from the world),[4] then such flight, when the world is the Nazi holocaust, is necessary if even a shred of sanity is to remain. Jewish prayer, however, cannot achieve this sanity, for it cannot disconnect God from the world. Hence any Jewish prayer at Auschwitz is madness. Such is the terrible tale, such is the terrible Midrash of Wiesel's madman.

The Midrashic Framework and the Holocaust

This Midrash has no precedent in the ancient Midrash, for the Nazi holocaust has no precedent in ancient Jewish history—or medieval or modern. All history is full of unjust suffering; this term, when applied to Auschwitz, is hopelessly inadequate. Many past Jewish martyrs died for their faith; Hitler murdered Jews on account of their "race"[5]—believers and unbelievers alike. And if we can trace "racial" antisemitism as far back as medieval Spain (when converted as well as unconverted Jews were persecuted), we must also concede that "racial" antisemitism is one thing; the very thought of genocide, another. Nor did the Nazi genocide of European Jewry remain in the realm of mere thought. The Christian theologian, J. Coert Rylaarsdam, deliberately using hyperbole in order to shock Christian conscience, asserts that for Christians there have generally been only two "good Jews," and dead Jew and a Christian.[6] This suggests a connection between a Christian antisemitism which gives Jews a choice and a "racial" one which may lead to the thought of Jewish genocide.[7] Still, contemplation is not action. Long before Hitler the crime was contemplated.[8] Hitler executed it. And so carefully planned was the execution, so relentlessly and system-atically was it pursued, there is little doubt that, had he won the war, not a single Jewish man, woman and child would today be left alive on earth.

The Nazi genocide of the Jewish people has no precedent within Jewish history. Nor, once the necessary distinctions are carefully made, will one find a precedent out-side Jewish history. Today such distinctions are recklessly ignored. There is violent and indiscriminate talk of genocide, and an American college professor passes beyond the bounds of all decency when he compares the American campus to the Auschwitz murder camp.[9] Even actual cases of genocide, however, still differ from the Nazi hol-ocaust in at least two respects. Whole peoples have been killed for "rational" (however horrifying) ends such as power, territory, wealth, and in any case supposed or actual self-interest. No such end was served by the Nazi murder of the Jewish peo-ple. Fantastic efforts were often made to hunt down even a single Jew; Adolf Eich-mann would not stop the murder trains even when the war was as good as lost, and when less "sincere" Nazis thought of stopping them in an effort to appease the victor-ious Allies. The Nazi murder of Jews was an "ideological" project; it was annihilation for the sake of annihilation, murder for the sake of murder, evil for the sake of evil. Where would one find a counterpart, among any criminals, to Eichmann, who, with the third Reich in ruins and ashes, declared that he would jump laughing into his grave because he had sent millions of Jews to their death?[10]

Still more incontestably unique than the crime itself is the situation of the vic-tims. The Albigensians died for their faith, believing unto death that God needs mar-tyrs. Negro Christians have been murdered for their race, able to find comfort in a faith not at issue. The more than one million Jewish children murdered in the Nazi holocaust died neither because of their faith, nor despite their faith, nor for reasons unrelated to the Jewish faith. Since Nazi law defined a Jew as one having a Jewish grandparent, they were murdered because of the Jewish faith of the great-grand-parents. Had these great-grandparents abandoned their Jewish faith, and failed to bring up Jewish children, then their fourth-generation descendants might have been among the Nazi criminals; they would not have been among their Jewish victims. *Like Abraham of old, European Jews some time in the mid-nineteenth century offered a human sacrifice, by the mere minimal commitment to the Jewish faith of bringing up Jewish children. But unlike Abraham, they did not know what they were doing, and there was no reprieve.*[11]

The Hitler regime had a "research" institute on the "Jewish question,"[12] enlisting learned scholars in the task of thoroughly understanding Jews and Judaism in order to be able thoroughly to destroy both. We ask: *Has it succeeded in one part of its aim, though failing in the other?* Hitler failed to murder all Jews, for he lost the war. *Has he succeeded in destroying the Jewish faith for us who have?*

We hardly dare ask so appalling a question. Yet it forces itself upon us. Mid-nine-teenth-century European Jews did not know the effect of their action upon their remote descendants when they remained faithful to Judaism and raised Jewish children. What if they had known? Could they then have remained faithful? Should they? And what of us who know, when we consider the possibility of a second Auschwitz three generations hence. (Which would we rather have our great-grandchildren be—victims, or bystanders and executioners?) Yet for us to cease to be Jews (and to cease to bring up Jewish children) would be to abandon our millennial post as witnesses to the God of history.

In view of such terrifying questions which arise, it is not strange that until a few years ago Jewish theological thought has observed a nearly total silence on the subject of the holocaust. A recent questionnaire does not even include it among the questions, and few of the respondents refer to it in their replies.[13] Is this nothing but cowardice? Such is the view of a "radical" Jewish theologian, who asserts that "the facts are in," that the traditional theological "options" are clear-cut, obvious, and "will not magically increase with the passing of time," and that the conclusion is certain: the Midrashic framework is shattered forever by Auschwitz; the God of history is dead.[14]

But might it not be a well-justified fear and trembling, and a crushing sense of the most awesome responsibility to four thousand years of Jewish faith, which has kept Jewish theological thought, like Job, in a state of silence, and which makes us refuse to rush in where angels fear to tread, now that speech has become inevitable? The critic, who rightly states that it "remains emotionally impossible for most Jews to deal . . . with the trauma of Auschwitz," is quick to attribute the silence of others to a defense mechanism which makes them deny that Auschwitz ever happened.[15] What assures him of his own capacities to deal with the trauma—or stills his fear that some other mechanism may cause him to utter words which should never have been spoken? We need not go beyond his jarring expression "the facts are in." Will all the facts ever be in? And what, in this case, are the facts apart from the interpretation? The statistics? The novelist Manés Sperber, a survivor, writes:

> *Even if all the firmament were made of parchment, all the trees were pens, all the seas ink, and even if all the inhabitants of the earth were scribes, and they wrote day and night—they would never succeed in describing the grandeur and the splendor of the Creator of the universe.* Fifty years separate me from the child who learned to recite these opening lines of a long Aramaic poem that had been transmitted, with an unalterable oral commentary accompanying it, from generation to generation. I come back to the resonance of these phrases whenever I bring myself, once again, to the realization that we will never succeed in making the *hurban*—the Jewish catastrophe of our time—understood to those who will live after us. The innumerable documents that we owe to the indefatigable bureaucracy of the exterminators, the many narratives by witnesses who miraculously escaped, the diaries, chronicles and records—all these millions of words remind me that "even if all the firmament. . . ."[16]

Clearly the long theological silence was necessary. Silence would, perhaps, be best even now, were it not for the fact that among the people the flood-gates are broken, and that for this reason alone the time of theological silence is irretrievably past.

Even to begin to speak is to question radically some time-honored Midrashic doctrines; and, of these, one is immediately shattered. As we have seen, even the ancient rabbis were forced to suspend the Biblical "for our sins are we punished," perhaps not in response to the destruction of the Temple by Titus, but in response to the paganization of Jerusalem by Hadrian.[17] We, too, may at most only suspend the biblical doctrine, if only because we, no more than the rabbis, dare either to deny our own sinfulness or to disconnect it from history. Yet, suspend it we must. For however we twist and turn this doctrine in response to Auschwitz, it becomes a religious absurdity and even a sacrilege. Are "sin" and "retribution" to be given an individual connotation? What a sacrilegious thought when among the Nazis' victims were more than one million children! Are we to give them a collective connotation? What an appalling idea when it was not our Western, agnostic, faithless, and rich but rather the poorest, most pious, and most faithful Jewish communities which were most grievously stricken! As in our torment we turn, as an ultimate resort, to the traditional doctrine that all Israelites of all generations are responsible for each other, we are still totally aghast, for not a single one of the six million died because they had failed to keep the divine-Jewish covenant: they all died because their great-grandparents *had* kept it, if only to the minimum extent of raising Jewish children. Here is the point where we reach radical religious absurdity. Here is the rock on which the "for our sins are we punished" suffers total shipwreck.

Did Jews at Auschwitz die, then, because of the sins of others? The fact, to be sure, is obvious enough, and evidence continues to mount that these others were by no means confined to the Nazi murderers.[18] What is in question, however, is whether a religious meaning can be found in this fact—whether we, like countless generations before us, can have recourse to the thought of martyrdom.

We have already made reference to Abraham's sacrifice of Isaac. The Midrash (which, like the Bible itself, abhors human sacrifice) transfigures the story into one of martyrdom. Isaac was not a child but rather a grown-up man of thirty-seven years, and he was no unwilling sacrifice but rather a willing martyr—for *Kiddush Hashem*, the sanctification of the divine Name. This Midrashic interpretation continued to be alive in the Jewish religious consciousness, and during the crusades it sustained countless martyrs.[19]

Can it sustain the Jewish religious consciousness after Auschwitz?[20] When the crusading mobs fell upon the Jews of the Rhenish cities of Worms and Mayence (1096 C.E.) they left them, in theory if not in practice, with the choice between death and conversion, thus enabling them to choose martyrdom. At Auschwitz, however, there was no choice; the young and the old, the faithful and the faithless were slaughtered without discrimination. Can there be martyrdom where there is no choice?

Yet we protest against a negative answer, for we protest against allowing Hitler to dictate the terms of our religious life. If not martyrdom, there can be a faithfulness resembling it, when a man has no choice between life and death but only between faith and despair.

But could and did Jews at Auschwitz choose faithfulness unto death? There every effort was made to destroy faith where faith had existed. Torquemada destroyed bodies in order to save souls. Eichmann sought to destroy souls before he destroyed bodies. Throughout the ages pious Jews have died saying the *Shema Yisrael*—"Hear, O Israel, the Lord our God, the Lord is One" (Deut 6:4). The Nazi murder machine was systematically designed to stifle this *Shema Yisrael* on Jewish lips before it murdered Jews themselves. Auschwitz was the supreme, most diabolical attempt ever made to murder martyrdom itself and, failing that, to deprive all death, martyrdom included, of its dignity.

Hitler and Eichmann have won their victories. A museum in an Israeli kibbutz of death-camp survivors[21] demonstrates that, given the power, determination, machinery, and diabolical cunning, it is possible to murder a nation of heroes. It would, alas, be possible to show that, given these instruments, it is possible to degrade and dehumanize a community of saints. A good Christian suggests that perhaps Auschwitz was a divine reminder of the sufferings of Christ.[22] Should he not ask instead whether his Master himself, had He been present at Auschwitz, could have resisted degradation and dehumanization? What are the sufferings of the Cross compared to those of a mother whose child is slaughtered to the sound of laughter or the strains of a Viennese waltz? This question may sound sacrilegious to Christian ears. Yet we dare not shirk it, for we—Christian as well as Jew—must ask: at Auschwitz, did the grave win the victory after all, or, worse than the grave, did the devil himself win?

Yet we still insist, and this with certain knowledge, that pious Jews *did* die in faithfulness, their faith untouched and unsullied by all the sadism and the horror.[23] Even so, however, Jewish if not Christian[24] exaltation of martyrdom is radically shaken—perhaps forever. The Midrashic Abraham remonstrates with God after the trial is over, for he demands to know its purpose; and he is told that the idolatrous nations, not God Himself, had stood in need of his testimony.[25] The martyrs of Worms and Mayence remembered this Midrash when they saw their children slaughtered before their very eyes, or, worse, themselves laid hands upon them; yet even they must surely have asked themselves whether murder and idolatry had diminished since the times of Abraham, and whether any purpose was served by further Jewish martyrdom. After Auschwitz, however, ours is a far worse question. One would dearly like to believe that the shock of the holocaust has made impossible a second holocaust anywhere. Is the grim truth not rather that a second holocaust has been made more likely, not less likely, by the fact of the first? For there are few signs anywhere of that radical repentance which alone could rid the world of Hitler's shadow.

If this is indeed the grim truth, is not, after Auschwitz, any Jewish willingness to suffer martyrdom, instead of an inspiration to potential saints, much rather an encouragement to potential criminals? After Auschwitz, is not even the saintliest of Jews driven to the inexorable conclusion that he owes the moral obligation to the antisemites of the world not to encourage them by his own powerlessness? Such, at any rate, is the view of a novelist, himself a survivor, who asserts that the Warsaw Ghetto uprising and the Eichmann trail have brought to an end "the millennial epoch of the Jews' sanctifying God and themselves by their submitting to a violent death."[26]

We turn next to Midrashim of protest. There is a kind of faith which will accept all things and renounce every protest. There is also a kind of protest which has despaired of faith. In Judaism there has always been protest which stays within the sphere of faith. Abraham remonstrates with God. So do Jeremiah and Job. So does, in modern times, the Hasidic Rabbi Levi Yitzhak of Berdiczev. He once interrupted the sacred Yom Kippur service in order to protest that, whereas kings of flesh and blood protected their peoples, Israel was unprotected by her King in Heaven. Yet having made his protest, he recited the Kaddish, which begins with these words: "Extolled and hallowed be the name of God throughout the world. . . ."

Can Jewish protest today remain within the sphere of faith? Jeremiah protests against the prosperity of the wicked; we protest against the slaughter of the innocent. To Job children were restored; that the children of Auschwitz will be restored is a belief which we dare not abuse for the purpose of finding comfort. Job protests on his own behalf, and within the sphere of faith; we protest on behalf of others, and above all on behalf of those who would not or could not be or stay within the sphere of Jewish faith and yet were murdered on account of it. In faithfulness to the victims we must refuse comfort; and in faithfulness to Judaism we must refuse to disconnect God from the holocaust. Thus, in our case, protest threatens to escalate into a totally destructive conflict between the faith of the past and faithfulness to the present.

As we shrink from this conflict we seek refuge in Midrashim of divine powerlessness. However, here too we seem threatened with ruin. In the Midrash the fear of God still exists among the nations, and Israel survives, albeit powerless and scattered among the nations.[27] In Nazi Europe, however, the fear of God was dead, and Jews were hunted without mercy or scruple. In the Midrash, God goes into exile with His people and returns with them;[28] from Auschwitz there was no return. Hence, whereas in the Midrash God is only "as it were" powerless, in *Night*, Wiesel sees Him in the face of a child hanging on the gallows.

> One day when we came back from work, we saw three gallows rearing up in the assembly place, three black crows. Roll Call. SS all round us, machine guns trained: the traditional ceremony. Three victims in chains—and one of them, the little servant, the sad-eyed angel.
>
> The SS seemed more preoccupied, more disturbed than usual. To hang a young boy in front of thousands of spectators was no light matter. The head of the camp read the

verdict. All eyes were on the child. He was lividly pale, almost calm, biting his lips. The
gallows threw its shadow over him. . . .
The three victims mounted together onto the chairs.
The three necks were placed at the same moment within the nooses.
"Long live liberty!" cried the two adults.
But the child was silent.
"Where is God? Where is He?" someone behind me asked.
At a sign from the head of the camp, the three chairs tipped over. . . .
I heard a voice within me answer . . .:
"Where is He? Here He is—He is hanging on this gallows. . . ."[29]

To stake all on divine powerlessness today, therefore, would be to take it both
radically and literally. God suffers literal and radical powerlessness, i.e., actual death;
and any resurrected divine power will be manifest, not so much within history as
beyond it. A Jew, in short, would have to become a Christian. But (as will be seen)[30]
never in the two thousand years of Jewish-Christian confrontation has it been less
possible for a Jew to abandon either his Jewishness or his Judaism and embrace
Christianity.

Jewish faith thus seems to find no refuge in Midrashim of divine powerlessness,
none in otherworldliness, none in the redeeming power of martyrdom, and most of
all none in the view that Auschwitz is punishment for the sins of Israel. Unless the
God of history is to be abandoned, only a prayer remains, addressed to divine Power,
but spoken softly lest it be heard.

One refuge is still unexplored. Rabbi Akiba once taught that God, as it were powerless, shares Israel's exile. It will be recalled that Rabbi Eliezer responded differently
to the destruction of the second Temple and the paganization of Jerusalem. The gates
of prayer were closed, and only those of tears were still open. Israel was separated
from her Father in Heaven as by a wall of iron.[31] God was no longer present in
history. Was God absent at Auschwitz? Is He in eclipse even now? May pious Jews
pray as loudly as they like, because God cannot or does not hear?

We have seen that Buber's image of the eclipse of God can sustain Jewish faith
in its confrontation with modern secularism.[32] It now appears, however, that this image fails to sustain us in our confrontation with the Nazi holocaust. Why could Rabbi
Eliezer continue to pray when the gates of prayer were closed? Because the divine
Presence remained the object of hope, and because for this reason the root experiences of the past could continue to be reenacted. For the hero of Wiesel's *The Gates
of the Forest*, however, a Messiah who can come, and yet at Auschwitz did not come,
has become an impossibility;[33] and this impossibility, were it to be and remain total
and absolute,[34] would be of devastating consequence. A divine eclipse which was
total in the present would cut off both past and future. The pious Jew during the
Passover Seder has always reenacted the salvation at the Red Sea. The event always
remained real for him because He who once had saved was saving still.[35] And this

latter affirmation could continue to be made, even in times of catastrophe, because the divine salvation remained present in the form of hope. What if our present is without hope? The unprecedented catastrophe of the holocaust now discloses for us that the eclipse of God remains a religious possibility within Judaism *only if it is not total*. If *all* present access to God of history is *wholly* lost, the God of history is Himself lost.[36]

With this conclusion we have come face to face with the horrifying possibility mentioned at the beginning—that Hitler has succeeded in murdering, not only one-third of the Jewish people, but the Jewish faith as well. Only one response may seem to remain—the cry of total despair—"there is no judgement and no judge."

Jewish Secularism and the Holocaust

But this conclusion has been reached long ago by the Jewish secularist, albeit for totally different reasons and to a totally different effect.

Jewish secularism has been a possibility ever since the Age of Enlightenment, and its vitality has been confirmed in our time in the most dramatic possible way by the foundation of a secular Jewish state. Today we must ask whether secularism may not be now the common fate of all Jews who persist in their Jewishness. However, we shall find that, if the death camps threaten the Jewish faith, they threaten no less any secularism which would take its place. All religious faith is in crisis in our time. A Jew who confronts Auschwitz and reaffirms his Jewishness discovers that every form of modern secularism is equally in crisis.

We have previously considered the rational grounds for secularism. We must now inquire into the grounds of its attractiveness for modern Jews. The secularism which we have termed subjectivist reductionism dissipates all gods, destroys all meaning except what is humanly created, and deprives Jewish existence of its millennial distinctiveness. Why should Jews *want* to—rather than be *rationally compelled to*—accept such a creed?

Subjectivist reductionism has a general attraction. To the pious, a life without Absolutes may be meaningless and goalless. To the secularist such a life is one of liberty. To the believer, the divine Presence exalts as it gives life a focus. To the secularist it seems to tyrannize, for it stifles life's natural pluralism for him. The life of faith is abnormal, and the dissipation of faith ushers in human normalcy. Such is the creed of the secular city.[37]

If for modern Jews this creed has always had a special attraction, it is because of the vision of "normalcy" which is part of it. The modern Jew has become modern by virtue of the Emancipation, and the Emancipation has been a process of "normalization." Its Gentile donors may have often had in mind the end of the Jewish people;[38] its Jewish recipients wished to normalize the Jewish people even when they were determined to perpetuate it; and, after many centuries of religious discrimination and persecution, this is not surprising.

Nor in view of these many centuries it is surprising that "Jewish normalcy" has often been not *one limited* goal but rather *the ultimate* goal. This is true of many "religious" Jews when they categorize themselves as Jewish by "denomination" and British, French, or American by "nationality." It is more true of "secularist" Jews proper when they define themselves as a "nationality" like all others. Most of all it is true of those Zionist Jews who, when they embark on the most abnormal enterprise of restoring a nation after two thousand years, are committed to the goal of becoming a nation like all others. The assimilationist has wished all along to solve the so-called "Jewish problem"[39] by dissolving Jewish existence; the secularist, by depriving it of its millennial distinctiveness.

We cannot guess what might have happened to this modern Jewish secularist or quasi-secularist drive for normalcy had the Nazi holocaust never occurred. We must face the fact, however, that had normalcy remained the all-overriding goal, the Jewish response to the holocaust should have been the exact opposite of the one which actually was and is being given. For twelve long years Jews had been singled out by a hate which was as groundless as it was implacable. For twelve long years a power had held sway in the heart of Europe to which the death of every Jewish man, woman, and child was the one and only unshakable principle. For twelve long years the world had failed to oppose this principle with an equally unshakable principle of its own. Any Jew, then or now, making normalcy his supreme goal should have been, and still should be, in flight from this singled-out condition in total disarray. In fact, however, secularist no less than religious Jews have responded with a reaffirmation of their Jewish existence such as no social scientist would have predicted even if the holocaust had never occurred. Jewish theology still does not know how to respond to Auschwitz. Jews themselves—rich and poor, learned and ignorant, believer and secularist—have responded in some measure all along.

No doubt social scientists have their ready explanations. Persecution stiffens resistance. Humiliation causes pride in half-remembered loyalties. The ancient rabbis themselves suggest that Israel thrives on persecution. Such are the normal explanations, and in normal times they may well be right.

The times, however, are not normal times. A Jew at Auschwitz was not a specimen of the class "victim of prejudice" or even "victim of genocide." He was *singled out* by a demonic power which sought his death *absolutely*, i.e., as an end in itself. For a Jew today merely to affirm his Jewish existence is to accept his singled-out condition; it is to oppose the demons of Auschwitz: and it is to oppose them in the only way in which they can be opposed—with an *absolute* opposition. Moreover, it is to stake on that absolute opposition nothing less than his life and the lives of his children and the lives of his children's children.

The holocaust has thus placed the Jewish secularist into a position for which secularism has no precedent within or without Jewish existence. As a secularist, he views the modern world as a desacralized world from which all gods have vanished. As a Jewish secularist he knows that the devil, if not God, is alive. As a secularist he has relativized all former absolutes. As a Jewish secularist he opposes the demons of Auschwitz absolutely by his mere commitment to Jewish survival. Thus a radical contradiction has appeared in Jewish secularist existence in our time. As secularist, the Jewish secularist seeks Jewish normalcy; as Jewish secularist, he fragments this normalcy by accepting his singled-out Jewish condition. As secularist, he reduces all absolute to relative affirmations; as Jewish secularist, he opposes absolutely the demons of death with his own Jewish life. Throughout the ages the religious Jew was a witness to God. After Auschwitz even the most secularist of Jews bears witness, by the mere affirmation of his Jewishness, against the devil.[40]

The Jewish secularist cannot escape this contradiction; or rather, he could escape it only if he either pretended that the Nazi holocaust had never occurred or else fled from his Jewishness. Will Herberg has therefore rightly asserted that Jewish secularism has become illogical in our time—that, by the logic of his position, the Jewish secularist should abandon his Jewishness.[41] Herberg has failed to notice, however, a truth of far greater consequence which the Jewish secularist himself recognizes: the devil confounds our logic.

Still, not all Jewish secularism falls into immediate contradiction. We have seen that, beside a secularism which dissolves all religious absolutes, there is a secularism which internalizes and transforms these absolutes.[42] Hence a Jewish secularism is conceivable which opposes the demons of Auschwitz absolutely—but in behalf of "free," autonomous, post-religious humanity.

A Jewish secularism of this kind was always problematic. Either the ancient religious absolutes remained absolute in the process of internalization; but then they were universals such as Reason or Progress, and Jewish existence had become accidental. Or else they remained particularized enough to sustain Jewish existence in its particularity; but then they would become idolatrous unless they lost their absoluteness. Jewish romantics and pragmatists both perceived that any specifically "Jewish genius" could be but one instrument in an orchestra requiring many others, and that any Jewish loyalty to Jewish "peoplehood" required by such a genius could exist only within a "pluralistic" scheme in which many loyalties made their respective claims, and in which none was absolute. The God of Judaism—who was and remained other-than-man—could both be Himself universal and single out the Jewish people. The internalized God of secularism could only be either universal (and then not single out at all) or else particular (and then not single out absolutely).

After Auschwitz, both alternatives, always problematic within Jewish existence, are fragmented. Jewish opposition to the demons of Auschwitz cannot be understood in terms of humanly created ideals. Those of Reason fail, for Reason is too innocent of demonic evil to fathom the scandal of the particularity of Auschwitz, and too abstractly universal to do justice to the singled-out Jewish condition. The ideals of Progress fail, for Progress makes of Auschwitz at best a throwback into tribalism and at worst a dialectically justified necessity. Least adequate are any ideals which might be furnished by a specifically Jewish genius, for Jewish survival after Auschwitz is not one relative ideal among others but rather an imperative which brooks no compromise. In short, within the context of Jewish existence the secularism which we have termed subjectivist reductionism is breached by *absolute* Jewish opposition to the demons of Auschwitz; and the secularism which we have seen exemplified in Nietzscheanism and left-wing Hegelianism is breached because internalized absolutes either cannot single out or else cannot remain absolute. Jewish opposition to Auschwitz cannot be grasped in terms of humanly created ideals but only as an *imposed commandment*. And the Jewish secularist, no less than the believer, is *absolutely singled out* by a Voice as truly other than man-made ideals—an imperative as truly given—as was the Voice of Sinai.

According to the Midrash, God wished to give the Torah immediately upon the Exodus from Egypt, but had to postpone the gift until Israel was united.[43] Today, the distinction between religious and secularist Jews is superseded by that between unauthentic Jews who flee from their Jewishness and authentic Jews who affirm it. This latter group includes religious and secularist Jews. These are united by a commanding Voice which speaks from Auschwitz.

The Commanding Voice of Auschwitz

What does the Voice of Auschwitz command?

> Jews are forbidden to hand Hitler posthumous victories. They are commanded to survive as Jews, lest the Jewish people perish. They are commanded to remember the victims of Auschwitz lest their memory perish. They are forbidden to despair of man and his world, and to escape into either cynicism or otherworldliness, lest they cooperate in delivering the world over to the forces of Auschwitz. Finally, they are forbidden to despair of the God of Israel, lest Judaism perish. A secularist Jew cannot make himself believe by a mere act of will, nor can he be commanded to do so. . . . And a religious Jew who has stayed with his God may be forced into new, possibly revolutionary relationships with Him. One possibility, however, is wholly unthinkable. A Jew may not respond to Hitler's attempt to destroy Judaism by himself cooperating in its destruction. In ancient times, the unthinkable Jewish sin was idolatry. Today, it is to respond to Hitler by doing his work.[44]

Elie Wiesel has compared the holocaust with Sinai in revelatory significance—and expressed the fear that we are not listening. We shrink from this daring comparison—but even more from not listening. We shrink from any claim to have heard—but even more from a false refuge, in an endless agnosticism, from a Voice speaking to us. I was able to make the above, fragmentary statement (which I have already previously made and here merely quote) only because it no more than articulates what is being heard by Jews the world over—rich and poor, learned and ignorant, believing and secularist. I cannot go beyond this earlier statement but only expand it.

1. The First Fragment

In the murder camps the unarmed, decimated, emaciated survivors often rallied their feeble remaining resources for a final, desperate attempt at revolt. The revolt was hopeless. There was no hope but one. One might escape. Why must one escape? To tell the tale. Why must the tale be told when evidence was already at hand that the world would not listen?[45] Because not to tell the tale, when it might be told, was unthinkable. The Nazis were not satisfied with mere murder. Before murdering Jews, they were trying to reduce them to numbers; after murdering them, they were dumping their corpses into nameless ditches or making them into soap. They were making as sure as was possible to wipe out every trace of memory. Millions would be as though they had never been. But to the pitiful and glorious desperadoes of Warsaw, Treblinka, and Auschwitz, who would soon themselves be as though they had never been, not to rescue for memory what could be rescued was unthinkable because it was sacrilege.[46]

It will remain a sacrilege ever after. Today, suggestions come from every side to the effect that the past had best be forgotten, or at least remain unmentioned, or at least be coupled with the greatest and most thoughtless speed with other, but quite different, human tragedies. Sometimes these suggestions come from Jews rationalizing their flight from the Nazi holocaust. More often they come from non-Jews, who rationalize their own flight, or even maintain, affrontingly enough, that unless Jews universalize the holocaust, thus robbing the Jews of Auschwitz of their Jewish identity, they are guilty of disregard for humanity.[47] But for a Jew hearing the commanding Voice of Auschwitz, the duty to remember and to tell the tale is not negotiable. It is holy. The religious Jew still possesses this word. The secularist Jew is commanded to restore it. A secular holiness, as it were, has forced itself into his vocabulary.

2. The Second Fragment

Jewish survival, were it even for no more than survival's sake, is a holy duty as well. The murderers of Auschwitz cut off Jews from humanity and denied them the right to existence; yet in being denied that right, Jews represented all humanity. Jews after Auschwitz represent all humanity when they affirm their Jewishness and deny the Nazi denial. They would fail if they affirmed the mere *right* to their Jewishness, participating, as it were, in an obscene debate between others who deny the right of Jews to exist and Jews who affirm it.[48] Nor would they deny the Nazi denial if they affirmed merely their humanity-in-general, permitting an antisemitic split between their humanity and their Jewishness, or, worse, agreeing to vanish as Jews in one way, in response to Hitler's attempt to make them vanish in another. The commanding Voice of Auschwitz singles Jews out; Jewish survival is a commandment which brooks no compromise. It was this Voice which was heard by the Jews of Israel in May and June 1967 when they refused to lie down and be slaughtered.[49]

Yet such is the extent of Hitler's posthumous victories that Jews, commanded to survive as Jews, are widely denied even the right. More precisely—for overt antisemitism is not popular in the post-holocaust world—they are granted the right only on certain conditions. Russians, Poles, Indians, and Arabs have a natural right to exist; Jews must earn that right. Other states must refrain from wars of aggression; the State of Israel is an "aggressor" even if it fights for its life. Peoples unscarred by Auschwitz ought to protest when any evil resembling Auschwitz is in sight, such as the black ghettos or Vietnam. The Jewish survivors of Auschwitz have no right to survive unless they engage in such protests. Other peoples may include secularists and believers. Jews must be divided into bad secularists or Zionists, and good—albeit anachronistic—saints who stay on the cross.

The commanding Voice of Auschwitz bids Jews reject all such views as a monumental affront. It bids them reject as no longer tolerable every version—Christian or leftist, Gentile or Jewish—of the view that the Jewish people is an anachronism, when it is the elements of the world perpetrating and permitting Auschwitz, not its survivors, that are anachronistic. A Jew is commanded to descend from the cross, and in so doing, not only to reiterate his ancient rejection of an ancient Christian view but also to suspend the time-honored Jewish exaltation of martyrdom. For after Auschwitz, Jewish life is more sacred than Jewish death, were it even for the sanctification of the divine Name. The left-wing secularist Israeli journalist Amos Kenan writes: "After the death camps, we are left only one supreme value: existence."[50]

3. The Third Fragment

But such as Kenan, being committed and unrepentant lovers of the downtrodden, accept other supreme values as well, and will suspend these only when Jewish existence itself is threatened or denied. Kenan has a universal vision of peace, justice, and brotherhood. He loves the poor of Cuba and hates death in Vietnam. In these and other commitments such left-wing secularists share the ancient Jewish religious, messianically inspired refusal to embrace either pagan cynicism (which despairs of the world and accepts the *status quo*) or Christian or pseudo-Christian otherworldliness (which despairs of the world and flees from it). The commanding Voice of Auschwitz bids Jews, religious and secularist, not to abandon the world to the forces of Auschwitz, but rather to continue to work and hope for it. Two possibilities are equally ruled out:

to despair of the world on account of Auschwitz, abandoning the age-old Jewish identification with poor and persecuted humanity; and to abuse such identification as a means of flight from Jewish destiny. It is precisely *because* of the uniqueness of Auschwitz, and *in* his Jewish particularly, that a Jew must be at one with humanity. For it is precisely because Auschwitz has made the world a desperate place that a Jew is forbidden to despair of it.[51] The hero of Wiesel's *The Gates of the Forest* asserts that it is too late for the Messiah—and that for exactly this reason we are commanded to hope.[52]

4. The Fourth Fragment

The Voice of Auschwitz commands the religious Jew after Auschwitz to continue to wrestle with his God in however revolutionary ways; and it forbids the secularist Jew (who has already, and on other grounds, lost Him) to use Auschwitz as an additional weapon wherewith to deny Him.

The ways of the religious Jew are revolutionary, for there is no previous Jewish protest against divine Power like his protest. Continuing to hear the Voice of Sinai as he hears the Voice of Auschwitz, his citing of God against God may have to assume extremes which dwarf those of Abraham, Jeremiah, Job, Rabbi Levi Yitzhak. (You have abandoned the covenant? We shall not abandon it! You no longer want Jews to survive? We shall survive, as better, more faithful, more pious Jews! You have destroyed all grounds for hope? We shall obey the commandment to hope which You Yourself have given!) Nor is there any previous Jewish compassion with divine powerlessness like the compassion required by such a powerlessness. (The fear of God is dead among the nations? We shall keep it alive and be its witnesses! The times are too late for the coming of the Messiah? We shall persist without hope and recreate hope—and, as it were, divine Power—by our persistence!) For the religious Jew, who remains within the Midrashic framework, the Voice of Auschwitz manifests a divine Presence which, as it were, is shorn of all except commanding Power. *This* Power, however, is inescapable.

No less inescapable is this Power for the secularist Jew who has all along been outside the Midrashic framework and this despite the fact that the Voice of Auschwitz does not enable him to return into that framework. He cannot return; but neither may he turn the Voice of Auschwitz against that of Sinai. For he may not cut off his secular present from the religious past: the Voice of Auschwitz commands preservation of that past. Nor may he widen the chasm between himself and the religious Jew: the Voice of Auschwitz commands Jewish unity.

As religious and secularist Jews are united in kinship with all the victims of Auschwitz and against all the executioners, they face a many-sided mystery and find a simple certainty. As regards the minds and souls of the victims of Auschwitz, God's presence to them is a many-sided mystery which will never be exhausted either by subsequent committed believers or by subsequent committed unbelievers, and least of all by subsequent neutral theorists—psychological, sociological, philosophical, theological—who spin out their theories immune to love and hate, submission and rage, faith and despair. As regards the murderers of Auschwitz, however, there was no mystery, for they denied, mocked, murdered the God of Israel six million times—and together with Him four thousand years of Jewish faith. For a Jew after Auschwitz, only one thing is certain: he may not side with the murderers and do what they have left undone. The religious Jew who has heard the Voice of Sinai must continue to listen as he hears the commanding Voice of Auschwitz. And the secularist Jew, who has all along lost Sinai and now hears the Voice of Auschwitz, cannot abuse that Voice as a means to destroy four thousand years of Jewish believing testimony. The rabbis assert that the first Temple was destroyed because of idolatry. Jews may not destroy the Temple which is the tears of Auschwitz by doing, wittingly or unwittingly, Hitler's work.

5. The Clash Between the Fragments

Such is the commanding Voice of Auschwitz as it is increasingly being heard by Jews of this generation. But how can it be obeyed? Each of the four fragments described—and they are mere fragments, and the description has been poor and inadequate—is by itself overwhelming. Taken together, they seem unbearable. For there are clashes between them which tear us apart.

How can the religious Jew be faithful to both the faith of the past and the victims of the present? We have already asked this question, but are now further from an answer than before. For a reconciliation by means of willing martyrdom is ruled out by the duty to Jewish survival, and a reconciliation by means of refuge in otherworldly mysticism is ruled out by the duty to hold fast to the world and to continue to hope and work for it. God, world and Israel are in so total a conflict when they meet at Auschwitz as to seem to leave religious Jews confronting that conflict with nothing but a prayer addressed to God, yet spoken softly lest it be heard: in short, with madness.

But the conflict is no less unbearable for the secularist Jew. To be sure, the space once occupied by God is void for him or else occupied by a question mark. Only three of the four fragments effectively remain. Yet the conflict which remains tears him asunder.

Søren Kierkegaard's "knight of faith" was obliged to retrace the road which led Abraham to Mount Moriah, where Isaac's sacrifice was to take place.[53] A Jew today is obliged to retrace the road which led his brethren to Auschwitz. It is a road of pain and mourning, of humiliation, guilt, and despair. To retrace it is living death. How suffer this death and also choose Jewish life, which, like all life, must include joy, laughter, and childlike innocence? How reconcile such a remembrance with life itself?

How dare a Jewish parent crush his child's innocence with the knowledge that his uncle or grandfather was denied life because of his Jewishness? And how dare he not burden him with this knowledge? The conflict is inescapable, for we may neither forget the past for the sake of present life, nor destroy present life by a mourning without relief—and there is no relief.

Nor is this all. The first two fragments above clash with each other: each clashes with the third as well. No Jewish secularist today may continue to hope and work for mankind as though Auschwitz had never happened, falling back on secularist beliefs of yesterday that man is good, progress real, and brotherhood inevitable. Yet neither may he, on account of Auschwitz, despair of human brotherhood and cease to hope and work for it. How face Auschwitz and not despair? How hope and work, and not act as though Auschwitz had never occurred? Yet to forget and to despair are both forbidden.

Perhaps reconciliation would be possible if the Jewish secularist of today, like the Trotskys and Rosa Luxemburgs of yesterday, could sacrifice Jewish existence on the alter of future humanity. (Is this in the minds of "progressive" Jews when they protest against war in Vietnam but refuse to protest against Polish antisemitism? Or in the minds of what Kenan calls the "good people" of the world when they demand that Israel hand over weapons to those sworn to destroy her?) This sacrifice, however, is forbidden, and the alter is false. The left-wing Israeli secularist Kenan may accept all sorts of advice from his progressive friends, but not that he allow himself to be shot for the good of humanity. Perhaps he has listened for a moment even to this advice, for he hates a gun in his hand. Perhaps he has even wished for a second he could accept, feeling, like many of his pious ancestors, that it is better to be killed than to kill. Yet he firmly rejects such advice, for he is *commanded to* reject it; rather than be shot, he will shoot first when there is no third alternative. But he will shoot with tears in his eyes. He writes:

Why weren't the June 4 borders peace borders on the fourth of June, but will only become so now? Why weren't the UN Partition Plan borders of 1947 peace borders then, but will become so now? Why should I return this gun to the bandit as a reward for having failed to kill me?
I want peace peace peace peace, peace peace peace.
I am ready to give everything back in exchange for peace.
And I shall give nothing back without peace.
I am ready to solve the refugee problem. I am ready to accept an independent Palestinian state. I am ready to sit and talk. About everything, all at the same time. Direct talks, indirect talks, all this is immaterial. But peace.
Until you agree to have peace, I shall give back nothing. And if you force me to become a conqueror, I shall become a conqueror. And if you force me to become an oppressor, I shall become an oppressor. And if you force me into the same camp with all the forces of darkness in the world, there I shall be.[54]

Kenan's article ends:

> . . . if I survive, . . . without a god but without prophets either, my life will have no sense whatever. I shall have nothing else to do but walk on the banks of streams, or on the top of the rocks, watch the wonders of nature, and console myself with the words of Ecclesiastes, the wisest of men: For the light is sweet, and it is good for the eyes to see the sun.[55]

The conclusion, then, is inescapable. Secularist Jewish existence after Auschwitz is threatened with a madness no less extreme than that which produces a prayer addressed to God, yet spoken softly lest it be heard.

Madness and the Commanding Voice of Auschwitz

The Voice of Auschwitz commands Jews not to go mad. It commands them to accept their singled out condition, face up to its contradictions, and endure them. Moreover, it gives the power of endurance, the power of sanity. The Jew of today can endure because he must endure, and he must endure because he is commanded to endure.

We ask: whence has come our strength to endure even these twenty-five years—not to flee or disintegrate but rather to stay, however feebly, at our solitary post, to affirm, however weakly, our Jewishness, and to bear witness, if only by this affirmation, against the forces of hell itself? The question produces abiding wonder. It is at a commanding Voice without which we, like the Psalmist (Ps. 119:92), would have perished in our affliction.

Witness unto the Nations

When the Israelite maidservants at the Red Sea and Mount Sinai saw what neither Isaiah nor Ezekiel nor all the other prophets were to see, they found themselves to be, to their own radical astonishment, witnesses unto the nations. Had this been otherwise, their astonishment at the divine Presence would have been itself neither radical nor abiding. The divine saving Presence at the Red Sea was sole Power: hence it required recognition of all the nations and promised salvation for all the nations. The divine commanding Presence at Mount Sinai, too, was sole Power: hence it required action of all human creatures and promised a covenant with all human creatures. Yet, the divine Presence was fragmentary and occurred *in history*: hence it did not dissolve Israel into the nations but rather made her a singled out witness unto the nations.

This fact of being a witness was never questioned throughout the millennia of the Jewish faith. Yet the nature of the required testimony was prey to recurring puzzlement with the change of historical circumstances. Thus in Biblical times the testimony was against idolatry; yet it was clear even then that not all Gentiles were idolaters; As for the rabbis, they formed a firm concept of a divine covenant with the children of Noah, as well as of "righteous Gentiles" among the nations, who required neither conversion to Judaism nor instruction in it in their achievement of righteousness. What then was the nature of the required testimony?

At times it could seem to be between God, Israel, and the nations. This was true, negatively, of the testimony against idolatry. It was true, positively, of the testimony to the One God which led to Christian and Muhammadan monotheism. It could be accepted as true also when in modern times Jews invoked their faith in partial or total support of social progress and secularist Messianism. It could seem true even when Jewish martyrs recalled the Midrashic account of Isaac's sacrifice, persisting in the belief that Jewish martyrdom had an effect on the world.

At other times, however, Jewish testimony, albeit to the nations, was between God and Israel alone, if only because to hold otherwise would have led to despair. Thus the Jews behind medieval ghetto walls could not seriously believe that the nations on the other side knew or cared about their faithfulness or faithlessness to the Torah; nor could the martyrs of Worms and Mayence seriously think that the crusading mobs would be moved by their martyrdom. And while it is a documented fact that countless pious Jews died at Auschwitz with the *Shema Yisrael* on their lips, no less documented is the fact that, while the Nazi murder machines on occasion broke down, the murderers themselves did not.[56] Nor, to judge by contemporary historians, novelists, philosophers, and theologians, does it seem that the world cares even now.

Even so, pious Jews believed themselves to be witnesses unto the nations. In the medieval ghettoes they believed that by studying the Torah they helped preserve the whole world, since if it were not for the Torah, the world would again become "without form and void" (Gen. 1:2)[57] The martyrs of Worms and Mayence continued to hold fast to the Midrashic Abraham whose sacrifice had been needed not by God but by the world. But what, in their final moments, the pious Jews of Auschwitz believed or did not believe is a mystery which can only be revered but which will never be fathomed.

After Auschwitz does a Jew remain a witness unto the nations, and, if so, what is his testimony? Even the first of these questions is fraught with peril. We shrink from an affirmative answer lest we stifle impulses for sheer survival and elementary normalcy with unnecessary or impossible burdens. Yet we shrink even more from a negative answer lest we cut off any part of the Jewish past, break up kinships of the present, or deny or obscure the universal significance of contemporary Jewish destiny.

What, then, when we hardly dare answer the first question, may be said of the second? The world which is a desperate place for the Jew after Auschwitz is becoming increasingly desperate for all men. Hope is being overwhelmed by despair; love by hate; commandment by loss of direction; and never far below consciousness is the spectre of a nuclear holocaust—the universal Auschwitz. This is an age in which former believers seek refuge in secularity, even as formerly self-confident secularists seek old or new gods. The only universal seems to be an apparent unwillingness or incapacity to *endure* through the present worldwide crisis; to cherish and nurture what needs to be saved as the foundations are shaking; to work and hope with unyielding stubbornness for a time when our present crisis may have passed, and a new, possibly post-"religious" and post-"secular" age may come in sight.

The Jew after Auschwitz is a witness to endure. He is singled out by contradictions which, in our post-holocaust world, are worldwide contradictions. He bears witness that without endurance we shall all perish. He bears witness that *we can* endure because we *must* endure; and that we must endure because we are *commanded* to endure.

Longing, Defiance, Endurance

Can the miracle at the Red Sea still be reenacted? Can the religious Jew still recall it twice daily in his prayers? After Auschwitz can we continue to celebrate the Passover Seder?

How can even the secularist, who has long abandoned the celebration, not reinstate it? When at Jerusalem in 1967 the threat of total annihilation gave way to sudden salvation it was because of Auschwitz, not in spite of it, that there was an abiding astonishment. Nothing of the past was explained or adjusted, no fears for the future were stilled. Yet the very clash between Auschwitz and Jerusalem produced a moment of truth—a wonder at a singled out, millennial existence which, after Auschwitz, is still possible and actual.

But the ancient Passover has acquired a new quality. Always mixed with longing, the celebration is, after Auschwitz, mingled with defiance as well. There has always been the longing for a future when salvation would no longer be fragmentary, when the angels need no longer refrain from singing, when men everywhere, at last reconciled, would see what once the Israelite maidservants saw. Astonishingly, this longing survived even at Auschwitz itself. We dare not destroy it but must keep it alive. A prayer of remembrance, added by Jews throughout the world to the Passover service, reads as follows:

> On this night of the Seder we remember with reverence and love the six millions of our people of the European exile who perished at the hands of a tyrant more wicked than the Pharaoh who enslaved our fathers in Egypt. Come, said he to his minion, let us cut them off from being a people, that the name of Israel may be remembered no more. And they slew the blameless and the pure, men, women and little ones, with vapors of poison and burned them with fire. But we abstain from dwelling on the deed of the evil ones lest we defame the image of God in which man was created.

Now, the remnants of our people who were left in the ghettos and camps of annihilation rose up against the wicked ones for the sanctification of the Name, and slew many of them before they died. On the first day of Passover the remnants of the Ghetto of Warsaw rose up against the adversary, even as in the days of Judah and Maccabee. They were lovely and pleasant in their lives, and in their death they were not divided, and they brought redemption to the name of Israel through all the world.

And from the depth of their affliction the martyrs lifted their voices in a song of faith in the coming of the Messiah, when justice and brotherhood will reign among men:

"Ani ma'amin b'emunah sh'lemah b'viat ha-mashiah, v'af al pi sh'yi-tmahmeah im kol ze ani ma'amin"

"I believe with perfect faith in the coming of the Messiah, and though he tarry, nevertheless I believe."

Maimonides, the author of this statement of faith and the wisest of Jewish philosophers, had included the words "though he tarry," knowing they would be necessary.[58] We ask how at Auschwitz, even with these words, this statement of faith remained possible. We shall never know. We do know that the age-old Jewish longing had become mingled with a new defiance and that only thus was there endurance. The old song of longing and hope had become united with a new song of defiance in the midst of hopelessness[59]—the song of the Warsaw Ghetto Jewish Underground:

Dos lid geshribn iz mit blut un nit mit blay
S'iz nit kayn lidl fun a foygl oyf der fray;
Dos hot a folk ts'vishn falndike went
Dos lid gezungen mit naganes in di hent.

Zog nit keynmol az du geyst dem letstn veg
Chotsh himlen blayene farshsteln bloye teg
Kumen vet noch undzer oysgebenkte sho
S'vet a poyk ton undzer trot: mir zeinen do.

This song is written not with lead but with blood,
It is not the song of birds upon the wing
But of a people upon whom the walls came crashing down
Who sang it, weapon in hand.

Do not ever say you go the last road.
Leaden skies may hide the blue day.
Yet the hour we have longed for will arrive.
Our footsteps confirm: we are here.

"Mir zeinen do"—we are here, exist, endure, witnesses to God and man even if abandoned by God and man. Jews after Auschwitz will never understand the longing,
defiance, endurance of the Jews at Auschwitz. But so far as is humanly possible they
must make them their own as they carry the whole Jewish past forward into a future
yet unknown.

Endnotes

[1]William Hamilton's "The New Optimism—From Prufrock to Ringo" takes a consciously Judaic stance when it sides with Saul Bellow against T. S. Eliot:

> Saul Bellow recently has written about the end of pessimism, and he has significantly spoken of the
> end of the Wasteland era, the end of the hollow men. Moses Herzog, in Bellow's novel, singlehanded-
> ly takes on the whole fashionable pessimism of modern intellectual life. He lashes out against those
> who tell you how good dread is for you; he speaks of the "commonplaces of the Wasteland outlook,
> the cheap mental stimulants of Alienation, the cant and rant of pipsqueaks about Inauthenticity and
> Forlornness." Perhaps the most thoroughly post-modern, post-pessimistic act Herzog commits is his
> decision, at the close of the novel, not to go mad—his decision for human happiness (159).

However, Hamilton's optimism is only pseudo-Judaic, for it is in the end concerned, not with
the world, but only with an optimistic attitude toward the world.

> This is not an optimism of grace, but a worldly optimism. . . . It faces despair not with the conviction
> that out of it God can bring hope, but with the conviction that the human conditions that created it
> can be overcome, whether those conditions be poverty, discrimination, or mental illness. It faces
> death not with the hope for immortality, but with the human confidence that man may befriend death
> and live with it as a possibility always alongside. I think that the new optimism is both a cause and
> a consequence of the basic theological experience which we today call the death of God (169). (Both
> excerpts from *Radical Theology and the Death of God*, copyright © 1996 by Thomas T. J. Altizer
> and William Hamilton, reprinted by permission of the publishers, The Bobbs-Merrill Company, Inc.)

Absorbed as he is by the conflict between theological "pessimism" and secular "optimism,"
Hamilton shows no signs of the kind of realism vis-á-vis the dark places of the contemporary world
which is as necessary for a "worldly" optimism as for one of "grace." Can the holocaust be classi-
fied with poverty, discrimination, or mental illness? Can one "befriend" death at Auschwitz or Hiroshima? So long as questions such as these are not asked, the "decision not to go mad" is a cheap
decision, and Eliot's spiritualizing "pessimism" is opposed by nothing better than a spiritualizing
"optimism." The dread of Auschwitz is assuredly not "good for you"; yet to avoid it for this reason
remains a form of unworldly escapism no matter how loudly it proclaims its worldliness.
 [2]A more precise identification would depend on whether A. Roy Eckhardt is right when he includes the words italicized by us in his definition of Christianity: "The acceptance, through the Holy
Spirit, of Jesus as Messiah means beholding him as the one who transforms and will transform the
world." (*Elder and Younger Brothers* [New York: Scribners, 1967] 107.)
 [3]See above, 51.

[4]The poet Hölderlin laments that the gods have fled, referring to the Greek gods who were nothing if not present in the world and asserting the impossibility of finding them in the modern world. Heidegger takes up Hölderlin's.

[5]I put "racial" antisemitism into quotation marks to indicate that it is pseudo-racial only, from the standpoint of both the persecutors and the persecuted. With the latter aspect I shall deal subsequently. As regards the former, it must here suffice that my point is not the obvious one that the "racial science" which such antisemitism may invoke is pseudo-science, but rather that it focuses its energies on the fact that whereas one becomes a Christian through baptism one becomes a Jew through birth and, unlike Christian antisemitism, denies that a Jew is redeemable through baptism.

> Over the centuries Christians have generally lived with the tacit assumption that a "good Jew" is either a dead Jew or a Christian. So, alternately, they have consented to the death of Jews and prayed for their conversion. . . . Christians have never really said that God loves the Jew for what he is now. (Quoted by Eckhardt, *op. cit.*, 171.)

Eckhardt does not give the reference to the issue of the *Christian Century* in which Rylaarsdam's article originally appeared.

[7]The connection is not merely theoretical. Nazi "racial" antisemitism could certainly never have arisen except for a long history of "religious" antisemitism. Moreover (as is only to be expected), "religious" antisemitism did not always stay within the bounds erected by theological theory. Thus, in 1298 the Jews of the German town of Röttingen were charged with profanation of the Host. The charge produced a massacre, not only of the Jews of that particular town, but also of those of countless other towns whom no one had even charged with any connection with the supposed crime. Leon Poliakov writes:

> What is new about the incident is that for the first time all the Jews of the country were held responsible for a crime imputed to one or at most several Jews. It is quite likely that as usual the accusation was a pretext for a large-scale pillaging. But heretofore incidents of this nature, numerous as they were, had remained in a sense localized. This one spread, and we may say in modern terms that apart from the excesses of the Crusaders it was the first case of Jewish "genocide" in Christian Europe. (*The History of Antisemitism*, I [New York: Vanguard, 1965] 100.)

[8]See especially Norman Cohn, *Warrant For Genocide* (London: Eyre and Spottiswoode, 1967), a work which thoroughly refutes the idea that pre-Hitler Germany—and Europe—is guiltless of all connection with Auschwitz.

[9]Jerry Farber, in an article entitled, "The Student as Nigger." This article was widely reprinted in student newspapers throughout North America.

[10]I have dealt more fully with the uniqueness of the Nazi holocaust in "Jewish Faith and the Holocaust," *Commentary*, 1967. (See also *Quest for Past and Future*, 17 ff.) I feel constrained to stress once again that I assert only that the Nazi genocide of European Jews is unique, not that it is a greater or more tragic crime than all others. Thus, for example, the fate of the Gypsies at the hand of the Nazis (itself an "ideological" project) is at least in one sense more tragic—that no one seems to bother to commemorate them. Even this example of genocide, however, though itself a product of Nazi ideology, still differs from the Nazi genocide of European Jewry: no comparable hate propaganda was directed by the Nazis against the Gypsies. Whence this groundless, infinite hate, indiscriminately directed against adults and children, saints and sinners, and so relentlessly expressed in action?

[11]I have quoted the preceding paragraph almost verbatim from the article cited in note 10. What is said in this passage is crucial, and I am unable to express it better now than in my earlier statement.

[12]I put "Jewish question" or "problem" into quotation marks to indicate that the question or problem is created by antisemitism and does not exist where there is no antisemitism.

[13]See "The State of Jewish Belief: A Symposium," *Commentary* (August 1966) 71-160; reprinted as *The Condition of Jewish Belief* (New York: Macmillan, 1966).

[14]See R. L. Rubenstein, "Homeland and Holocaust," *The Religious Situation 1968* (Boston: Beacon, 1968) 110.

[15]*Op. cit.*, 57.

[16]. . . . *than a Tear in the Sea* (Bergen Belsen Memorial Press, 1967) vii.

[17]See above, 26 ff.

[18]See most recently A. D. Morse, *While Six Million Died* (New York: Random House, 1967).

[19]For this Midrash and its medieval use see Shalom Spiegel, *The Last Trial* (New York: Pantheon, 1967). Spiegel shows the element of protest among the medieval chroniclers which is prominent above all because, while Isaac had been reprieved, no reprieve had occurred for the many Isaacs during the Crusades.

[20]We say "after" and not "at" Auschwitz because any opinion as to what was or was not religiously possible at Auschwitz itself is ultimately permissible, if for anyone, only for an actual survivor.

[21]*Kibbutz Lohamay Ha-getaot.*

[22]In the article cited in note 10, I have already characterized this attempt to find a purpose in Auschwitz as reflecting "a moving sense of desperation, and an incredible lapse of theological judgement." Since the passage I criticize was part of a sermon which was not published but only mimeographed and privately distributed, I feel obligated to withhold the name of the well-known author.

[23]Secularist Jews, too, died with Jewish faithfulness; but we are not presently concerned with Jewish secularism.

[24]See note 25.

[25]This contrasts with Søren Kierkegaard's *Fear and Trembling*, in which God needs to have Abraham's testimony and Abraham needs to give it. Whether Christian (like Jewish) resort to martyrdom is decisively affected by Auschwitz depends on whether worldly effectiveness, however remote or improbable, is part of its meaning, Kierkegaard to the contrary notwithstanding.

[26]Manés Sperber, *op. cit.*, xiv. I am constrained to quote this remarkable passage in full:

Genocide, whatever its extent, never succeeds completely. That perpetrated by the Nazis failed more than any other, because it provided the main reasons for the creation of the State of Israel. Encouraged by the way Hitler had practiced genocide without encountering resistance, the Arabs surged in upon the nascent Israeli nation to exterminate it and make themselves its immediate heirs. The military and political leaders of the Arab states, along with Foreign Minister Bevin and his advisers in the Colonial Office, did not understand that the *millennial epoch* of the Jews' sanctifying of God and themselves by their submitting to violent death had just come to an end with the *Warsaw Ghetto* uprising. With this conclusive experience of European Jewry there also came to an end the illusion that they could count on other men to defend them. The Arab armies were cut to pieces and thrown beyond the borders by men who, in going to battle with no thought of retreat, meant also to avenge a people murdered and not buried, whose brothers, sons or nephews they were. They meant to teach the world that the long hunting season was over forever, and that one could no longer kill Jews easily or with impunity. To be sure, the soldiers of this new Hebrew army, Zionists for the most part, were fighting for the land that their labor had redeemed, for the villages, towns and kibbutzim that they had brought into being out of nothingness, and for the lives of all of them. But they were fighting above all—particularly since 1945 and beyond the spring of 1948—to deliver their people from a degradation that threatened to encourage exterminators, their sons and their grandsons, as well as their innumerable silent accomplices the world over.

For the greatest boon that can be brought to peoples tempted by aggressive anti-Semitism is to make the crime that it inspires dangerous for the instigators and executors themselves. Between 1933 and 1945, the whole world provided Hitler—who moved only step-by-step at first—with proof that he could undertake anything he pleased against the Jews, with nothing to fear but verbal protestations never followed up with the slightest reprisal. This is why the abduction of Eichmann by agents of the State of Israel and his trial in Jerusalem are events of *major significance* (xiii-xiv).

The less than ten pages of which this passage is part were written in 1964; Sperber states that it took him weeks to write them, "every time escaping anew from the shadows of a past whose memory threatens the present" (xvi).

[27]See above, 29.

[28]See above, 28.

[29]Elie Wiesel, *Night* (New York: Pyramid Books, 1961) 78.

[30]Only briefly and indirectly, since Jewish-Christian relations after the holocaust are not part of my concern in this discourse. (See the article cited in note 10). I here merely wish to state my conviction that the holocaust calls for a new dimension in Jewish-Christian relations—one which cannot be reached until the subject is confronted.

[31]See above, 27 ff.

[32]See above, 49, 61.

[33]*The Gates of the Forest* (New York: Holt, Rinehart and Winston, 1966) 225.

[34]For Wiesel on this question, see below, 88.

[35]See above, ch. 1, note 13.

[36]Buber himself sees this with the utmost clarity. See the weighty passage quoted at the end of the preceding chapter.

[37]To have caught the mood of this creed is the greatest accomplishment of Harvey Cox's *The Secular City* (New York: Macmillan, 1965).

[38]Kant expected the "euthanasia" of Judaism. His intentions at the time were benevolent; but today the very phrase sounds obscene.

[39]See above, note 12.

[40]For my interpretation of Nazism as the supreme and unsurpassable modern idolatry, see "Idolatry as a Modern Religious Possibility," *The Religious Situation 1968* (Boston: Beacon, 1968) 254-87.

[41]In a public address heard by the author.

[42]See above, 49 ff.

[43]*Midrash Tanhuma*, ed. Buber (Wilma, 1885) Yitro, 37b.

[44]Once again I quote from the article cited in note 10, for the reason stated in note 11.

[45]See especially Elie Wiesel, "A Plea for the Dead," *Legends of Our Time* (Holt, Rinehart and Winston, 1968) 174-97.

[46]See especially Yuri Suhl, *They Fought Back* (New York: Crown, 1967).

[47]Wiesel is dismayed to discover that some critics of Nelly Sachs' poetry try to minimize its Jewishness and contract a "universal vision" with a merely Jewish one. He comments:

> Her greatness lies in her Jewishness, and this makes it belong to all mankind. It is perhaps only natural that there are those who try to remove her, if not to estrange her, from us. But this will never

happen. She has many Jewish melodies left to sing. . . . What disturbs me is that strangers have stolen them. ("Conversation with Nelly Sachs," *Jewish Heritage* [Spring 1968] 33.)

[48]In recent years some North American TV stations and university groups have seen fit to furnish American Nazis and German neo-Nazis with a forum, and even invited Jews to debate with them, apparently utterly oblivious to the obscenity of such invitations.

[49]See a letter by Professor Harold Fisch of Bar Ilan University quoted in the article cited in note 10, and also note 26.

[50]"A Letter to all Good People—To Fidel Castro, Sartre, Russell, and All the Rest," *Midstream*, October 1968 (This article originally appeared first in *Yediot Aharonot* and was republished in *The New Statesman*). Here and in the following, I single out this article, not only because of its excellence, but also (a fact doubtless largely accounting for this excellence) because its author is a left-wing secularist (who cannot and will not abandon his universalistic ideals) and an Israeli (who cannot and will not condone collective Jewish suicide).

[51]I distinguish with the utmost sharpness between (a) the view that because of Auschwitz the justification of Jewish existence depends on Jews behaving like superhuman saints towards all other peoples ever after and (b) the view that because of Auschwitz Jews are obligated to (i) Jewish survival as an end which, less than ever, needs any justification (ii) work for oppressed and suffering humanity everywhere. I accept the second view, and (as will be seen) the inevitably painful conflicts that go with it. The first view is totally unacceptable.

[52]P. 225. See above, 78 and note 33.

[53]See *Fear and Trembling* (Garden City NY.: Anchor, 1954).

[54]*Op. cit.*, 35.

[55]*Op. cit.*, 36.

[56]Simon Wiesenthal writes:

Once Himmler was present when experiments using the exhaust gases of submarine engines for extermination had proved highly unsatisfactory. Himmler had been furious, and there had been drastic punishment. Machines broke down, but the people handling them never did. How could it be that the people operating the gas chambers and ovens were more reliable than the machines? (*The Murders Among Us* [New York: McGraw-Hill, 1967] 315.)

Wiesenthal's revelations about Nazi schools for mass murder give a partial answer to the question.

[57]*Midrash Deut. Rabbah*, Nizzabim, VIII, 5.

[58]This passage is the twelfth of Maimonides' thirteen principles of Jewish faith.

[59]Manés Sperber states that it was not hope but rather despair that inspired the Warsaw Ghetto uprising, and quotes the non-Jewish Polish writer Tadeusz Borowski, an inmate of Auschwitz who committed suicide at the age of twenty-nine:

It is hope that provokes men to march indifferently to the gas chambers, and keeps them from conceiving of an insurrection. . . . Never has hope provoked so much ill as in this war, as in this camp. We were never taught to rid ourselves of hope, and that is why we are dying in the gas-chambers (*op. cit.*, xi, xiii).

Chapter 9

The Human Condition after Auschwitz: A Jewish Testimony One Generation After*

Emil L. Fackenheim

1

A Midrash in Genesis Rabba disturbs and haunts the mind ever more deeply. It begins as follows:

> Rabbi Shim'on said: "In the hour when God was about to create Adam, the angels of service were divided. . . . Some said, 'Let him not be created,' others, 'Let him be created.'. . . Love said, 'Let him be created, for he will do loving deeds.' But Truth said, 'Let him not be created, for he will be all falsity.' Righteousness said, 'Let him be created, for he will do righteous deeds.' Peace said, 'Let him not be created, for he will be full of strife.' What then did God do? He seized hold of Truth, and cast her to the earth, as it is said, 'Thou didst cast Truth to the ground.' "[Dan 8:12][1]

No Midrash wants to be taken literally. Every Midrash wants to be taken seriously. Midrash is serious because its stories and parables address the reader; they are not confined to the past. It is religious because, while it may contain beauty and poetry, its essential concern is Truth. And when, as in the present case, a Midrash tells a story of human origins, the religious truth it seeks to convey is universal. Its theme is nothing less than the human condition as a whole.

Why does this Midrash disturb and haunt us? Not simply because it is realistic rather than romantically "optimistic" about man. Midrash is always realistic. We are haunted because Truth is cast to the ground. This climactic part of the story (as thus far told) does not say that all is well, that the good Lord has the power, so to speak, of indiscriminately silencing all opposition. Were this its message, then Peace as well as Truth should be cast to the ground. That Truth alone is singled out for this treatment suggests the ominous possibility that *all* that might be said in favor of the creation of man is nothing but pious illusion; that Truth is so horrendous as to destroy *everything* for us unless we shun it, avoid it, evade it; that *only* after having cast Truth to the ground can God create man at all.

But then we ask: whom does God deceive? Surely one thing even God cannot do is, as it were, fool himself. Are we the ones, then, who are fooled? Are we

---

*From *The Jewish Return into History*. Copyright © 1978 by Emil L. Fackenheim. Reprinted by permission of Georges Borchardt, Inc. for the author.

radically deceived in our belief that at least *some* of that which we undergo, do, are, is *ultimately* worthwhile—a belief without which we cannot endure?

But such a divine deception (if a deception it is) does not succeed. We can see through it. The midrashic author *knows* that Truth is cast to the ground. So do all the devout Jews who have read his story throughout the generations. But what is the effect of this knowledge? Can it be other than despair?

The Midrash itself deals with this question when it repudiates despair. It ends as follows:

> Then the angels of service said to God, "Lord of the universe, how canst Thou despise Thy seal?[2] Let Truth arise from the earth, as it is said, 'Truth springs from the earth.' " [Ps. 85:12]

Somehow it is possible for man to face Truth and yet to be. But do we know how?

II.

Without doubt to say yea or nay to existence is the ultimate question in all religion and all philosophy. Judaism is firmly committed to being when it sees God himself as Creator of the world, and the Creation as good. Yet many a deep religious and philosophical spirit has chosen nonbeing, and has considered the tragic ultimate. And the most vocal of these in the West, Arthur Schopenhauer, blames all the "vulgar" Western "optimism" on Judaism and its creation story. Is Jewish "optimism" vulgar? Is it blind to the tragic? Must we follow Schopenhauer when he suggests that Jewish and indeed all optimism reflects but a self-congratulatory human "egoism" which is blind to all except our all-too-frail human goals and aspirations?[3] Our Midrash suggests a very different view. Not until Truth is cast to the ground is God able to create man. And not even God himself can despise his own "seal" of Truth. "Jewish optimism" affirms existence while at the same time confronting a Truth that is tragic. Yet, in our Midrash at least, the grounds for this togetherness remain inscrutable. "Jewish optimism" is not a "vulgar" optimism. It is an enigmatic optimism.

III.

When Judaism came to North America the enigma became obscured. Faith in God often became faith in ever-evolving Reason, with idolatry becoming superstition gradually vanishing in an age of enlightenment. Halakha—the discipline of divine commandments that recognizes both the greatness and the misery of man—moved toward "customs and ceremonies" that had no discipline and no authority, and that stood in no need of them since man himself stood in no need of them. Radical evil, if recognized at all, was considered to have been left behind in Europe. Wars and colonialism were European affairs; poverty was an evil progressively conquered by

American conscience, initiative, and know-how; antisemitism shrivelled into a "medieval prejudice."

In retrospect, this American Jewish optimism simply is a version of American optimism. Who but an American political leader could ever have seriously and sincerely waged a war to end all wars, when all experience shows that even "just wars" serve at best but limited ends? Who except Americans could still hope, in this century, that the complex Arab-Israeli conflict would vanish if only American know-how came on the scene and irrigated the Jordan waters?

That this and indeed all American optimism was always shot through with illusion is obvious today. Indeed, to scorn it as superficial has become the fashion. Yet the paramount task of the hour is not a rehearsal of the obvious, but rather a discriminating search for such truth as may remain behind all the superficialities and illusions. For a robust, ebullient affirmation of life is of the American essence. And if "American optimism" were ever *wholly* lost, America itself would be lost.

That such discrimination is hard to come by is evident on every side. If traditional American optimism was sweeping and indiscriminate, it has not found a nemesis that shows these same qualities. No political, religious or philosophical quarter has remained exempt. Only in a single camp does the old American optimism seem to survive wholly intact, and this, ironically, is the camp that would destroy America. Where except in America has a group of revolutionaries arisen which does not ask what social forces might be available to build the new world on the ruins of the old which speaks and acts as though, with the act of destruction accomplished and "the system" destroyed, paradise will come of itself? Perhaps alone of all the present groupings, the American New Left has not abandoned the American Dream. It has merely transformed and postponed it.

IV.

No professional historical expertise is required for the discovery of the causes of our present crisis. Hiroshima made known that America had lost her political innocence; and while the Vietnamese war was a daily, tragic reminder that indiscriminate international involvement is neither politically nor morally tenable, retreat to the idyllic isolationist view that the problems of power politics are confined to Europe has become, in a shrinking world, quite impossible. At home, all America now recognizes that in her collective affirmation that all men are created equal the Black man was somehow forgotten; and the nemesis of this past forgetfulness is a racial conflict that seems insoluble. For all their traumas, these two experiences are overshadowed by yet a third, for this assails at its roots the very mainspring of the traditional self-confidence of America. No nation has matched America in the modern certainty that, whatever nature and history have set wrong, human ingenuity and initiative can set right. No nation has staked greater faith in modern technology or has shown greater ability to develop it. Indeed, to this day the word "know-how" has American connotations. Yet this know-how, in no way diminished in energy and ability, has not produced a nemesis of which we read daily in our newspapers. Nature, subdued for human use, is becoming increasingly unusable. The city, built for human habitation, is becoming increasingly uninhabitable. Man himself, the sovereign creator of all the machinery, is himself being turned into part of it: as his power over nature and society increases, so diminishes his ability to be human. And we somehow seem unable to stop the process or to alter its course.

The search into causes is the task of the historian. The search for remedies is the task of the leaders of society. The philosopher's task is the critical examination for our collective human self-image. *A virtually all-pervasive human self-deprecation is today abroad in the land. It is as indiscriminate, or even enthusiastic, as was the former human self-elevation. And just as the one once called for philosophical discrimination and criticism, so, now, does the other.*

Two illustrations must suffice. Once the characteristically American movie was the cowboy picture. With clear villains and clear heroes, it was a morality play whose happy end was foreordained. (In Europe it used to be a bit of a joke that all American movies, cowboy or not, had to end happily.) Today, only the midnight cowboy remains. And foreordained are gloom, disaster, and every kind of degradation and depravity. The odd movie may still dare to portray heroism. It then still remains foreordained that, regardless of the merits of the movie, the critics will pan it. Are there no heroes left?

From the down-to-earth sphere of popular culture we turn to the rarefied sphere of theology—nearly always a sound indicator of the general consciousness even when it is bad. That Harvey Cox's celebration of the secular city[4] should have seen a theological bestseller is hard to believe slightly more than ten years later, when this very city is obviously so near to the core of our technological despairs. The phenomenon clearly reflects a religious consciousness that runs hither and thither in search of hope and light but seems unable to find it. Hence, in quick succession, the God-is-dead theology, itself already dead except for one lone, dark voice which moves us but cannot guide us;[5] the theology of hope which, arousing hope if only because its place of origin was post-Nazi Germany, could find no grounds for hope because the grounds of our despair were not confronted;[6] and, finally, a political theology which, deriving as it does most of its strength from the well-warranted militancy of Black Americans, seems at best either a confession of guilt on the part of the ex-Constantinian white Christian, or else a mere theological endorsement of a Black American militancy that is able to dispense with all theological endorsements. In short, current American theology (its core, of course, is Protestant, but Catholic and Jewish representatives are not lacking) may seek to transcend our present crisis; in fact, however, it seems merely to reflect that crisis.

V.

The above observations should be taken as a description of our present state of affairs, and not without further ado as a criticism arrived at from some superior standpoint—as if such a standpoint were readily available.

For many centuries this availability was taken for granted. Theologians would resort at once to the Word of God, with or without the help of ecclesiastical authority. Philosophers would affirm a human "nature" immune to the vicissitudes of history—an immunity which in turn guaranteed a timeless access to the True, the Good, and the Beautiful. And a long alliance between these two disciplines produced a firm stand in behalf of "eternal verities" against perpetually shifting "arbitrary opinion."

These centuries are past. Theologians (Jewish and Christian) should always have known that the Word of their God is manifest *in* history if it is manifest at all: because of the historical self-consciousness of contemporary man, this knowledge can now no longer be evaded. If nevertheless seeking refuge in the eternal verities of philosophy, they find that these, too, have vanished. For modern philosophy has found itself forced to abandon the notion of a permanent human nature—and along with this all timelessly accessible visions of the True, the Good, and the Beautiful.

This fact is most profoundly if not uniquely manifest in the philosophies arising from the work of Immanuel Kant. These philosophies do not deny aspects of the human condition that remain more or less permanent throughout human history. Such aspects, however, are not confined to man's natural constitution. What makes man *human* (we are told) is neither given nor permanent, but rather the product of his own individual or collective activity. *Man qua man is a self-maker.* This formula sums up the deepest of all the many revolutions in modern philosophy. We may wish to quarrel with its central thesis. We may wish to qualify it. We may even wish to reject it outright. One thing, at any rate, seems for better or worse impossible—the return to the premodern philosophical wisdom.

Not so long ago theologians of liberal stamp greeted this revolution in philosophy with rejoicing. Who has not heard sermons (and in particular American sermons) about the "infinite perfectibility of man?" The notion of man as a self-maker seemed (and in some respects surely is) far more grandiose than the notion of a human nature given by another—even if this Other was not (rather vaguely) "Nature" or "the Universe," but the Lord of Creation himself. Add to this what was said above about the American tradition of optimism, and it is not surprising that for a considerable period of time all talk about "the nature of man" and "*the* True, *the* Good, and *the* Beautiful" seemed in many circles to be timidly conservative, if not downright reactionary.

But now the crisis of American optimism has disclosed for us that the concept of man as a self-maker gives us ground for apprehension and dread as well as for hope. The lack of a permanent nature may hold the promise that unforeseeable ways of human self-perfection are possible; since this lack is an unlimited malleability, however, it implies the possibility of unforeseeable negative as well as positive developments. And thus the specter comes into view that man, *qua* unlimited maker, may reach the point of making his whole world into a machine, while at the same time, *qua* infinitely malleable, himself being reduced to a mere part of the machine, that is, to a self-made thing. Nor is this possibility today a mere unsubstantial fancy confined to philosophers. For some of our futurologists have begun to conjure up a future in which man, the proud self-maker, will have lost control over the world he had made, and the reduction to self-made thinghood will be complete. Indeed, even popular consciousness is haunted by the prospect that the whole bold and exciting story of the one being in the universe capable of making his own nature—the story of the only truly *free* being—will come to an end, the pathos of which is matched only by its irony.

With prospects so terrifying, it is no wonder that some simply opt out of history; that others hanker after a simpler, more innocent past; and that, as if anticipating catastrophe, we are all tempted even now to deprecate indiscriminately all things human.

The philosopher may not yield to the temptations of escapism or indiscriminate despair. Nor may he simply throw in his lot with the futurologists, for (as we shall show at least in part) their entire approach calls for considerable philosophical suspicion. At this point, we shall be well advised to suspend the future and confine ourselves to the present. Is a genuinely *human* existence possible *even now*? Or, in order to make it possible, must we cast Truth to the ground? Must we suppress all knowledge of a future that is sure to come and force Truth to *stay* cast to the ground?

VI.

We have thus far made no reference to Jewish experience in this century. We do so at this point because the direst predictions any futurologist might make have already been fulfilled and surpassed at Auschwitz, Mauthausen, Bergen-Belsen and Buchenwald. One shrinks from speaking of these unspeakable places of unique horror in any context that might invite false generalizations and comparisons. Yet one simple statement may safely be made. In the Nazi murder camps no effort was spared to make persons into living *things* before making them into dead things. And that the dead had been human when alive was a truth systematically rejected when their bodies were made into fertilizer and soap. Moreover, the criminals themselves had become living *things*, and the system, run by operators "only following orders," was well on the way toward running itself. The thoughtful reader of such a work as *The Holocaust Kingdom*[7] reaches the shocking conclusion that here was indeed a "kingdom," that is, a society organized to a purpose; that, its organization near-perfect, it might in due course have dispensed with the need for a "king"; and that such was its inner dynamic and power for self-expansion that, given a Nazi victory, it might today rule the world. This "society," however, was an antisociety, indeed, *the* modern antisociety *par excellence:* modern because unsurpassably technological, and antisociety because, while even the worst society is geared to life, the Holocaust Kingdom was geared to death. It would be quite false to say that it was a mere means, however depraved, to ends somehow bound up with life. As an enterprise subserving the Nazi war effort the murder camps were total failures, for the human and material "investment" far exceeded the "produce" of fertilizer, gold teeth, and soap. The Holocaust Kingdom was an end in itself, having only one ultimate "produce," and that was death.

It is not without *prima facie* plausibility that Richard Rubenstein, Jewish theologian long preoccupied with the Holocaust, should in his more recent spoken utterances have characterized the Nazi murder camp as simply the extreme technological nightmare. Taking his cue from Lewis Mumford[8] and others, he in these utterances understands Auschwitz as but the extreme of a technological dehumanization which, to varying degrees, may in the end become the fate of us all. Nazism was simply the machine radically dehumanized, and its millions of victims, its "waste products."[9]

In this view, Richard Rubenstein, the Jewish theologian overwhelmed by the Holocaust, is at one with Martin Heidegger, the German philosopher who, so far as is known to us, never mentions the Holocaust in any of his writings. Heidegger omits this subject. He makes much, however, of "world wars" and their "totality," of the human "raw material" of technology, and of *Führers*. Of all these he writes:

> "World wars" and their "totality" are mere consequences of a loss of Being. It is only as consequences of this loss that they drive toward securing a stable form of dissipation-through-use. Man himself is drawn into this process, and his condition of being the most important raw material of all is no longer concealed. . . . The moral indignation of those who do not yet recognize what is the case often concentrates on the arbitrariness and claim-to-power made by *Führers*. This, however, is the most fatal way of lending them dignity. . . . In truth, the *Führers* are merely the necessary consequences of the fact that what-is [cut loose from Being] has gone astray, has spread itself out into the emptiness that has come to pass, and demands a single order and a making-secure of what-is.[10]

In linking Rubenstein with Heidegger we pay Rubenstein a tribute, for of all the philosophical thinking that has thus far been done about the involvement of modern man's very being with modern technology, Heidegger's is doubtless the deepest. Heidegger goes beyond the mere external manifestations of technology. He goes to man, the autonomous self-maker, who stands behind these manifestations. Moreover, he goes beyond this self-maker's purported "autonomy" to a modern loss of an original presence of Being, to a *Seinsvergessenheit* and a *Seinsverlassenheit* of which that autonomy, for better or worse, is but a derivative result. And the reward for this search in depth is that, unlike all the far more superficial futurologists, Heidegger offers us at least a glimmer of justified hope.

Yet we are forced, equally by the very depth of Heidegger's philosophy and by the very agony of Rubenstein's preoccupation with the Holocaust, to ask of both thinkers essentially the same question. Can either Nazism or its murder camps be understood as but one particular case, however, extreme, of the general technological dehumanization? Or (to use language which theologians are equipped to understand) does not a scandal of particularity attach to Nazism and its murder camps which is shied away from, suppressed or simply forgotten when the scandal is technologically universalized? To be sure, there have been "world wars"—but none like that which Hitler unleashed on the world. There have been (and are) "total" political systems— but none like Nazism, a truth suppressed when "fascism" is used as a generic term in which Nazism is included. And while there have been (and are) "cults of personality," there have been no *Führers* but only one *Führer*.

Nor is it possible to distinguish between the goals of Nazism-in-general, as one system, and those of the murder-camp-in-particular, as a second system subserving the first. In essence, Nazism *was* the murder-camp. That a nihilistic, demonic celebration of death and destruction was its animating principle was evident to thinkers such as Karl Barth from the start; it became universally revealed in the end, when in the Berlin bunker, Hitler and Goebbels, the only true Nazis left, expressed ghoulish satisfaction at the prospect that their downfall might carry in train the doom, not only (or even at all) of their enemies, but rather of the "master race." The mind shrinks from systematic murder that serves no purpose beyond murder itself, for it is ultimately unintelligible. Yet in Nazism as a whole (not only in the murder camps) this unintelligibility was real. And except for good fortune this diabolical celebration might today rule the world.

Even this does not exhaust the scandalous particularity of Nazism. The term "Aryan" had no clear connotation other than "non-Jew,"[11] and the Nazis were not antisemites because they were racists, but rather racists because they were antisemites.[12] The exaltation of the "Aryan" had no positive significance. It had only the negative significance of degrading and murdering the "non-Aryan." Thus Adolf Eichmann passed beyond the limits of a merely "banal" evil when, with nothing left of the Third Reich, he declared with obvious sincerity that he would jump laughing into his grave in the knowledge of having dispatched six million Jews to their death. We must conclude, then, that the dead Jews of the murder camps (and all the other innocent victims, as it were, as quasi-Jews, or by dint of innocent-guilt-by-association) were not the "waste product" of the Nazi system. They were *the* product.

VII.

Despite all necessary attempts to comprehend it, the Nazi system in the end exceeds all comprehension. One cannot comprehend but only confront and oppose. We can here attempt to confront only one minuscule manifestation.[13] When issuing "work permits" designed to separate "useless" Jews to be murdered at once from "useful" ones to be kept useful by diabolically contrived false hopes and murdered later, the Nazis on occasion issued two such permits to able-bodied Jewish men. One was untransferable and to be kept for himself; the other was to be given *at his own discretion* to his able-bodied father, mother, wife, or one child. On those occasions the Nazis would not make this choice, although to do so would have resulted in a more efficient labor force. Jewish sons, husbands and fathers themselves were forced to decide who among their loved ones was—for the time being—to live and who to die at once.

The mind seeks escape in every direction. Yet we must confront relentlessly the Nazi custom of the two work permits, recognizing in this custom not the work of some isolated sadists, but rather the essence of the Nazi system. Hence we ask: where here was Heidegger's "dissipation-through-use?" Where was Rubenstein's technological dehumanization with its human "waste products?" Had utility been the principle of Nazism it would not have left the choice between "useful" and "useless" Jews to its victims. Not utility (however dehumanized), but rather torture and degradation was the principle. Indeed, there is no greater contrast between the technological exaltation of utility (even when out of control) and a celebration of torture *contrary* to all utility when it is not incidental but rather *for torture's sake*.

Why is this scandalous particularity overlooked, denied, or repressed by Rubenstein and Heidegger, not to speak of all the other writers who lack the agony of Rubenstein and the profundity of Heidegger? The theologian (Jewish or Christian) may hazard a guess if he falls back on his own authentic resources. For he is himself acquainted with scandalous particularity, for better (in the presence of God) and for worse (in the presence of the demonic). Moreover, he is acquainted with our all-too-human desire to evade or deny each and every scandalous particularity, and he knows this tendency to be pagan. And if he modernizes what he already knows he will understand that in a scientific age the characteristic form of evading or denying scandalous particularity is to explain it away. Hence it may be no coincidence that Heidegger's later thought is pagan,[14] that Rubenstein advocates a Jewish return to paganism; and that the dire predictions of the futurologists have a strong resemblance to ancient pagan fatalism.

We cannot be sure how the ancient rabbis, were they alive, would respond to the death camps. We *can* be sure that they would not explain them away. In their own time, they knew of idolatry, and considered groundless hate to be its equivalent. They knew, too, that it could not be explained but only opposed. Alive today, they would reject all fatalistic futurological predictions as so many self-fulfilling prophecies which leave us helpless. Instead, they would somehow seek to meet the absolute evil of the death camps in the only way absolute evil can be met—by an absolute opposition on which one stakes one's life.[15]

The authentic Jew after Auschwitz has no privileged access to explanations of the past. He has no privileged access to predictions of the future, or to ways of solving the problems of the present. He is, however, a witness to the world. He is a witness against the idolatry of the Nazi murder camps. This negative testimony is *ipso facto* also the positive testimony that man shall *be*, and shall be *human*—even if Truth should be so horrendous that there is no choice but to cast it to the ground.

VIII.

The Jew in whom this testimony is unsurpassably manifest is the survivor of the two-work-permit custom. When the torture occurred he had no choice but compliance. Armed resistance was impossible. So was suicide. So was the transfer of his own work permit to another member of his family. Any of these attempts would have doomed the one member of his family who was to live. To save this one member, he was forced to become implicated in the diabolical system that robbed him of his soul and made him forever after innocently guilty of the murder of all his family except one member.

We ask: having survived (if survive he did), why did this Jew not seek blessed release in suicide? Choosing to live, why did he not seek refuge in insanity? Choosing to stay sane, why did he not do all he could to escape from his singled-out Jewish condition but rather affirmed his Jewishness and indeed raised new Jewish children? How could even one stay with his God?

These are unprecedented questions. They required unprecedented responses. Why not suicide? *Because after the Nazi celebration of death, life has acquired a new dimension of sanctity.* Why not flight into madness? *Because insanity had ruled the kingdom of darkness, hence sanity, once a gift, has now become a holy commandment.* Why hold fast to mere Jewishness? *Because Jewish survival after Auschwitz is not "mere," but rather in itself and without any further reasons or theological justifications a sacred testimony* to all mankind *that life and love, not death and hate, shall prevail.* Why hold fast to the God of the covenant? Former believers lost him in the Holocaust Kingdom. Former agnostics found him. No judgement is possible. All theological arguments vanish. Nothing remains but the fact that the bond between him and his people reached the breaking point but was not for all wholly broken. Thus the survivor is a witness against darkness in an age of darkness. He is a witness whose like the world has not seen.

We do not yet recognize this witness, for we do not yet dare to enter the darkness against which he testifies. Yet to enter that darkness is to be rewarded with an altogether astonishing discovery. *This may be an age without heroes. It is, however, the heroic age* par excellence *in all of Jewish history.* If this is true of the Jewish people collectively (not only of the survivor individually), it is because *the survivor is gradually becoming the paradigm for the entire Jewish people.*

Nowhere is this truth as unmistakable as in the state of Israel. The state of Israel is collectively what the survivor is individually—testimony on behalf of all mankind to life against death, to sanity against madness, to Jewish self-affirmation against every form of flight from it, and (though this is visible only to those who break through narrow theological categories) to the God of the ancient covenant against all lapses into paganism.

We ask: having survived, why did the survivor not seek both safety and forgetfulness among such good people as the Danes, but rather seek danger and memory in the nascent and embattled state of Israel? Indeed, why do not even now Israeli Jews in general, survivors or not, flee by the thousands from their isolated and endangered country, in order that they might elsewhere find peace and safety—not to speak of the world's approval? Why do they hold fast to their "law of return"—the commitment to receive sick Jews, poor Jews, oppressed Jews, rejected by the immigration laws of every other state? A world that wants no part of Auschwitz fails to understand. Indeed, perpetuating antisemitism, despite Auschwitz or even because of it, it often does not hesitate to resort to slander. Yet the truth is obvious: the state of Israel is a collective testimony against the groundless hate which has erupted in this century in the heart of Europe. Its watchword is *Am Yisrael Chai*—"the people Israel *lives*." Without this watchword the state of Israel could not have survived for a generation. It is a watchword of defiance, hope, and faith. It is a testimony to all men everywhere that man shall *be*, and be *human*—even if it should be necessary to cast Truth to the ground.

And now, astonishingly, this watchword has come alive among the Jews of the Soviet Union. What makes these Jews affirm their Jewishness against the overwhelming odds of a ruthless system, when they could gain peace and comfort by disavowing their Jewishness? Though we can only marvel at their heroism and not understand it, its mainspring is obvious enough. No American Jew has experienced the Holocaust as every Russian Jew has experienced it. Hence every Russian Jew must have felt all along that to be denied the right to his Jewishness is not, after what has happened, a tolerable form of discrimination or prejudice but rather an intolerable affront; it is, as it were, a secular sacrilege. And if now these Jews increasingly dare to convert secret feeling into public action, it is because of the inspiration incarnate in the spirit of Israel.

Is heroism in evidence among ourselves, the comfortable, mostly middle-class Jews of North America? In order to perceive any trace of it, we must break through the false-but-all-pervasive categories of a world that does not know of Auschwitz and does not wish to know of it.

In America this is a time of identity crisis. Among these there is a specific Jewish identity crisis which springs from the view that a Jew must somehow achieve a "universal" transcendence of his "particular" Jewishness if he is to justify his Jewish identity. Thus it has come to seem that a Jew shows genuine courage when he rejects his Jewish identity, or when he at least seeks a "universal" justification of that identity by espousing all noble causes except the Jewish. And the North American Jewish hero may seem to be he who actually turns against his own people, less because he seeks the creation of a Palestinian Arab state than because he seeks the destruction of the Jewish state.

Such may be the appearances. The truth is otherwise. Just as the Black seeking to pass for white has internalized racism, so the Jew joining al-Fatah has internalized antisemitism, and this is true also (albeit to a lesser degree) of the Jew espousing all except Jewish causes. Where is the universalism in this exceptionalism—a "universalism" that applies to everyone with one exception—Jews? There is only sickness. To the extent to which the world still wants the Jew either to disappear or at least to become a man-in-general, it still has the power to produce Jews bent on disappearing, or at least on "demonstrating" their exceptionalist "universalism."

These may seem harsh judgements. They are necessary because Jewish identity crises such as the above have become a surrender to Auschwitz. For a Jew after the Holocaust to act as though his Jewishness required justification is to allow the possibility, after Hitler murdered one-third of the Jewish people, that the rest should quietly pass on. But merely to allow these possibilities is *already* a posthumous victory for Hitler. It is *already* an act of betrayal. And the betrayal is as much of the world as of the Jewish people.

Is there any trace of Jewish heroism among ourselves? The question transcends all conventional distinctions, such as between old and young, "right" and "left," and even "religious" and "secular." The North American Jewish hero is he who has confronted the demons of Auschwitz and defied them. It is the Jew who has said "No!" to every form, however mild or disguised, of antisemitism without and self-rejection within. It is the Jew at home in his Jewish skin and at peace with his Jewish destiny. It is the Jew who is whole.

IX.

But if this is the age of heroism in the history of the Jewish people, it is, after all, also an age of unprecedented darkness in world history, and Jewish heroism itself is possible only at the price of perpetually verging on despair. The question therefore arises what meaning the Jewish *Am Yisrael Chai* might have for contemporary man.

One shrinks from so large a question for two opposite reasons. At one extreme, the singled-out Jewish testimony may all-too-easily dissipate itself into a vacuous and thus cheap and escapist universalism. At the other extreme, it may express its universal significance at the false price of deafness to quite different, and yet not unrelated testimonies, such as might come from Vietnam, Czechoslovakia and Bangladesh. Perhaps one avoids both dangers best by concretizing the question. Earlier we dwelt on the American tradition of optimism, which is now in a state of crisis, and stressed that, while much in this optimism was always false, America itself would be lost if American optimism were wholly lost. What may the Jewish *Am Yisrael Chai* reveal about American optimism? What was always false about the American Dream? What —if anything—remains true?

Always false was precisely the "Dream." The innocence that produced that dream is lost. If the saving of America were dependent upon the recapturing of the innocence and the Dream, there would be no hope. However, the Midrash that has furnished the test for the present discourse is not the product of a dream. Truth may be cast to the ground. The midrashic author *knows* that it is cast to the ground. He knows, too, that in the end Truth must rise again from the earth.

When dreams are shattered, men are wont to seek refuge in wishful thinking. Our age is no exception. In a half-hearted version, collective make-believe is manifest in our current, self-enclosed, middle-class apotheosis of psychoanalysis. (Within its sober bounds, that discipline gives limited help to disturbed individuals, and quite possibly we are all disturbed. Expanded into systematic wishful thinking, it turns into a panacea for all the ills of our world.) In a radical version, collective make-believe is manifest in a self-enclosed ideologizing which would refashion all reality in its own image, while being itself out of touch with reality.

Being self-enclosed, collective make-believe can survive for a long period of time. Yet its nemesis is sure to come, and by dint of its greater honesty it is the radical version which is bound first to experience it. To be sure, ideology seeks to refashion reality. Being divorced from reality, however, it in fact refashions only ideology, and the conflict between ideality and reality in the end becomes so total as to result—when Truth springs from the earth—in despair.

Is despair, then, the only *truthful* outcome? Richard Rubenstein does not lack the courage of radically opposing the entire Jewish tradition with his affirmation that the only messiah is death. Long before him Arthur Schopenhauer wrote as follows:

> Death is the greatest reprimand which the will to life, or more especially the egoism which is essential to it, receives through the course of nature; and it may be considered as a punishment for our existence. Death says: thou are the product of an act which should not have been; therefore to expiate it thou must die.[16]

Once the sentiment expressed in this passage was attractive only to idle drawing room speculation. Today one can detect on every side a veritable fascination with every kind of negation and death itself. Once the denial of the will to live could seem to be a noble rejection of "egotism." Today it stands revealed as the foe, nothing short of obscene, of a will to live which, far from "egotistic," is a heroic act of defiance. And the revelation is nowhere as manifest as in the survivor of the Nazi custom of the two work permits. He is not blind to the shadows of death but has walked through its valley. He does not cling to life but rather affirms it by an act of faith which defies comprehension. He relives, in a form without precedent anywhere, that great "nevertheless" which has always been the secret of the enigmatic optimism of Judaism. His testimony is a warning to men everywhere not to yield to death when Truth springs from the earth. It is an admonition to endure Truth and to choose life. It is a plea, anguished and joyous, to share in a defiant endurance which alone reveals that Truth, despite all, remains the seal of God.

Endnotes

[1] Midrash Genesis Rabba, VIII:5.

[2] Truth is the seal of God.

[3] Arthur Schopenhauer, *Works*, trans. R. B. Haldane and J. Kemp (London: Kegan Paul; Trench; Trübner & Co., 1909) vol. III, 305 ff., 446 ff.

[4] Harvey Cox, *The Secular City: A Celebration of Its Liberties and an Invitation to Its Discipline* (New York: Macmillan Co., 1965).

[5] See T. J. J. Altizer, *The Gospel of Christian Atheism* (Philadelphia: Westminster, 1966); *The Descent into Hell* (Philadelphia: Lippincott: 1970).

[6] See e.g., J. Moltmann, *The Theology of Hope* (New York: Harper & Row, 1967).

[7] Alexander Donat, *The Holocaust Kingdom* (New York: Holt, Rinehart & Winston, 1963; New York: Holocaust Library, 1978).

[8] Mumford writes: "Well before the first atom bomb was tested, the American Air Force had adopted the hitherto "unthinkable" practice of wholesale, indiscriminate bombing of concentrated civilian populations: this paralleled, except for the distance of the victims, the practice employed by Hitler's sub-men in extermination camps like Buchenwald and Auschwitz." (*The Myth of the Machine* [New York: Harcourt, Brace & World, 1970] 256.)

In the following it will emerge that, despite admittedly terrifying similarities, this "parallel" is totally false. Mumford's (unexplained) use of the word "sub-men" in the above passage already suggests that, rather that *argue* for a parallel, he simply begs the question. Elsewhere he even lapses into self-contradiction. His case for Nazism as *nothing but* a megamachine requires that (following Hannah Arendt) he must view Eichmann as a "banal" bureaucrat (279), while at the same time murder-camps serving no end except murder itself require an (unexplained) "pathological hatred" in the Nazi leaders (250). If even Eichmann was a mere banal bureaucrat, who were the "pathological" leaders? How many? In the end, perhaps just one? And what made all those "merely following orders" follow orders *such as these*—with a "faith" not shrinking from total self-sacrifice? Nazism was a demonic compact between *Volk* and *Führer* in which each exalted the other in an orgy of death and destruction—with the consequence that the view of Nazism as *simply* the extreme megamachine lies in shambles.

[9] Ibid, 279.

[10] Martin Heidegger, "Oberwindung der Metaphysik," *Vorträge und Aufsätze* (Pfullingen: Neske, 1967) 84-85. (The translation is mine.) I deal more fully with these and related Heideggerian views in chap. 5 of my *Encounters Between Judaism and Modern Philosophy* (New York: Basic Books, 1973).

[11] Except only for "non-Gypsy." The fate of the Gypsies in Nazi Germany is in at least one respect more tragic than that of the Jews—no one seems to bother remembering it.

[12] "Antisemitism" itself is nothing but a synonym for "Jew-hatred," concocted in the nineteenth century when hatred of Jews was fanned without explicit recourse to its ancient theological rationalizations. A secret Nazi order, dated, May 17, 1943, reads as follows: "When the Grand Mufti visited *Reichsleiter* Rosenberg, the *Reichsleiter* promised to instruct the press that the word "antisemitism" was henceforth to be abandoned. This term seemed to include the Arab world which, according to the Grand Mufti, was overwhelmingly pro-German. The Allies utilize our use of that term in order to argue falsely that it is the nationalist socialist intention to view Jews and Arabs in

the same light. Poliakov-Wulf, *Das Dritte Reich und die Juden* (Berlin: Arami, 1955) 369. (The translation is mine.)

This secret Nazi order might be pondered by those who believe (or pretend to believe) that "anti-Zionism" by definition cannot be antisemitic, on the grounds that Arabs as well as Jews are "Semites."

[13]See above, 46. I have resisted the temptation to change the example to avoid repetition. The two-work-permit custom illustrates unsurpassably not only the demonic (as in the above context), but also (as in the present context) my contention that the Nazi murder camp was so far from being a utilitarian system as to be, on the contrary, fundamentally at odds with the principle of utility.

[14]See Hans Jonas, "Heidegger and Theology," *The Phenomenon of Life* (New York: Harper & Row, 1966) 235-61.

[15]For an attempt to bring rabbinic wisdom concerning idolatry to bear on Nazism, see chap. 4 of the work cited in note 10.

[16]Schopenhauer, *Works*, vol. III, 306.

Part Five
Summing Up

Chapter 10

Confronting the Holocaust*

Eugene B. Borowitz

Having followed the writing of the two great Holocaust theologians, we conclude with a survey of the theological issues viewed together and at once by the leading theologian of Reform Judaism in the twentieth century, certainly the most accomplished and important mind Reform Judaism produced in our times.

Borowitz traces the various sources for Holocaust theology, the writing of Eli Wiesel, the issue raised by Richard Rubenstein, the arguments and doctrines put forth by Emil Fackenheim, and the theology of faith affectingly spelled out by Eliezer Berkovits. Borowitz not only affords perspective on the views of others, seen in the proper perspective and proportion; he also introduces his own civil and reasonable, persuasive reading of matters—a fitting conclusion to this account of theologians' encounter with events of surpassing weight and meaning.

***

Since Abraham Heschel, no Jewish theologian has presented a full-scale, distinctive exposition of Judaism. (The work of Louis Jacobs, a possible exception to this rule, is discussed in Chapter 11.) The work of Jewish thought has continued, if anything, in a more varied vigorous and sophisticated form than previously, but it has been scattered and thematic rather than concentrated and systematic. No topic has drawn more attention and been discussed in greater depth than the theological implications of the Holocaust. Tracking this debate is more than technically difficult; it is humanly daunting. Most of the thinkers involved admit that the Holocaust overwhelms them. They also consider it their Jewish duty to try to come to terms with it, even tentatively. These factors make summarizing this discussion particularly difficult. Nevertheless, a number of basic intellectual positions, often identified with certain protagonists, have emerged over the years. Let us track these points of view and the debates to which they have given rise.

*From *Choices in Modern Jewish Thought: A Partisan Guide*. Copyright © 1983 by Eugene B. Borowitz. Reprinted by permission of Behrman House, Inc.

The Two-Decade Silence

We begin with a historical puzzle. What caused the hiatus in time between the end of the Holocaust and the beginning of the discussion? Not until the mid-1960's, twenty years after World War II, did the Holocaust become a central topic in Jewish religious thought. Elie Wiesel's *Night* appeared in 1960 to little notice and the articles which Richard Rubenstein wrote then (later gathered with others into *After Auschwitz*), awakened little debate. Why?

Most observers have given a psychological answer, one not without moral overtones. The Holocaust had so traumatized us that we repressed it as too painful to bear. As it receded in time and our anguish lessened, we could open up to the terrible hurt and let it into our consciousness. Surely this is true of the survivors. Only in recent years have they found the inner strength to speak out. With the exception of Elie Wiesel, none of the thinkers presented in this chapter was in the death camps though several fled Europe before the mass murder began.

For most American Jews, the silence resulted as much from guilt at their inaction as from their identification with those who suffered and died. American Jewry had all too readily followed the advice of their leaders who, despite evidence of unprecedented mass extermination, acquiesced to the government's demands for silence and concentration on the war effort. For two decades guilt grew as they realized how great an evil they had abetted. The therapy for that festering wound was exposure— and the new Jewish devotion manifest through the 1970's.

The Cultural Context of the Change

The psychological analysis is persuasive but I believe it improperly isolates Jewish experience from its American context. Though I agree with Irving Greenberg's plea that the Holocaust should lead Jews to break their fawning dependence on modernity, I do not see our change, as he apparently does, as an internal Jewish community affair. I believe our Jewish turn inward substantially arose as part of a shift in the American ethos which made it socially acceptable for Jews to face up to the Holocaust and its implications. Against Greenberg, I view our very discussion of the Holocaust not as a withdrawal from modernity but as another sign of our continuing involvement in it.

As a result of the civil rights movement, the United States entered a period of ethnic reassertion in the early 1960's. Black civil disobedience shattered the notion that minorities had to be well behaved. Etiquette was revealed to be a means of keeping the underprivileged powerless. Polite silence at one's continuing disabilities was no longer considered a reasonable price to pay for having been granted some rights. Blacks, Indians, Poles and other groups became conscious of their guilt and anger at the servility they had gratefully undertaken. Public complaint and hostility to leaders became common; attacks on supposed friends who deserted others in a time of need were heard; and comparisons with Nazis and the Holocaust were a steady theme of minority invective.

American Jews had arrived at the mid-1960's with a new self-confidence. They were unexpectedly influential in the society and probably its single most affluent religio-ethnic community. Once that status would have enjoined a more neurotic conformity. Now it meant being secure enough to speak out.

In my opinion, the old Jewish inhibitions were finally dissolved by the popular acceptance of the Protestant death-of-God movement. Most Americans—and Jews—considered the American Jewish community a religious group. With Judaism one of the country's three great religions, the Jews, despite small numbers and endemic unbelief, had extraordinary social position. Consciously and unconsciously, they tended to emulate the dominant, Protestant mood. In the leading liberal churches this now shifted from a pronounced theocentrism to a death-of-God theology that was quite different from the atheism of another time. Its adherents proposed to stay in the church and rebuild it, in Dietrich Bonhoeffer's words, "as if there were no God." Once religion without God became acceptable in the paradigmatic group, the Jewish release was complete. Jews were bold enough ethnically to attack all anti-semitism and religiously free to do so in terms of giving up belief in God. Richard Rubenstein writes that he was surprised when William Hamilton, the organizer of the death-of-God movement, identified him as the Jewish counterpart to the Protestant thinkers but soon recognized, within limits, what he shared with them. Once again, particular Jewish experience participated in, yet extended, what was happening in the civilization generally.

The Influence of Elie Wiesel

The pivotal figure in the resulting intellectual work is Elie Wiesel, though his works on the Holocaust are mainly fiction. They are not entertainments but learned and reflective narrative explorations of the range of responses one might make to the Holocaust. Wiesel has often characterized his role as that of a witness. His effort to give truthful testimony has been agonizing. How can an author avoid reducing the terror in order to have its horrifying message widely heard? Wiesel's painful effort not to bear false witness is the standard by which the integrity of all who discuss this topic is measured.

In only one of his books has Wiesel permitted himself to describe the suffering during the Holocaust. *Night* is autobiographical and depicts the reactions of a pious teenager as he goes from his sheltered village existence to Auschwitz and thence, astonishingly, to liberation. I will not say more for I do not want to give anyone an excuse for not reading the book nor contribute to lessening its impact. A number of its passages have already been cited so frequently they have become our Holocaust clichés, thus emptying them of meaning—exactly the problem of authenticity that so agitates Wiesel.

In *Night*, Wiesel enunciated many of the themes around which his writing centers. The death camp experience was unutterably evil. No previous human experience or imagination of suffering explains such horror. Auschwitz, the symbolic name for all the ghettos and camps, was a unique event in history. More, it was revelatory. Now everything in human life must be seen through its lens. That is not meant as hyperbole but as fact. Auschwitz is the new Jewish Sinai; it must set the context and content of contemporary Jewish views of God, humankind, religion and Judaism. By that standard we can no longer be satisfied with the old Jewish apologies for God's bungling of reward and punishment: Life after death, suffering out of love or for the sake of others, redemption by the Messiah, and the like. They are not utterly false, yet after the Holocaust they are empty. Nothing makes sense any more—even the very act of trying to make sense of things. In the face of such evil, one may well wonder why one should bother with the world of history. But despair, too, is wrong. It makes the Holocaust more reasonable than existence. We must live—but what can it mean not to despair after the Holocaust? The question haunts Wiesel's work and life.

Wiesel believes there are no "answers" to the Holocaust. He is not even certain we have the right questions. He restlessly moves from one aspect of it to another, afraid to come to rest at any intellectual point and by such relaxation betray the fathomless terror Jews knew. Again and again he suggests that a species of intelligent madness is the most appropriate response to the Holocaust. Were we capable of becoming appropriately deranged we might see in what now appears to us as blackest night. Philosophers who seek to "explain" the Holocaust are engaged in a self-contradictory project. Madmen are more truthful witnesses to the insanity we lived through.

The final word cannot be insanity, else how would we write fiction or try to face life? A cruel duty is laid upon the survivor, not to forget, and not to let the world forget, as it would dearly like to do.

Continuing the Work of the Survivor-Witness

Night is the first book of a trilogy whose second volume is *Dawn* and whose final part, "Day" in French, is entitled *The Accident* in English. The increasing light is intentional. *Dawn* treats the partial answer to suffering of a people's national revival in its own homeland—an "explanation" made almost as irrational as the Holocaust by the violence it precipitates. In *Day*, the protagonist confronts the redemptive kindness of a doctor who fights death with all his might and thereby shows the goodness yet to be found in life. *The Town Beyond the Wall* contrasts helping a human being with the iniquity of spectatorship. In acknowledging the power of personal responsibility, Wiesel finds himself open to a positive relation with the God with whom he remains in conflict. By the end of *The Gates in the Forest*, the survivor, racked by the ambiguities of life and the guilt he bears, becomes sufficiently positive in his ambivalent relationship to God to recite the *kaddish*, that extravagant praise of God Jewish mourners offer. And having faced the dead and the God who brings death, he is able to take up marriage and procreation, the primal burdens of life.

Each novel discloses a partial truth and leaves one recognizing how fragmentary our understanding must remain. The ultimate irrationality of existence was given unusual expression in *A Beggar in Jerusalem*. This novel interprets one of the most joyous events in Jewish history, the return of the Old City of Jerusalem to Jewish sovereignty in 1967. It is the only one of Wiesel's novels not written in a realistic style. The swirling, uncertain, dreamlike narration communicates the madness which alone can cope with the paradox. The generation of ultimate suffering has been granted unexpected happiness.

In the late 1960's, Wiesel began publishing in other forms. His addresses and articles on the Holocaust, his response to contemporary Jewish issues, most notably a powerful book on the resurgence of Jewish life in the Soviet Union, and his retelling of biblical, talmudic, and Hasidic tales now were increasingly brought to the public. This continuing Jewish devotion puts into relief the one question which never occurs in his work: Should the Jewish people and tradition continue? Wiesel's categorically positive stance toward Jews and Judaism is no narrow self-assertion of ethnicity. His quest is thoroughly universal. He wonders how anyone can affirm life after the Holocaust. He takes it for granted that if there is any proper human response to Auschwitz, it will also be true for Jews. At the same time, since no one knows human suffering better than the Jews, their wisdom is humankind's best source of insight into the mystery called existence. To Wiesel, every Jew and the Jewish people itself, is holy. Promoting Jewish survival is an unshakable dogma after the Holocaust.

Issues Posed by Richard Rubenstein

For all the influence of Wiesel's work, the theological discussion of the Holocaust has not centered about it because its format is intentionally ambiguous. Instead, Richard Rubenstein's book, *After Auschwitz*, focused the significant controversies of the late 1960's and shaped the form in which they developed. That volume collects articles written over the six years when Rubenstein was evolving his radical Jewish theology. Readers today sometimes find it difficult to determine the position at which he ultimately arrived, though his later writings partially clarify this. Rubenstein agrees with Wiesel that Auschwitz is our Sinai. The refusal of contemporary Jewish theologians to listen to its voice is a damning indictment of anything they might now be shocked into saying about it. Rubenstein proposes instead to make its revelation about the human situation the basis of his illusionless Judaism.

The evil the Nazis perpetrated upon the Jews requires, at the very least, that Jews give up any claim to be chosen. In the western mind, as in much Jewish teaching, chosenness means suffering for God's sake. Persecutors may then have an easy conscience because suffering is the divinely appointed Jewish role. After Auschwitz such attitudes are intolerably offensive. Rather than give any comfort to the oppressor and validate indifference to the victims, Jews should renounce the notion of their appointment as God's suffering servant.

Rubenstein's opposition to chosenness did not arouse much conflict. It had long been reinterpreted, as in Mordecai Kaplan's case, to the point of repudiation. Such connection as it had retained with suffering had largely been severed by the events of the Holocaust. Some traditionalists, such as Harold Fisch, Eliezer Berkovits, and Irving Greenberg, have tried to recast the doctrine of necessary Jewish suffering without legitimizing persecution, but none of these views has been widely discussed or accepted.

A major controversy broke out over Rubenstein's rethinking of belief in God. He argued that the Holocaust invalidated all the classic Jewish positions regarding God and evil and requires us to reject classic Jewish faith in God. Rubenstein remained a religious thinker, albeit one whose idea of the Holy Nothing was disturbing to the average Jew, though his reworked understanding of the Jewish people and of Jewish practice was far more recognizable.

The First, Negative Assertions

Rubenstein denies that any of the old Jewish theodicies, the defenses of God despite evil, are tenable after Auschwitz. On occasion he remarks that the death of one innocent child should have been enough to refute them. (Such comments imply, against his normal stand, that *all* evil refutes theism; the Holocaust is not unique but merely gross.) That the Nazis' bestiality was just compensation for Jewish sins; that God must allow such evils so as to preserve human freedom; that it taught a valuable lesson to the world; that God tests our faith; that God has compensated the Jews for their suffering by giving them the State of Israel; or that the Holocaust brutality can be expunged by the bliss of the world-to-come, are all morally unbearable notions. No God who did such things would be worth worshipping. Further, to take refuge in traditional humility and say that God's ways are infinitely beyond us, is an utter abdication of our human judgement and of the victims' human dignity.

Rubenstein calls on us to reject the God of traditional Jewish theology. He makes two quite different statements of his position, one doctrinal, the other a social observation. The former was most concisely put this way:

> Traditional Jewish theology maintains that God is the ultimate, omnipotent actor in the historical drama. It has interpreted every major catastrophe in Jewish history as God's punishment of a sinful Israel. I fail to see how this position can be maintained without regarding Hitler and the SS as instruments of God's will. The agony of European Jewry cannot be likened to the testing of Job. . . . The idea is simply too obscene for me to accept.

In a number of other places Rubenstein similarly objects to what he understands to be the normative Jewish teaching about God's control of history.

Rubenstein does not equate giving up an old doctrine of God with denying God's reality. Atheism involves a metaphysical certainty, a negative one, which is incompatible with Rubenstein's existentialist, person-based thought. Instead, he makes a temporal, immediate judgement concerning our post-Holocaust period. He continues, "No man can really say that God is dead. How can we know that? Nevertheless, I am compelled to say that we live in the time of 'death of God.' This is more a statement about man and his culture than about God. The death of God is a cultural fact." This, too, became a steady theme in his thought. Most Jewish thinkers considered these two assertions faulty but I think it will clarify Rubenstein's total position better if we immediately consider his positive teachings.

Recreating Judaism Around the Holy Nothingness

Auschwitz should lead us to agree with the French existentialists Sartre and Camus that "We stand in a cold, silent, unfeeling cosmos, unaided by any purposeful power beyond our own resources." But Rubenstein is not an atheist. There is, after all, not *no*thing but *some*thing. The source of that being is the focus of Rubenstein's religiosity. He is wary of applying positive terminology to it lest he mask the negativity revealed by Auschwitz and the death that awaits all created things. Borrowing a theme from Jewish and general mysticism, he terms the object of his reverence the Holy Nothingness. "In the final analysis, omnipotent Nothingness is Lord of all creation."

An inverted messianism results from this. In discussing Christian death-of-God theories, he wrote, "There is only one Messiah who redeems us from the irony, the travail, and the limitations of human existence . . . the Angel of Death. Death is the true Messiah and the land of the dead the place of God's true Kingdom. . . . We enter God's Kingdom only when we enter His Holy Nothingness." Rubenstein does not seek that Kingdom "because I prefer the problematics of finitude to their dissolution in the nothingness of eternity."

Though no supernatural basis for Jewish continuity exists, the Jews, compelled by history to be Jews, should now affirm their Jewishness to attain self-protection and mutual caring. The State of Israel models a transformed Jewish identity because it reasserts the naturalness of being a Jew and gives proper attention to one's body and a connection to the soul. With chosenness abandoned, the State need reflect no special standard of quality. It rightly does whatever it must to ensure its survival in an amoral universe.

The Jewish religion should continue as a means of helping individual Jews meet life's inevitable traumas. In so unfeeling a cosmos, people need to share with one another to gain the human strength required to face the existential challenges of life. Human beings, having great emotional depths, will benefit from a religious life rich in ritual and myth, particularly those which do not neglect their primitive impulses. If Jewish theology and practice can be transformed, Judaism has much to offer Jews.

Why These Were Not the Relevant Issues

Rubenstein has often expressed surprise that, as the Jewish death-of-God discussion developed, he became increasingly marginal to it. At first, many Jews responded positively to the morality of his attack on the silence of other thinkers and the inadequacies of the traditional theodicies. Ever since modernization had taken hold, Jews had cared far more about ethics than about God. But the death-of-God discussion soon moved off in other directions.

Rubenstein's first argument, the rejection of a rigidly controlling God, was never disputed because modern Jews had not espoused it. Some sages of the "*yeshivah* world" and some Hasidic leaders, such as the Lubavitcher Rebbe or the Satmarer Rebbe, have declared that the Holocaust was God's punishment of the Jews for their non-observance. Almost all modern Jews agree with Rubenstein that such a view of God and the Holocaust is utterly unacceptable.

This judgement is not a new one. Modern Jewish thinkers had been revising their concepts of God through much of the twentieth century to avoid any mechanical connection between God and human suffering. The God of Cohen, Baeck, Kaplan, Rosenzweig, Buber and other such thinkers was not the "ultimate, omnipotent actor of history." No one who accepted their ideas had a God-concept which required Rubenstein's radical revision after the Holocaust. Except at some atavistic level, even the masses of modernized Jews no longer had believed in a God who operated every historical occurrence. The major response of modernized Jews to the Kishinev pogrom of 1903—the "holocaust" of its day—was a call for Jewish action, not cries of self-incrimination or arguments justifying God.

By 1966, when Rubenstein's book appeared, most American Jews were so thoroughly secularized that, in my opinion, their "faith" was usually some variety of agnosticism. The announcement of God's death only added a historical-moral proof to those other arguments which modernization had long since convinced them were cogent. To that extent, Rubenstein's second statement of his case, that we live in a time of the death-of-God, confirmed their experience. Since then, another cultural change has taken place. For much of the 1970s, not the absence of God but God's immediate, felt presence in charismatic movements, cults and mysticism has characterized American religious life. "The time of the death-of-God" passed rather quickly. Most Jews consider the lessons to be derived from Auschwitz less ephemeral than that and so their search moved elsewhere.

The Failure to Provide an Adequate Ground of Value

I have argued that the most significant Jewish religious phenomenon of the 1970's was the erosion of Jewish agnosticism. Intellectually, I ascribe it to the confrontation with nihilism which Rubenstein's thought generated. In the heady days of confidence in human rationality, we were comfortable being unbelievers for we could count on the eternal validity of ethics. But Rubenstein's cosmos was utterly devoid of moral standards or values. In that respect he accurately reflected post-World War II secularity. Unlike Hermann Cohen's era, human rationality no longer implied ethical commitment. Reason meant logic and tight thinking, not moral law. As Sartre taught, values were now only what a person chose wholeheartedly to do. By that standard, one had every right to be a Nazi, an outcome utterly unacceptable to those morally outraged at Auschwitz. Any theory of ethics that reduces the distinction between the murdered and the murderers to a social or historical accident is contemptible. The difference between a Nazi and a Jew testifies not merely to our upbringing but to something in the ultimate nature of reality itself. Against the drift of much of modern life and thought, many Jews found themselves believing in the claims of a realm of human value that no longer had a rational foundation. Confronted with Rubenstein's claim that the Holy Nothingness is indifferent to good and evil, a good portion of our community had to acknowledge it believed in a trans-rational, commanding absolute good. For us, that meant a belief in something very much like what previous Jewish generations called God. Astonishingly, the very discussion that sought to lead Jews away from God, led them, like many others in the 1970s, back to God.

Rubenstein sought to meet this problem of the loss of moral standards by arguing that a commanding ethics may be derived from the human body and the self. Had that project succeeded, he would have solved one of the most pressing intellectual problems of western civilization, namely, providing a secular justification for stringent obedience to moral imperatives. Rubenstein's book on this topic, *Morality and*

Eros, convinced few thinkers. With the ethical consequences of his thought nullifying the very moral outrage it had raised against Auschwitz, Rubenstein's ideas increasingly lost their appeal in the Jewish community.

The social factor in this change of perspective must not be overlooked. Gross immorality invaded much of American life in the 1970s, manifesting itself most dramatically in sexual license, drug abuse, and wanton violence. Few people could avoid the problem of a compelling ground of moral values. An amoral universe validates doing anything one can get away with, even holocausts. Many Americans knew they must reject any view of reality which taught no serious set of limits and had few standards of quality. With rationalism and other forms of secularism unable to deal persuasively with this intuition, a turn to religion began and grew during the 1970s. We shall return to this topic at the end of this chapter and in Chapter 10.

Fackenheim and the Modern Loss of Revelation

Emil Fackenheim's essay soon became a source of the most significant themes of the continuing Jewish discussion of the Holocaust. Ever since the late 1940's he had been a leader of the existentialist revolt against the rationalist establishment of liberal Jewish theology. Fackenheim, who teaches modern philosophy at the University of Toronto, utilized his considerable technical expertise to criticize the generally accepted axiom that a modern Judaism had to be a religion of reason. He argued that all authentic religion, certainly Judaism, is based on revelation. Religious rationalism, by basing itself on human reason, had grossly overestimated our human powers and paid too little attention to God's reality. Until the mid-1960s, Fackenheim's most influential work focused on restoring God to an appropriately prominent place in the liberal Jewish religious consciousness.

Fackenheim largely accepted Martin Buber's theory of revelation for he particularly admired the way the I-Eternal Thou encounter preserved individual autonomy while yet making God an active, independent partner in the process. Buber had suggested that God gave presence, not works; people provided the language and content. Because God was available, the Divine-human relationship could arise and engender a compelling but non-Orthodox variety of revelation. The reality and immediate presence of God was therefore a critical element of Fackenheim's two-decade battle with the theological rationalists.

Confronted by the issues raised by Wiesel and Rubenstein, Fackenheim felt he must substantially rethink his position. The biographical background is pertinent: a German, one of the last men ordained a liberal rabbi in Berlin and briefly confined in Sachsenhausen after the November 1938 Nazi outbreak, the *Kristalnacht*, he barely escaped to Canada because the war broke out. Opening himself up now to the Holocaust, Fackenheim conceded that Wiesel and Rubenstein were right: God was not present in the Holocaust. What, then, was one to make of this event or of the understanding of Judaism?

In our bewilderment, tradition offers little help. After previous catastrophes, great Jewish spirits have written of God's presence in judgement or in consolation. We cannot do that, not because of some lack of spiritual capacity on our part, but because the Holocaust was a unique act of evil. Here, too, Wiesel and Rubenstein were right. Auschwitz exposes us to a qualitatively new and unprecedented dimension of suffering. Fackenheim is therefore intellectually outraged by the liberal sentimentality which brackets the Holocaust with any human disaster we seek to condemn. For all their moral odiousness, calling either Hiroshima or *apartheid* another Holocaust betrays an effort to avoid the uniqueness of Nazi barbarity.

Arguments for a New Level of Evil

No other Jewish thinker has explored as has Fackenheim what we might mean by saying the Holocaust is without parallel and what follows from that assertion. Obviously, we are not referring merely to numbers or its unexpectedness or its methodical execution. All such matters amplify common cruelty; they do not specify what constitutes the Holocaust as a unique evil. Fackenheim identifies two factors in the Holocaust which newly transform the old problem of suffering. The one stems from the charge leveled against the Jews. Their alleged guilt was independent of their conduct or beliefs. In previous persecutions-say, in the Middle Ages—Jews could often save their lives by conversion. The Nazis condemned the Jews because of their biology. Having one Jewish grandparent became a sentence of death. Being itself was made a capital crime and there was nothing one could do about it. That, Fackenheim argues, was a uniquely evil act.

His other line of argument points to the will of the persecutors. The Nazis knew the evil they were doing. They were educated people whose moral consciousness was shaped by a Christian culture, yet they calmly, routinely proceeded to process the mass murder of Jews. They even did so after continuing the extermination made no sense. During the last stages of the war, when trains were desperately needed for immediate military purposes, the Nazis refused to divert them from transporting Jews to the death camps. The hatred of Jews transcended the drive to self-preservation. They must have kept killing from a demonic desire to do evil for evil's sake, to commit the ultimate sin, a thoroughly evil act done for a thoroughly evil purpose. Nothing like that had ever happened in human history.

With God withdrawn and inaccessible—no small part of the agony—and in the face of this incomparable evil, one might have expected the Jews to despair. But the events of Jewish history, as theologians read them, are often more numinous than Jewish thoughts. Though the Holocaust itself discloses no transcendent meaning,

Fackenheim detects a new "revelation" at the base of the Jewish people's response to it. By what logic can one explain why the Jews did not turn their backs on life after the Holocaust? Why despite all that they had seen and suffered, did not survivors insist on resuming Jewish existence? And, most surprisingly, why did they choose to be Jews in a more self-conscious, manifest way than they had before? On some unconscious, spiritual level, they *had to do* what they did. For them to allow the Jewish people to die would have been, themselves, to complete the Holocaust. That was inconceivable. Individual Jews might be so traumatized they could not care any more about being Jewish. The people itself somehow summoned—or was given —the strength to deny Hitler the ultimate triumph. Absolute evil had aroused absolute commitment.

The Nature of Post-Holocaust Judaism

Fackenheim provides an explanation of this incredible act of self-transcendence. Though God was utterly silent, the Jews heard an absolute command come forth from Auschwitz. To emphasize its Torah-like status, Fackenheim has termed it the 614th commandment (though he seems to consider it the most fundamental of all the commandments today). He hears it as having four components. Jews are forbidden "to hand Hitler posthumous victories." Rather, they must survive as Jews. They must remember the victims. They must not despair of God "lest Judaism perish." In this formulation Fackenheim explained to the Jewish community the impetus which motivated its extraordinary postwar return to Jewishness and which continues to energize the best of Jewish life today.

Fackenheim drew three consequences from his reoriented belief and these remain basic to his community leadership and intellectual work. First, he no longer finds it useful to distinguish between religious and secular Jews. Earlier, when arguing for the centrality of revelation in Judaism, he had demeaned Jewish secularism. Seeking to come to terms with the Holocaust, his criterion of Jewish loyalty had changed. Though God is no longer present to reveal, Jews respond to the "commanding voice" of Auschwitz. Any Jew, regardless of label, who helps preserve and maintain, or, better, enriches the life of the Jewish people, fulfills the supreme Jewish responsibility of our time.

The second consequence he derives from emphasizing peoplehood is a new regard for the State of Israel. It is the ultimate fulfillment of the 614th commandment. Nothing else Jews have done so fully sums up, expresses and symbolically projects the Jewish people's rejection of death, its return to life, its willingness to face the ambiguities of history and its insistence on remaining visibly, demonstrably, proudly Jewish. The State of Israel is the incomparable answer Jews have given to the incomparable evil of the Holocaust. Fackenheim therefore considers the State of Israel incomparably sacred and demands that every threat to its existence be fought with the utmost Jewish dedication.

This faith is easily misinterpreted. Fackenheim is *not* suggesting that the founding of the State of Israel was God's way of compensating the Jewish people for its suffering. He spurns any such suggestion as morally repugnant, as does Wiesel. He considers such compensation theodicies another effort to compromise the radically unique evil of the Holocaust. The two events have a bearing on one another but each must be understood in its own distinct terms.

Third, Fackenheim concludes that the test of good faith of Gentiles who enter discussions on Jewish matters is their willingness to face up to the Holocaust. When people admit that they were, or are, prejudiced against Jews, one knows with whom one is dealing. Far more pernicious is the attitude of those who are so proud of their decency and good will that they are blind to their complicity in Jew-hate. We must never forget how the liberal democracies impeded the entry of refugees to their countries and later would not bomb death camps. Non-Jews must make plain their attitudes toward the Holocaust and the State of Israel if they would truly talk to Jews.

Christianity must stand under special scrutiny in this regard. The Nazis were not Christians in any normal sense but had it not been for centuries of Christian anti-Jewish teaching, the Holocaust could not have happened. Worse, the church as an institution did not oppose the Nazi degradation of Jews or later, when it became known, their extermination. Occasionally Christians behaved nobly, sometimes even giving their lives to help Jews or call attention to their plight. Most Christians quietly accepted what happened, thereby condoning and abetting absolute evil. Until Christians are willing to come to terms with the anti-semitism implicit in much of the church's teaching and confess the guilt the church bears for its sinfulness during the Holocaust, Jews cannot give any spiritual credence to Christianity or its leaders.

The Debate over Fackenheim's Position

Much of the thinking which arose in response to Fackenheim's point of view has sought a way to restore the dead or absent God to post-Holocaust Judaism. Michael Wyschogrod's trenchant criticism of Fackenheim's arguments is an important case in point. Wyschogrod, himself a professor of philosophy at Baruch College, New York, points out the logical difficulty involved in inferring a positive command from a negative experience. Boldly paraphrasing the Jewish experience, he asks if stamp collectors were subject to a Holocaust, would the remaining stamp-collectors be required not to hand the tyrant posthumous victories? Would they be under a command to carry the special burdens which come from competent stamp-collecting?

Wyschogrod wants to focus our attention on the way a happening might become a commandment of overriding power and authority. In the Jewish case, he does not see why we must say that Jewish secularists heard a "commanding voice" from Auschwitz. Yiddishists, Hebraists, and Zionists may now want to go on being Jewish for many of the same reasons as before the Holocaust. Only people who believe in a Transcendent Commander will divine in the decision to-be-a-Jew-despite-everything a response to an absolute, categorical command. The Torah-like imperative is a result of one's prior perspective. It does not stem from the historical experience of Auschwitz or the response to it. In themselves, they remain as ambiguous as all events. The notion that Jews are hearkening to an absolute command makes sense only when one begins with belief in a commanding God. We may not understand God's relation to evil but we nonetheless know what we must do in response to it—a human situation with many precedents in Jewish history.

Wyschogrod also rejects the notion that the Holocaust is a qualitatively unique event of evil. He can understand why Fackenheim is particularly concerned with the Holocaust and why, as against the many monstrous occurrences in recent history, a Jew would want to assert the special quality of Jewish fate. From an ethical point of view, that is, from the standpoint of universal human suffering, Wyschogrod does not see how Fackenheim can substantiate the moral individuality of the Holocaust.

I believe the argument can be carried a step further. Fackenheim's two efforts to validate the singularity of the Holocaust seem faulty to me. That no other people has been singled out for destruction, simply for existing rather than for what they did, seems incorrect. In the history of tribal and national antagonism, one people not infrequently proscribes the members of another people merely for not belonging to its kin.

Less easy to decide is the proper interpretation of the will of the Nazis who carried out the Holocaust. I do not mean to detract from either the perversity of the crime or from its unique significance for the Jewish people when I say that I do not find the charge of the unprecedented Nazi will to do evil convincing. The Germans often made what I consider irrational, because self-damaging, decisions in order to continue the Holocaust. I do not see that they did so to do evil as such. Rather, they obsessively pursued their murderous project because they believed their propaganda that the destruction of the Jews was more important than the possible defeat of the Reich. They persisted in their paranoid devotion to ridding the world of its major enemy. Their words and acts fully accord with this interpretation. Like others who have administered terror, they acted in dedicated pursuit of what they, with demonic misjudgment, saw as the greatest good. I despise what they did but my revulsion is insufficient reason to transform their acts into a uniquely qualitative evil which might in consequence thereby attain uniquely commanding power.

Greenberg's Radically Reinterpreted Orthodoxy

Irving Greenberg has approached the issue of the uniqueness of the Holocaust only indirectly. He insists that Auschwitz is the transforming religious experience of our time but he does not give it precedence over Sinai, as do Wiesel, Rubenstein and Fackenheim. He retains the major categories of classic Jewish faith but subjects them to radical reworking in terms of the Holocaust. His thinking is therefore dialectical, balancing the claims of Orthodoxy and Auschwitz one against the other.

Though Rubenstein asserts that traditional Judaism is no longer believable after Auschwitz, Greenberg finds no reason to explain why the Holocaust does not shatter rather than reshape his Orthodoxy. He only suggests that the contemporary traditional Jew believes in a modern fashion, on the basis of "moment faiths." Explicitly crediting Buber, Greenberg says there remain times when God is known and present, though there are others when one finds oneself in the cruel world of the Holocaust. In Greenberg's case, the occasions of validation still supply the context for coming to terms with the times of doubt and disbelief.

Additional ground for the assertion of a dynamic traditional Jewish faith may be found in Greenberg's vigorous, continually reiterated polemic against modernity. The first lesson which he would have Jews—and all others—learn from the Holocaust is that our wholehearted embrace of modernity was a major blunder. Western secular civilization has shown itself to be deeply demonic and capable of the most monstrous inhumanity. The form and operation of the Holocaust are the consummation of centuries of western religion, intellectuality, science and technology (a theme also dear to Rubenstein). For Jews to have given up their tradition for such spiritual trash, seems to Greenberg unutterably tragic and in need of thoroughgoing reversal. Somewhat like Fackenheim's argument that utter tragedy can be converted into energetic devotion, Greenberg hopes that convincing Jews to give up their dependency on western culture will lead them back to traditional observance. The logic of his case is even less compelling than Fackenheim's. Many Jews, like many other Americans, merely withdraw from all groups to concentrate on the one thing they know they are genuinely committed to, self-gratification.

Aspects of the New Belief and Duty

Greenberg agrees that we are in a post-secular time and that compelling moral affirmation can only be based on a relationship to God. He goes further, arguing that the establishment of the State of Israel validates continued faith in God. As Jewish tradition should have led us to expect, a redeeming act has "matched" the catastrophe.

Almost all Jews consider the State of Israel central to their Jewishness and most believe it to be a balance for the horror of the Holocaust. These sentiments do not lead to belief in God by any large number of Jews, particularly the Israelis who remain resolutely secular. Were Greenberg's argument more than a statement of his personal faith, Fackenheim would not need to inveigh so against continuing the distinction between secular and religious Jews.

To revise his traditional faith in God, Greenberg utilizes models derived from Job and Lamentations. These justify, in ways quite familiar from liberal theologies, the *search* for faith against confidence in establishing doctrine and find argument with God a legitimate Jewish way of maintaining a relationship. Despite Rubenstein's strictures, Greenberg offers a defense of the Jewish people as God's suffering servant. Anti-semitism's eerie quality derives from its satanic theological basis. Because the Jews are a witness to God and testify that the world remains unredeemed, the nations hate them. On a practical level as well, the Jews are a likely target for whatever demonic impulses inhere in a culture. Jewish suffering is not therefore senseless but an active part of the Jewish people's service of God. A limit to such suffering must be invoked, for, as the Holocaust showed, "when the suffering is overwhelming, then the servant must be driven to yield to evil. . . . The redemptive nature of suffering must be in absolute tension with the dialectical reality that it must be fought, cut down, eliminated."

Positively, Greenberg maintains that after Auschwitz our central religious affirmation is the creation of life. By having and properly rearing a child, one shows a primal hopefulness and decisively rejects all that the death camps stood for. For Jews, whose numbers have been radically depleted, propagation is a primary obligation. Simultaneously, any cultural or religious activity which devalues the worth of human beings or any group among them, must be adjudged anathema. From there it is a simple step to the elimination of the secular-religious dichotomy. Anyone who desists from murder or exploitation or, better, who is dedicated to the care of people, must now be regarded as a God-fearer. With humanism now an acceptable piety, Greenberg can identify the State of Israel, despite its committed secularity, as a religious institution. Like Fackenheim, he sees it as the Jewish people's supreme, life-generating response to the Holocaust. He goes beyond Fackenheim by suggesting that in itself—the Holocaust aside—the founding and continuation of a Jewish state on the sacred land is numinous. It must become a generative premise for the construction of an adequate modern Jewish theology.

Berkovits' Argument for a Holocaust Theology of Faith

Eliezer Berkovits, also an Orthodox rabbi, has sought to do more than revise traditional faith as a result of the Holocaust. His new philosophy of rabbinic Judaism is still in process and I must therefore limit this presentation to his special contribution of the discussion of the Holocaust.

Berkovits cannot understand why so many thinkers insist that God was not to be found in the death camps. Many people who were there had the opposite experience. To be sure, a good number did lose their old beliefs and values but numerous others did not; some few even found faith there or later. For them, God was available and this knowledge enabled them to bear their suffering, often with nobility. If anything, the records indicate that in these dire circumstances traditional belief stood up better than modernist and liberal world views, which rather easily collapsed. The Jewish death-of-God theologians have simply ignored this data. Berkovits lays down the principle that those who were not there, but passed the murder era miles away in safety, should be most restrained in making dramatic, negative claims about its lessons.

Berkovits contends that our Holocaust theology has begun with the wrong premise. It has extrapolated from the experience of the disillusioned to create a vision of the cosmos which necessarily then had no God. Surely there is nothing new and certainly not revelatory in evil's producing a loss of faith. Disbelief is the common situation of secular humankind; under the blows of the Holocaust, modernized unbelievers would naturally lose whatever faith lurked in their psyches. What naivete about the human condition has led our thinkers to suggest that negation ought to awaken our awe?

Should we not, however, be astonished by the many people who maintained their faith despite everything the Nazis did to them? Their spiritual accomplishment in our time, in their situation, is breathtaking. In this argument Berkovits does not indulge in pathos. He does not try to wring from sentimentality what intelligence and conscience deny. Rather, he reverently calls our attention to the common saints and everyday heroes of the ghettos and death camps. Their unwavering devotion is awesome by any standards. And Berkovits demands to know why they should not be the foundation of our religious reconstruction after Auschwitz. If the commanding voice of Auschwitz calls us to maintain faith with the victims, they, above all, should be our models. We should remember them in the most significant possible way, by trying to emulate their faith. Should we find belief difficult—Berkovits admits understanding is utterly beyond us—we ought to give their affirmations more credence than our doubts and honor their memories by patiently awaiting the return of faith.

The full force of Berkovits' negative feelings as a result of the Holocaust is directed against Christianity. Fackenheim and Greenberg have felt a positive obligation to challenge Christians (who would speak to Jews) to acknowledge the depth of Christian religious anti-semitism and its role in making the Holocaust possible. They have made the repudiation of any vestige of Christian anti-Jewishness, the acknowledgement of Christian guilt for the Holocaust and an appreciation of the State of Israel to post-Auschwitz Jews, the conditions of contemporary Christian-Jewish dialogue. Berkovits denies that Jews and Christians can have any significant interchange whatsoever in our generation. The obloquy and persecution of pre-Hitler years should themselves be sufficient to prevent any self-respecting Jew from taking seriously present-day Christian declarations of a change of heart. After Auschwitz and the Christian silence during it and the subsequent threats to the State of Israel, how can any rational person take Christian declarations of good will as anything more than desperate efforts to bolster what is left of their decaying self-image? That some Christians still seek to convert Jews to their faith rouses him to fury. His cry, "All we want of Christians is that they keep their hands off us and our children!", must rank as one of the strongest rejections of interchange with Christians to appear before the English-reading public.

A Limited God, the One Rational Religious Answer

Rationalistically-minded Jews have not been impressed by any of these arguments for continued belief in God today. They do not see how thinking people can be asked to believe what they cannot understand. For them, reestablishing faith depends on finding a new conception of God, one which establishes value while making intelligible the occurrence of evils such as the Holocaust. (Rationalists cannot, in principle, accept the notion of the Holocaust as a radically unique act of evil since terming it unique excludes it from universal categories of explanation.)

The alternatives for a rational theodicy are limited. Thinkers after the Holocaust can hardly say that evil is unreal, and claim to be realistic. They might follow Rubenstein and deny that God is good, but that destroys the ultimate qualitative distinction between Nazis and Jews—an unacceptable position for those morally indignant at the Holocaust. That leaves only the possibility that God does not have sufficient power to stop all evil. Instead of being thought of as omnipotent, God should be conceived of as finite or limited. God cannot "do all things" as Job thought, and thus great evil sometimes occurs. With God's powers limited, human moral action becomes all the more important if the world is to be redeemed.

Belief in a limited God is not without warrant in the Jewish tradition. The Bible unequivocally states that God granted the very first human being the power to do or not do God's commands to them. The biblical authors thereby implied that they believed there were limits as to what God could, perhaps would do. Various rabbinic statements and some of the ideas of Jewish philosophers and mystics similarly restrict the Divine power. None of the modern thinkers we have previously discussed, except Heschel, makes an unequivocal claim for God's omnipotence. Mordecai Kaplan, at the other extreme specifically, identifies God as referring only to the helping powers in nature, thus resolving by definition the classic problem of evil. A number of other pre-Holocaust thinkers taught that God was finite. Henry Slonimsky had elegantly described God as growing in history through human moral acts.

Hans Jonas' Construction of a Limited God

One intriguing outline of a finite God is that of Hans Jonas, who taught philosophy at the New School for Social Research with a particular concern for the philosophy of science. In his Ingersoll Lecture, "Immortality and the Modern Temper," Jonas describes a God in keeping with the naturalistic view that all causes must be internal to the world. Unlike Kaplan's God, who is entirely immanent in natural processes, Jonas suggests that God created the world but, once having ordered it and its values, God allowed it full independence. After creation, God is never a natural cause. But unlike the Deists' God who no longer is involved with the creation, this God, because of values, remains "concerned" with what happens. God's own future, so to speak, has become conditional upon what transpires in creation, particularly once human beings evolve who are free to determine its outcome by their action. Jonas' God may be said to be dependent on creation, as against biblical faith in which all created things depend on God. Jonas can also say that God "cares" what takes place in history for the future of values depends on it. In this context, metaphorical by contrast to Heschel's literalism, God suffers with every ethical defeat in human history.

When, then, the Nazis abuse the freedom natural evolution gave them, we cannot hold God responsible. That God did not act to stop the Holocaust, or did not take away the Nazi's freedom to do evil, or did not miraculously save the Jews, or did not manifest the Divine presence in some spectacular way in the death camps, is not irrational. A God who violates or vitiates human freedom is not the sort of God morally dedicated people would want the world to have. We are overwhelmed by what our people suffered but can take some consolation from knowing that God's own future was damaged by the Nazi bestiality. We can also understand why Jews and others ought to respond to the Holocaust by fighting every vestige of Nazism or sign of its reappearance. Jonas' lecture does not develop the particular Jewish consequences of his idea of God but it could easily ground a defense of the State of Israel as a major agent of God's work in history.

For all their intellectual appeal, finite doctrines of God have been difficult to accept. In Jonas' case, the rationalistic appeal of limiting God is compromised by the inexplicable reversal of God's energy after creation. By having the creator God suddenly withdraw from nature, Jonas saves God from utter immanence while giving the cosmos independence and people freedom, yet establishing the transcendent authority of immanent values. Jonas himself is forced to admit that the expansion-contraction description of creation involves a mythic, not a rationalistic model of creation, specifically the Jewish notion of *tzimtzum*, God's self-concentration.

Substantively, too, finite theories of God undermine Jewish messianism. Can we still believe that the ideal will one day be made reality if we must depend on human-kind to achieve it? After all, the Holocaust has taught us about the limited moral steadfastness of even good people: Should not those whose God has limited power to overcome evil join Rubenstein and despair of human history? Classic Judaism had faith in people because they were in covenant with God. What their righteousness could not accomplish, God's power would ultimately complete. Can any doctrine of hope today dispense with God's help even though we cannot explain just how God acts or why God's saving influence is seen only sporadically and after long delay?

Was It God We Had Lost Faith In?

Let me add a few further observations of my own on the death-of-God controversy. In retrospect, the decade-plus discussion taught us little about God we did not already know. For nearly a century Jewish modernists have given up their traditional beliefs out of respect for science and in response to Nietzsche's cultural arguments for athe-ism. Then, as our confidence in human capability became less absolute, our atheism dwindled to the agnosticism which, for some time, has been the nearly universal atti-tude of sophisticated Jews to God. Long before mid-century, there was little of God left to bury.

For modernized believers, as we have seen, modern Jewish thinkers had long since removed God far enough from the world to allow for the human ethical inde-pendence they all so highly prized. Even the notion of a finite God was widespread. From the early 1930's on, Mordecai Kaplan and Henry Slonimsky had expounded it to their Conservative and Reform rabbinical school students. In my opinion, the Holocaust discussion has yielded only some variations of the well-known modern arguments about God.

If so, why did our theological discussion of the Holocaust so agitate us?

I suggest that the Holocaust did undermine our true faith but the term *God* did not indicate what we believed in, only how important our underlying belief was. We can uncover our true concern by applying Ludwig Feuerbach's rule about theology, though in a way he never imagined. In the nineteenth century, Feuerbach said that all our assertions about God are really about ourselves; they speak of our vision of humankind. He hoped then to convert supernatural religion, which no modern could accept, into a humanism that would then be believable. Since then, Feuerbach's in-sight has seemed the definitive refutation of religion, for what we claim to be saying about the reality of God can be called only a projection of human ideals.

But what if the central religious assertion of the mid-1960's was that God-is-dead? What if the religious implication of the Holocaust is that no good God rules the universe? Translated by Feuerbach's rule, these are statements about humankind.

And that, I take it, was the utterly unsettling truth buried under the Holocaust talk about God: after Auschwitz we could no longer maintain our modernist faith in humankind.

For *that* was the operative religion of American Jews. We believed in the goodness of people and trusted that education and culture would guide them properly, while psychotherapy remedied their flaws. We counted on politics to bring the Messiah, with an assist from social science. We followed the commandments of self-realization and looked forward to perfecting humankind. Sitting in our homes, walking on the way, lying down and rising up, we spoke of human progress and put our faith in new projects. For us, humanity sat on God's old throne. The debate of Auschwitz gradually has made us acknowledge our covert religion and confess its untenability. And with that recognition, death-of-God theology lost the vitality it had once displayed.

More Realism about People
Leads to New Openness to God

We have not, of course, stopped talking about the religious implications of the Holocaust. Only for some years now the once fashionably radical calls for non-belief and the once shocking rabbinic admissions of atheism or agnosticism seem old-fashioned and irrelevant. It seems a triumph of illusion today to suggest we should still place our ultimate faith in humankind. The death of our faith in human omni-competence has been shatteringly conformed by the continuing disillusionments of the past decade and a half. The 1970's made plain to our mounting disgust that nothing human beings have long been involved with remains untainted by moral failure. Our government is suspect, our economy exploitative, our ecology destructive, our families troubled and we ourselves conflicted to the point where avoiding depression is a major species of fulfillment. Humanity is no longer the answer but the problem.

Ironically, as we have become strong enough to face the loss of our old covert faith in ourselves, we have discovered that, despite everything, we probably are far less agnostic than we thought we were. When, in moral revulsion against the vulgarity of our society or in rejection of its temptations to paganize, we insist on living on another level of quality, we can be led to ask: Whence this stubborn devotion to high human value? For us, being Jewish is the likely source of our ethical stubbornness and our most likely resource for its perpetuation in a society indifferent or antithetical to moral excellence. When we insist that our values, for all that they are difficult to define or apply, are no arbitrary acts of our will or the accidents of our upbringing, but fundamental to the universe itself, we base our lives on a transcendent claim of quality laid on human beings, one that our society largely dismisses and to which contemporary rationality gives little credence. If we are determined not to lose our intuition of proper human dignity but to pursue it despite the burdens that quest will impose upon us, we are ready to join those other Jews who now searchingly inquire what being a Jew can mean to them (even as Christians are finding a way back to heartfelt Christian faith). Most Jews moving in this direction are satisfied by a return to the Jewish community, some institutional involvement of *havurah* face-to-face exploration, some study, some folk culture, some ritual, perhaps even some prayer. All these well-documented paths of activity comprise the new search for Jewish identity which has been the surprise and promise of the 1970's.

But if I am right that the central human experience of our generation has been the collapse of our humanistic faith and the loss of our old ground of values, then a choice confronts us. We may say with Rubenstein that the universe is, at best, neutral, and order our lives accordingly. Or we may stubbornly insist that righteousness, not nothingness, is ultimately real and therefore properly worthy of our lives' devotion. Taking that latter stance, we are likely at some quiet or critical moment to ask about the root of this crucial belief. What is it, then, that we are trusting in? And more than likely we shall find ourselves realizing that we, in our modern way, are responding to the same commanding presence in the universe to which previous generations of Jews hearkened. In recovering our Jewish identity in depth, we find ourselves on new terms with what our tradition called God. The almost unbelievable, dialectical outcome of our attention to the Holocaust has been that a sizable minority in the Jewish community is now involved in exploring the dimensions of their personal relationship with God. Through mysticism or the study of texts, in liturgy or Jewish activism, some Jews are seeking to draw closer to what they dimly sense is the still living God of the universe. They do not claim to understand God or to explain God's erratic way in history. The Holocaust remains as disturbing as ever—if anything, more so, for the God on whom they base their lives is also the God of the six million. They only know that God is real and the Covenant continues, and they propose to build their lives on these commitments. Theirs is a fragmentary faith but in this empty era even a partial belief is a lot to have gained.

Can one believe when one does not understand? How can God now be present, and then, and often, terrifyingly absent? How could God, the God who grounds all values, not have done something, anything to stop the Holocaust, the antithesis of all value?

Why do the good suffer?